FINDING JESUS

ALSO BY DAVID GIBSON

*The Coming Catholic Church: How the Faithful Are Shaping
a New American Catholicism*

*The Rule of Benedict: Pope Benedict XVI
and His Battle with the Modern World*

ALSO BY MICHAEL MCKINLEY

It's Our Game

Hockey Night in Canada: 60 Seasons

Hockey: A People's History

Ice Time: The Story of Hockey

Facetime: A Novella

The Penalty Killing: A Martin Carter Mystery

Putting a Roof on Winter: Hockey's Rise from Sport to Spectacle

The Codebreakers: The Battle for Intelligence 1914–18 (June 2015)

FINDING JESUS

FAITH. FACT. FORGERY.

SIX HOLY OBJECTS THAT TELL

THE REMARKABLE STORY

OF THE GOSPELS

DAVID GIBSON and
MICHAEL McKINLEY

St. Martin's Press New York

www.stmartins.com

Designed by Steven Seighman

The Library of Congress Cataloging-in-Publication Data is available upon request.

ISBN 978-1-250-06910-8 (hardcover)
ISBN 978-1-4668-7790-0 (e-book)

St. Martin's Press books may be purchased for educational, business, or promotional use. For information on bulk purchases, please contact the Macmillan Corporate and Premium Sales Department at 1-800-221-7945, extension 5442, or write to specialmarkets@macmillan.com.

First Edition: February 2015

10 9 8 7 6 5 4 3 2 1

For our families

CONTENTS

Authors' Note

The following experts appeared in the CNN series *Finding Jesus*, and we have used quotations from their interviews throughout this book: Nicholas Allen, Rev. Bruce Chilton, Kate Cooper, Annelise Freisenbruch, Camil Fuchs, Rabbi Joshua Garroway, Oded Golan, Mark Goodacre, Mark Guscin, Israel Hershkovitz, Tom Higham, Shimon Ilani, John Jackson, Matthew Kalman, Georges Kazan, Noel Lenski, Fr. James Martin, Byron McCane, Candida Moss, Elaine Pagels, Jonathan Pagis, Joan Taylor, and Ben Witherington III.

All Scripture references in the book are taken from the New Revised Standard Version of the Bible.

Last, in keeping with current practices, we have used BCE ("Before the Common Era") and CE ("Common Era") throughout the book, rather than BC and AD.

FINDING JESUS

WHO IS JESUS?

The question must be posed in the present tense because, for believers, Jesus is God and he exists in the here and now every bit as much as he ever did: "Jesus Christ, the same yesterday, today, and forever," as the New Testament says. To be a Christian is to have a relationship with a Jesus who is alive in heaven and with us at every moment of every day.

Yet Jesus is also profoundly present for today's agnostics and even die-hard skeptics, who are engaged with Jesus of Nazareth, in their own way, almost as devoutly as Christians are.

Just look at the reaction to any new artifact excavated from the Holy Land, or every scrap of papyrus that emerges from the sands of Egypt or the sometimes shadowy antiquities markets that operate throughout the West. Each is accompanied by astounding claims and a wave of boldface headlines, and each prompts a new round of global fascination with a man who died two thousand years ago, crucified by the Romans on a dusty hill near Jerusalem.

It was a fate inflicted on countless others deemed enemies of the state. Yet Jesus was different. For believers, he rose from the tomb on the third day, on that first Easter morning, bringing a message of eternal life and galvanizing a small band of followers who would go on to create a church and spread a faith that would reach every corner of the globe. Those who dismiss such claims must contend with the reality of Jesus's afterlife in this world, with the historic forces he unleashed, forces that remain undiminished even in this supposedly secular age. It's not surprising that the entry on Jesus in the open-source encyclopedia Wikipedia is the fifth-most-edited page among the more than thirty million articles on the site.

Everyone seems to have a stake in who Jesus is, and in what we should believe about him—but to prove their claims, they have to know who Jesus was.

Exploring that mystery, and that history, is the goal of this book and the CNN series *Finding Jesus*. It is a fascinating adventure into theology; archeology; our contemporary preoccupations with sex, religion, and the meaning of life; and our age-old love of relics. In six chapters we examine six relics—or artifacts, if you will—that provide a window onto the past, opening up our understanding of first-century Judea, of the men and women around Jesus, and of those who later followed the man they believed to be the Messiah—the Christ (*Christos*, in Greek, or the "anointed one").

These investigations take us deep into history, and modern scholarship on the Bible, and demonstrate again that finding the truth about Jesus is no easy task. It never has been. When Jesus was brought before Pontius Pilate, the Roman governor of Judea wasn't sure what to make of him. "Are you the King of the Jews?" Pilate asked him.

Jesus said, "You say so." But when he was accused by the chief priests and elders, he did not answer.

Then Pilate said to him, "Do you not hear how many accusations they make against you?"

But he gave him no answer, not even to a single charge, so that the governor was greatly amazed.

This famous exchange, with slight variations, is present in all four canonical gospels—Matthew, Mark, Luke, and John—which recount the life, and death, of Jesus. Yet the gospels are not biographies in the commonly understood sense of the word. They tell the story of Jesus, but above all with the aim of conveying the "why" of his life (the message of his teachings) as much as the who, what, when, and where. That is why different gospels cover different aspects of Jesus's life: Two give versions of his birth; two do not. Only one mentions anything about Jesus between his life as an infant and his emergence as a public figure at about the age of thirty. They vary in details and sometimes recount the same stories in different ways, or even contradict one another on particular details.

For centuries this was not much of a problem. The life of Christ was taken for granted. The different versions just meant preachers had a deeper well of material upon which to draw, and a greater reservoir of meaning to explore. Elaboration, even embroidering the stories, was not necessarily a bad thing. Bible stories, and the myriad images in stone and on canvas that depict them, could lead people to the essence of the faith. Christianity was mainly a matter of belief, and that's what believers argued about—often with deadly results. Yet when the wars of religion that raged across Europe in the seventeenth century gave way to the Age of Reason in the eighteenth century, everything changed. Tradition was subjected to rational inquiry, dogma to scientific scrutiny—and if they didn't withstand the Enlightenment's standards, they were tossed out.

The stories about Jesus in the gospels were a special focus. Thus was born the so-called First Quest for the historical Jesus, an endeavor led by German Protestants who brought the critical eye of modern scholarship to holy writ, and wound up rewriting the New Testament in ways that often scandalized the faithful. Everything that could not be proven was called into question, and much of what had mattered to believers for centuries was cast aside. Perhaps the most famous, and graphic, example of this approach is the Jefferson Bible, a version of the New Testament that Thomas Jefferson, an accomplished child of the Enlightenment, created in his later years by (literally) cutting out all the Scripture passages about miracles and supernatural claims and leaving Jesus's ethical teachings, which Jefferson thought were just fine.

The First Quest effectively ended in 1906, with the publication of a volume that gave the phenomenon its name, Albert Schweitzer's *The Quest of the Historical Jesus*. Schweitzer, a Lutheran who later won renown as a humanitarian in West Africa and was awarded the Nobel Peace Prize in 1952, ultimately concluded that "the historical Jesus will remain a stranger and an enigma to our time."

Yet Jesus would not be dismissed so easily. A 1953 lecture by another German scholar, Ernst Käsemann, titled "The Problem of the Historical Jesus," launched what is called the Second Quest, one that brought textual criticism and other modern scholarship tools to attempt yet again to find solutions to this "problem." The Second Quest was bolstered by a number of remarkable archeological finds that did for the Bible what the 1922 discovery of the tomb of King Tutankhamen did for all things Egyptian. Suddenly, biblical archeology was hot.

Until it was not. The Second Quest seemed to run its course by the 1970s, but the historical Jesus, again, continued to pique the Western imagination, and by the 1980s a whole new generation of scholars, using a whole new range of tools and technologies, launched what has come to be called the Third Quest. This one shows no signs of slowing, for several reasons.

One is that Christian scholars are themselves more engaged than ever in this research, using science and history not simply to try to prove their beliefs—that has too often ended in intellectual embarrassment—but also to inform their faith and to show a suspicious public that faith and reason can work in harmony. Previous quests for the historical Jesus tended to be dominated by critics of Christianity who sought to debunk the faith, or by Christians focused on brushing away the film of myth in order to dig deeper and recover the solid nuggets of truth that had been buried, to recover the original Jewish prophet who could speak anew to the modern world.

These efforts led to some questionable projects, such as the Jesus Seminar, a loose collective of some 150 scholars who, during the 1980s and '90s, used a system of colored beads to vote on how much of the gospels was reliable. In the end, they cast serious doubt on 82 percent of the sayings attributed to Jesus and 84 percent of his deeds—a worse result than even the Jefferson Bible, and with a methodology that mainstream experts found wanting.

Some scholars, bloggers, and conspiracy theorists have even taken to reviving the theory that Jesus did not exist, or was nothing like the man the gospels portray, and that his life, death, and Resurrection were pretty much a hoax. The arguments have become so insistent that, in 2012, Bart Ehrman, a leading New Testament scholar at the University of North Carolina at Chapel Hill, wrote a book to refute them. Ehrman has no dog in this fight; on the contrary, though he was raised an evangelical, he later became a convinced agnostic. Yet, as he writes, "The reality is, whatever else you may think about Jesus, he did exist."

Ironclad proof of his existence, however, remains hard to come by. Jesus left no writings of his own, and no bodily relics (outside of a few implausible artifacts, such as the famous foreskin of Jesus, another tale altogether). His existence is mentioned in passing by a couple of historians from the first century, but other than that, we rely largely on the gospels.

So what do we know of him for sure? Even after all the questing and testing, the most reliable answer is a brief one: Jesus was a Jewish man from Nazareth who lived, and was crucified, in the Roman province of Judea, the land of Israel, a restive region on the eastern border of the empire, situated at a dangerous crossroads of the ancient world.

What did he look like? No one can say for sure. Even the language he spoke remains a matter of dispute. When Pope Francis met Israeli prime minister Benjamin Netanyahu during the pontiff's visit to Jerusalem in June 2014, Netanyahu sought to make a connection with the leader of the world's largest Christian church by noting that Christianity and Judaism drew from the same sources, and indeed Jesus himself spoke Hebrew. "Aramaic!" the pope gently corrected him, referring to the Semitic tongue that is closely related to Hebrew and was commonly used in Jesus's day. "He spoke Aramaic but he knew Hebrew," Netanyahu said diplomatically.

Well, Greek was also widely used at the time, and often mixed together with Hebrew and Aramaic. "Ancient Jewish language use resembled Spanglish, switching languages depending on what they were saying and who they were talking with," Seth Sanders, a religion professor at Trinity College and author of *The Invention of Hebrew*, wrote at the time.

This uncertainty, this relative lack of hard facts, is at the heart of the problem. As the *New Yorker* writer Adam Gopnik wrote about the unending obsession with trying to uncover the real-life story of William Shakespeare, whose biography remains opaque four hundred fifty years after his birth, "The easy answer is the disproportion between the mountainous heights of his reputation and the fragmentary shards of his biography: the tallest mountains produce the most abominable of snowmen, Yetis crowd the slopes of Everest."

Indeed, it can seem that the field of biblical archeology produces as many hoaxes, or exaggerated claims that look much the same, as sightings of Bigfoot or Elvis. The greater the shock value, the greater the appeal; the more outlandish the find, the more believable it will be.

It has also been conventional wisdom in Jesus studies that the lack of precise data on Jesus means that we wind up filling in the portrait so that the man from Galilee looks suspiciously like us. An old joke illustrates the point. Question: How do we know Jesus was Jewish? Answer: Because he went into his father's business, he lived at home until he was thirty, he thought his mother was a virgin, and his mother thought he was God. Add a couple variations—he had wine at every meal or he loved to tell stories—and Jesus becomes Italian or Irish, and so on.

Our present-day concerns tend to be a bit different, and so is our Jesus, who at any given time is found to be a proto-Marxist or an anti-tax Tea Partyer, a simple-living peasant or a model businessman, a freedom-loving zealot or a detached Greek philosopher, a gay man or a happily married one—with kids.

Focusing on artifacts associated with Jesus can be a way around some of these pitfalls. To be sure, relics can lead to their own kind of literalism, a shortcut to hard thinking about faith by believers and skeptics alike. The genuinely remarkable discoveries that have come to light in recent decades often lead one to think that, any day now, the real truth will emerge and some piece of papyrus will show that, yes, Jesus was a feminist; or an engraving will show that he had a brother; or a piece of cloth will show us, finally, what he really looked like.

Even the most jaundiced nonbelievers can seize on relics to prove their point, every bit as much as Christian apologists did in the past. More than ever we live in a winner-take-all world, and we want to be proven right—we need to be proven right. We don't like ambiguity; we don't like doubt. Who does? One of Jesus's own apostles, Thomas, would not believe in the Resurrection until "I see the mark of the nails in his hands, and put my finger in the mark of the nails and my hand in his side." Fortunately for Thomas, he had that chance when Jesus appeared to him. We have to content ourselves with other objects, no less fascinating.

In this book, we look for answers in bits of bones from Jesus's contemporaries, in papyrus texts that may or may not give new insights into events not recorded in the gospels, and in a limestone funerary box that may have held the bones of Jesus's brother. We examine pieces of what may be the cross on which Jesus was crucified, and the burial shroud that may have enfolded his corpse—and recorded his rebirth to this life. We dig into the lives of John the Baptist, Mary Magdalene, and Judas Iscariot to see what the biographies of those closest to Jesus tell us about the Nazarene.

Objects associated with Jesus have always held an allure. The gospels recount how a woman who had been suffering from hemorrhages for twelve years worked her way through the crowds around Jesus, convinced that "If I only touch his cloak, I will be made well." And so it happened. People today seem no less drawn to objects associated with famous athletes or celebrities, and if they are relics connected to the dead, they are that much more powerful.

Yet the objects we examine in the following pages—with the possible exception of the Shroud of Turin—are not necessarily miraculous relics of the sort adored by the faithful or dismissed by nonbelievers such as eighteenth-century Scottish philosopher David Hume, who famously defined a miracle as "a violation of the laws of nature."

Rather, these objects are themselves of the natural world, and evidence of what happened at a particular time and place in history. These objects have the capacity to take us out of ourselves, to transport us to a time and place not our own as we hope to discover something about Jesus that is not filtered through the distorting lens of time and our own desires.

Artifacts are, in a way, a rare patch of common ground between skeptics and believers, a place where science and religion can come together, not as foes but as pilgrims on a shared journey—wherever it leads.

In telling the story of these objects, we want to ask, and answer, two central questions: Are they real? And what do they mean?

"Everyone who belongs to the truth listens to my voice," Jesus told Pilate as he stood before him awaiting his sentence. "What is truth?" Pilate asked him. Jesus was silent, according to the Gospel of John. Yet finding an answer to Pilate's question is at the heart of the Jesus quest, and this book.

ONE

JOHN THE BAPTIST

Rival Messiah, Bones of Contention

Human bones discovered in a Bulgarian church have been tested to reveal that they come from a Middle Eastern man who lived in the first century CE. Could they be the bones of John the Baptist? *(Getty Images)*

The island of Sveti Ivan does not immediately strike a visitor as the likeliest place to solve one of the most puzzling mysteries of Christian history.

Just a quarter-mile square, the hardscrabble patch of land sits in the Black Sea, near the coast of Bulgaria, half a mile from the resort town of Sozòpol and nearly fourteen hundred long miles from Jerusalem. Yet the island always had a rather outsize strategic and cultural importance. After the Romans conquered the area in 72 BCE, they built a lighthouse on the island, and next to an ancient Thracian sanctuary they constructed a temple that featured a forty-three-foot-tall bronze statue of Apollo.

The complex of buildings around the temple eventually fell, along with the fortunes of the empire, and in the fifth century CE, as Christianity began arriving in the region and filling the vacuum left by the Romans, a monastic complex was built on the ruins, and the low-lying island was christened Sveti Ivan, or St. Ivan—or, as the English-speaking world would translate the name, St. John, as in John the Baptist.

In the New Testament, John is known as the Baptizer, or the Immerser, because of his fame for drawing repentant souls to his river baptisms. Yet Christians also know him as the Precursor, or the Forerunner, the man who famously predicted the coming

Messiah and then identified Jesus as that man when he baptized him in the River Jordan. John was a plainspoken prophet, a fearless herald of the coming Kingdom of God, the original street preacher who instead of a sandwich board screaming "Repent!" wore camel's hair as his only garment and subsisted on locusts and wild honey.

John lived by the words he proclaimed, and was imprisoned by Herod Antipas, Rome's puppet king in Judea, for denouncing Herod's incestuous remarriage to Herodias, his own niece. John then famously lost his life when Herod agreed to grant his daughter, traditionally identified as Salome, anything she wanted if she danced for his dinner party guests. She did so, apparently quite convincingly, and asked for the Baptist's head on a platter, which Herod delivered.

Sveti Ivan, St. John's Island, suffered various tribulations over the centuries. The original basilica was abandoned and then reconstructed in the tenth century, and it flourished in the 1200s along with the growing devotion to John the Baptist. Two patriarchs of Constantinople may have been buried there, a great honor for such a small site. The Ottoman Muslims who would overrun Christian Byzantium sacked St. John's Island, in 1453, though a church was rebuilt on the site. Then, in the 1600s, Cossack pirates used the island as a refuge, and the church as a feasting hall. The Ottomans eventually leveled all the buildings in order to deprive the pirates of any sanctuary, and the island was last used as a field hospital for Russian soldiers in the nineteenth century.

In the 1980s there was some talk of turning the island into a tourist destination, with a hotel and shops and such. Yet that stalled, and for the most part Sveti Ivan is home only to wildlife, chiefly dozens of species of birds, some of them endangered. Even the rare monk seals that once populated the island's rocks, their name an echo of the island's monastic past, are gone.

So it was something of a leap of faith when archeologists began excavating the island's old ruins, and truly astonishing when, in July 2010, they discovered beneath the ruins of the original altar a small marble reliquary (or box for relics) that contained a number of bones. Three of the bones were from livestock—one each from a sheep, a cow, and a horse. "The animal bones are the biggest of the group, and they may have just been put there to bulk up what looks like a pretty minimal collection of bones," Thomas Higham, a professor of archaeological science at the University of Oxford, told Reuters. Higham was a member of the team brought in to test the DNA of the bones to determine if there were any way they could actually belong to John the Baptist.

Along with the animal bits were five human bones: a knuckle-bone from the right hand, a tooth, part of a skull, a rib, and an ulna, which is a bone from the forearm. Higham and the team took these bones back to the Oxford Radiocarbon Accelerator Unit, one of the world's top laboratories for carbon-dating archaeological mate-rial, and two years later produced a result that left even Higham astounded: the human bones dated right to the middle of the first century CE, the time of Jesus. Testing of the genetic material by experts at the University of Copenhagen showed that the bones all came from the same man, and he apparently came from the Middle East.

Moreover, buried in an older part of the church was a small box made of volcanic stone. The box is inscribed with the name of "Saint John," in Greek, and the feast day of John the Baptist, June 24, the day tradition says he was born. The stone from which the box was made, called tuff, came from an area in modern-day Turkey, along one of the routes used to take relics from the Holy Land to Con-stantinople (now Istanbul), where Roman emperors and various aris-tocrats, as well as patriarchs and bishops, were eager to acquire them.

"They were often bestowed as a sign of favor. The monastery of Sveti Ivan may well have received a portion of relics as a gift from a patron, a member of Constantinople's elite," said Oxford archaeologist Georges Kazan, who wrote his doctoral thesis on the movement of relics in the fifth and sixth centuries. He noted that the island was an easy distance from the Byzantine capital, on a major Black Sea trading route.

"It's really stretching it to think that material from the first century can end up all the way in this church in Bulgaria and still be there for archaeologists to excavate," Higham said. "But stranger things have happened." Higham, a professed atheist with no motive to make religious claims look good, told reporters that when he first heard about the relics in 2010, "I thought it was a bit of a joke, to be honest." Going into the testing phase, he thought the age of the original church (about the fifth century) would give a likely age for the material. "We thought that perhaps these bones would be fourth or fifth century as well. But we were surprised when they turned out to be much older than that."

Could these be the bones of John the Baptist? So far there is no way to be sure, since there is no DNA database to compare, no genome for the Baptist's family—which tradition says would include his first cousin Jesus of Nazareth. Even so, just finding these bones—all from the middle of the first century, all from one man who lived in the Middle East—stands as a remarkable discovery.

John the Baptist was in many ways the Humpty Dumpty of martyrs. He was beheaded, and over the centuries so many different churches and shrines and mosques—John is a revered prophet in Islam—claimed his skull and various bones that church wags liked to quip that John must have had six heads and twelve hands. Putting a single John the Baptist together again may be impossible, though the task and the popularity of his remains provide a window onto the truly important questions: Who was John the Baptist and why was he so important to Jesus of Nazareth? Why did Jesus go to John to be baptized? Was John really a more popular figure than the Son of God? And why did John's movement fade away, as he himself predicted it would, while Jesus's movement became a global religion?

"NOT TO UNDERSTAND THE BAPTIST IS NOT TO UNDERSTAND JESUS"

What John the Baptist provides to the Christian story above all is a historical and religious context, and that context is vitally important to understanding Jesus. Yet it can also be profoundly threatening to many of his followers.

The threat emerged in the seventeenth and eighteenth centuries with the rise of "biblical criticism," the academic movement to examine the Scriptures from a dispassionate, scholarly, "just-the-facts" perspective rather than viewing the Christian texts chiefly as a fulfillment of Old Testament prophecies, an account about the one true God sending his only son into the world to live and die as a man for the sins of the world, and to rise from the tomb and point the way to eternal salvation. Along the way, this divine man, Jesus Christ, also demonstrated and instructed his followers on how to live. For centuries, the New Testament was taught as a set of beliefs one must follow to get to heaven and a handbook of morality to guide one's life in this world. For most believers, science only got in the way of meaning, and historical context only diminished the uniqueness of Jesus.

Scholars increasingly thought otherwise, and most of them were viewed as debunkers who highlighted inconsistencies or outright contradictions among the gospels and who dismissed the accounts of the miracles (the Resurrection first among them) as obvious myths that were outright inventions by early Christians, a misinterpretation of natural phenomena, or a mass hallucination.

Some Christian scholars have tried to use science to support the Scriptures and confound the biblical skeptics. One of the earliest examples was a seventeenth-century Anglican archbishop, James Ussher, whose complex calculations based on the Bible established the time and date of the Creation as the night preceding Sunday, October 23, 4004 BCE. Other have followed in Ussher's footsteps in efforts to explain away scientific theories that appear to conflict with the Bible's claims, or to divine the exact date and time of the end of the world.

Such efforts have tended to end badly or have wound up a mirror image of the views of rationalists, focusing so intently on justifying the Scriptures scientifically that they have obscured the higher purpose and theology of Christianity.

When it came to Jesus of Nazareth, the fear for many believers was that by portraying him as a Jewish man living in first-century Judea, a rabbi and prophet among the many who populated the land in those tumultuous days of the Roman Empire, Jesus as the Christ would be compromised. Better to see him solely as the Son of God, the first Christian, emerging in the pages of holy writ fully formed, starting a new faith, and dying for it.

The structure of the gospels themselves fostered this view: two of the four gospels, Mark and John, begin abruptly with Jesus starting his public ministry in Galilee, an unmarried man around thirty years of age. Luke and Matthew begin with the so-called infancy narratives, retelling the beloved Christmas story of the birth in a manger in Bethlehem, and the Holy Family's flight into Egypt to escape the terrible edict from Herod that every male child under two be slain in order to snuff out the Messiah before he could grow up and pose a danger to Roman rule.

The Gospel of Luke mentions the story of Jesus at the age of twelve accompanying Mary and Joseph to Jerusalem for Passover. On that visit, they lose track of the boy, only to find him three days later in the Temple discussing Jewish teaching with the elders, who were astounded by his learning and wisdom.

Other than that episode, which also shows Jesus as preternaturally mature, the gospels jump from Jesus as infant to Jesus as full-grown Savior, and skip any growing pains or backstory. Hence the proliferation of fanciful theories about "the lost years" of Jesus. Believers in the Middle Ages loved the stories that Jesus visited Britain in those gap years, while believers with modern sensibilities prefer theories that he went to India (like the Beatles visiting an ashram) and maybe even discovered Buddhism, which would explain what these latter see as the "eat, pray, love" vibe of his teachings.

Yet modern believers who dismiss any such musings also need not fear efforts to understand Jesus, and the faith he preached, by understanding the historical context of his upbringing. And this starts with his mentor, John the Baptist.

"All too often in books on the historical Jesus, the Baptist, like the miracle stories, gets a perfunctory nod and short shrift," the Rev. John P. Meier writes in his sweeping multivolume survey, *A Marginal Jew: Rethinking the Historical Jesus.* "Yet one of the most certain things we know about Jesus is that he voluntarily submitted himself to John's baptism for the remission of sins, an embarrassing event each evangelist tries to neutralize in his own way." As Meier notes, the very first followers of Jesus were apparently eager that he not be "contextualized" out of his uniqueness. Yet that's not a desirable approach, Meier says, nor possible: "Not to understand the Baptist is not to understand Jesus."

And understanding John the Baptist starts with the four canonical gospels of the New Testament. That John the Baptist appears in Matthew, Mark, Luke, and John is a record of consistency that undergirds claims that he was a real historical figure. That he receives extensive treatment by Josephus, the Jewish historian of the first century, as we will see later, makes the fact of his existence a veritable slam dunk. Meier has several criteria for determining the historical reliability of a person or statement or story recounted in the New Testament, a chief one being the "criterion of multiple attestation"—that is, if someone or something is mentioned in various sources, it is likely true, and John the Baptist fits that bill.

Yet the Baptist also fits under Meier's "criterion of embarrassment," which holds that if something or someone in the New Testament creates embarrassment or theological difficulties that Jesus's followers have to explain, then it is likely true because it's not something early Christians would have invented—on the contrary. This criterion of embarrassment will also come into play in discussions of Mary Magdalene (a woman as the first witness to the Resurrection!) and Judas Iscariot (all-knowing Jesus chooses an apostle who will betray him!).

John the Baptist fits that bill given that he baptized Jesus, who ostensibly had no need to be cleansed of sin. Explaining this theological conundrum in part accounts for why John is portrayed differently in different sources.

By way of background: three of the gospels (Matthew, Mark, and Luke) are so close in form and content that they are called the synoptics, from the Greek word meaning "to look at from the same point of view." Scholars believe these three gospels were written first, starting a few decades after the Crucifixion, and were based on oral accounts that had been circulating since the days of Jesus's public ministry, which would have begun about 30 CE.

The Gospel of Mark was likely the earliest of the three, composed between 65 and 75 CE, with Matthew and Luke taking their cues from its narrative. The fourth gospel, the Gospel of John, was written later, perhaps as late as 100 CE, and has a markedly different style. Tradition (which is disputed by many if not most scholars) attributes this last gospel to the apostle John, the "beloved disciple" who, custom holds, also composed the Book of Revelation as an aged man living in exile on the island of Patmos, off the coast of what is modern-day Turkey.

Mark, the earliest gospel, opens without a preamble, diving straight into the story of Jesus by starting with John the Baptist: he is introduced as fulfilling the Old Testament prophecy of Isaiah, "a voice of one crying out in the desert," preparing the way of the Lord to "make straight his paths." Mark continues:

John the baptizer appeared in the wilderness, proclaiming a baptism of repentance for the forgiveness of sins. And people from the whole Judean countryside and all the people of Jerusalem were going out to him, and were baptized by him in the river Jordan, confessing their sins. Now John was clothed with camel's hair, with a leather belt around his waist, and he ate locusts and wild honey.

All the chief elements of the Baptist's story are there: his prophetic voice, his role as a baptizer, his broad appeal, and his ascetic lifestyle. Yet lest anyone think John was too important, Mark immediately records the Baptist as announcing, "The one who is more powerful than I is coming after me; I am not worthy to stoop down and untie the thong of his sandals. I have baptized you with water; but he will baptize you with the Holy Spirit."

On cue, Jesus appears to be baptized by John, and Mark says that on coming out of the waters of the River Jordan—this was full immersion, mind you, no sprinkling—Jesus "saw the heavens torn apart and the Spirit descending like a dove on him." He adds: "a voice came from heaven, 'You are my Son, the Beloved; with you I am well pleased.'" Whether anyone else saw that sign or heard that voice is not made clear.

This moment, this baptism, clearly launches Jesus's ministry. Like John might have done, Jesus heads straight out into the desert to endure the wild beasts and temptations by Satan, and then, after hearing that John has been arrested, Jesus begins his public ministry in the Galilee region in northern Judea, where he was raised.

Midway through Mark's gospel, Jesus returns to complete John's story, recounting the circumstances of John's imprisonment and grisly death: that John denounced Herod for marrying his brother's wife and was thrown in prison, but that Herod was afraid to kill John. His wife, Herodias, wanted him dead, but Herod knew that John was viewed as "a righteous and holy man," and Herod himself liked to listen to John preach, though he wasn't quite sure he understood what John was saying.

Then came the famous banquet, at which Herod's daughter, identified elsewhere as Salome, danced for the guests and in return was given the head of John the Baptizer on a platter, which she then gave to her mother. Herod was "deeply grieved," Mark says, and that may be one reason he allowed John's disciples to collect his body and lay it in a tomb—a story that in many respects prefigures the Passion of Jesus. John was so popular, in fact, that when Herod later hears about Jesus, he first thinks that John has been raised from the dead.

The Gospel of Matthew is more expansive. It picks up on Mark's narrative about John only after recounting the infancy story of Jesus. The Baptist is then introduced in much the same way, only Matthew has him specifically criticizing the Pharisees and Sadducees—two other Jewish groups that wielded power in Jerusalem at the time and were the focus of resentment by many prophets. John the Baptist denounces them as "a brood of vipers" and intimates that they will be cut down and cast into the fire.

When the Baptist predicts the coming Messiah, who will be Jesus, he also invokes the "unquenchable fire" that Jesus will bring to consume those who do not repent. When Jesus does show up at the Jordan River, John recognizes him as the One, and protests that

Jesus should be baptizing him, not the other way around. Jesus says no: "Let it be so now; for it is proper for us in this way to fulfill all righteousness." Then the baptism, the dove descending, and the voice of God confirming Jesus as his Son.

This is followed, as in Mark, by Jesus spending forty days in the desert, with some elaboration on the temptations, and then Jesus commencing his public ministry of preaching—repenting, as John did—and teaching, but also working wonders. These miracles are a key difference between John and Jesus, and in fact, later on in Matthew, when the imprisoned John hears what Jesus is doing, he sends two of his followers to ask for confirmation that he is the Messiah: "Are you the one who is to come, or are we to wait for another?"

Apparently John the Baptist did not see the dove or hear the voice of God there at the river, or still harbored doubts. Jesus instructs John's disciples, "Go and tell John what you hear and see: the blind receive their sight, the lame walk, the lepers are cleansed, the deaf hear, the dead are raised, and the poor have good news brought to them. And blessed is anyone who takes no offense at me."

Jesus then goes on a tear in praising John the Baptist to the crowds. "Truly I tell you," he says, "among those born of women no one has arisen greater than John the Baptist." He notes also that "the least in the kingdom of heaven is greater than he," but this is high praise coming from the Son of God.

The last reference to the Baptist in Matthew's gospel is one of the most telling and poignant moments in the story: after John is killed, his own disciples claim his body and bury it, and immediately go to tell Jesus. At the news, Jesus "withdrew from there in a boat to a deserted place by himself," apparently pained, and perhaps sobered by what might await him.

Luke's gospel fleshes out the backstory of John and Jesus even more, as Luke does with so many aspects of the story, though they are the sort of details on which scholars cast doubt. Chief among these claims is the story, which only Luke tells, of the elderly and infertile couple, Elizabeth and the priest Zechariah, who are visited by an angel, Gabriel. The angel announces that Elizabeth will bear him a son, and he will be called John and will be a seer prophet who will turn many of the people of Israel back to God. Elizabeth goes into seclusion, Luke says, until one day, when she is six months pregnant, she is visited by a young woman—she may even have been a teenage girl—named Mary, who announces to Elizabeth that she, too, is miraculously pregnant. The child in Elizabeth's womb immediately leaps, which Elizabeth announces as a sign that John recognized Jesus as the Son of God.

Luke says the women are related, and a tradition naturally grew up that the elderly Elizabeth and the young Mary were cousins. So, too, then, were John the Baptist and Jesus. The evangelist says that Mary stayed with Elizabeth for three months, which would have been until Elizabeth gave birth, a date traditionally named as June 24, exactly six months before the birth of Jesus, the first Christmas, which Luke recounts in splendid detail.

Luke later picks up the story of John in the wilderness "preaching the baptism of repentance for the remission of sins." John again denies he is the Messiah, but points to Jesus, whom he baptizes. Again the Holy Spirit "descended upon him in bodily form like a dove," God gives his approval, and Jesus begins his own public ministry after enduring forty days in the desert, while Herod locks John in jail and has him beheaded.

The Gospel of John, fourth in the New Testament and also the last to be written, begins like the first gospel, Mark, and dives right in with John as the herald of the Word, Jesus Christ: "He himself was not the light, but he came to testify to the light. The true light, which enlightens everyone, was coming into the world." John again protests that he is not the Messiah, as some wonder, but instead of describing his baptism of Jesus in the Jordan River, he tells his listeners that he saw the Holy Spirit descend on Jesus like a dove, and that Jesus was indeed the Son of God.

John the Evangelist is most focused on emphasizing the divinity of Jesus, with everything tailored to highlighting Jesus as the Christ, the Messiah, the Son of God—and that is what John the Baptist does. When the Baptist sees Jesus coming toward him, he tells his followers, "Here is the Lamb of God who takes away the sin of the world!" His disciples then go to off to follow Jesus. In the third chapter, some of John the Baptist's remaining disciples note that Jesus and his disciples are also baptizing, and they question him about why everyone is going to see Jesus. The Baptist again extols Jesus as the chosen one, and in a famous phrase says, "He must increase, but I must decrease."

John the Baptist then exits the narrative, and no reference is made to his death.

"GOD STOOD IN LINE"

If the evangelists were concerned here to show that Jesus was indeed greater than his mentor, and surpassed him both as a religious figure and a spiritual teacher, historians of the era show no such deference.

The greatest of these chroniclers was Flavius Josephus, a Jew who was born in 37 CE, just after the events recorded in the gospels, and who went on to fight for the Jewish people in the 66–70 CE revolt against the Romans. Captured by Roman forces and facing execution, he instead defected to the imperial camp and became Romanized, though he still considered himself Jewish.

After the defeat of the Jewish rebels and the destruction of the Temple in Jerusalem in 70 CE, an apocalyptic event that many later saw as a fulfillment of the dire warnings delivered to the people of Israel by John the Baptist, Jesus, and others, Josephus retired to Rome and wrote several extensive and excellent histories of the era. In them, he twice refers to Jesus, once only in passing, in discussing the death of Jesus's brother James; and once a bit more fully, when he describes Jesus as a "wise man" and "a doer of wonderful works" who was crucified by Pontius Pilate and rose again on the third day. Scholars believe that some of elements of that passage may have been embellishments by later Christian translators, but there is no doubt about Josephus's treatment of John the Baptist, who comes across as a more successful and more influential figure than Jesus.

In all extant manuscripts of his history, the *Jewish Antiquities*, Josephus writes about a battle that Herod fought against a rival who routed Herod's army:

> *Now some of the Jews thought that the destruction of Herod's army came from God, and that very justly, as a punishment of what he did against John, that was called the Baptist: for Herod slew him, who was a good man, and commanded the Jews to exercise virtue, both as to righteousness towards one another, and piety towards God, and so to come to baptism . . .*

Josephus goes on to explain that the Baptist was drawing large crowds around him, and that Herod feared John would use his influence over the people to start a rebellion, "for they seemed ready to do any thing [John the Baptist] should advise." So he decided, in a preemptive strike, to have John imprisoned in the Machaerus, a fortified palace on the other side of the Dead Sea, east of Jerusalem. There he put the Baptist to death. Josephus does not mention Herod's dancing daughter or the head on a platter, but he does provide the daughter's name, Salome.

All this information adds up to a fuller portrait than we have of many other central New Testament figures, such as Mary Magdalene or Judas Iscariot. Yet what does it tell us?

First, it is clear that the land of Israel in the first century was a powder keg with a short fuse. It always had been, to a great degree. The Jewish people were fiercely independent, and had a long, proud history as the chosen people of the one true God, an identity that was manifest in a fusion of religious tradition and nationalist fervor. Yet the province of Judea was also relatively small, and sat at the intersection of history, where great armies clashed and empires rose and fell. Often the Jews were collateral damage, but they could exploit any moment of inattention by the ancient world's superpowers to try to shuck off the oppressor's yoke.

In the second century before Jesus, in 164 BCE, the Maccabee clan led a rebel Jewish army that successfully established independence from the Seleucid Empire, an event recalled each year at Hanukkah, the Festival of Lights, which commemorates the rededication of the Temple in Jerusalem. Judea's autonomy lasted until 63 BCE, when a rising Roman Empire conquered Judea and established a malleable ruler, a client-king, to govern in Rome's name. That never sat well with the Jews, and periodically a rebel leader would rise—as Judas of Galilee did in 6 CE—only to be crushed.

This constant restiveness among the populace kept Judea's rulers in a state of perpetual paranoia. One clue to the state of mind of Rome's client-kings emerges in the gospel account of Herod the Great's order, after hearing the prophecy that baby who had been born in a manger would grow up to be King of the Jews, that all newborn boys be slaughtered. Herod the Great's son and successor, Herod Antipas, shared his father's anxious nature and took no chances, as the account by Josephus makes clear.

"When you get a popular leader arising in a particular context in time, it's because things have preceded that have made people desperate for some kind of change," says Joan Taylor, a professor of early Christianity at King's College in London. "And if you look at Josephus . . . and what he says, there was a tremendous amount of social upheaval and worry that the Romans were taking over."

Was John the Baptist really a threat? Nothing in the Baptist's actions, or those of his followers, would seem to support such a view. "As Josephus makes clear, any idea of revolt lay in Herod's ever-suspicious brain, not in John's message and deeds," says Meier.

Yet Herod's suspicions ruled, and John was killed—a fate that foreshadowed that of Jesus, except that Antipas evidently respected the Baptist enough to have him beheaded, a punishment normally reserved for Roman citizens because it was considered swift and merciful. Jesus of Nazareth, on the other hand, was crucified, a slow, cruel, and humiliating punishment meted out to lowly criminals, such as the two tortured to death on crosses with Christ.

Second, it's also clear that there was religious ferment in the land to match the political tumult. The 1979 Monty Python movie, *Life of Brian*, was a hugely controversial, and commercially successful, satire of the gospels—and, in a way, of the growing faddism of gospel scholars—that wrapped its blasphemies around kernels of truth. One of those insights comes in a scene in which Brian, who is mistaken for the Messiah, passes before a series of street-corner prophets and sages spouting hellfire or spinning incomprehensible parables. One senses that the Judea of John the Baptist's day was not terribly different, with Rome's heavy hand fueling not only political and military plots but also fevered dreams of divine deliverance.

"It's important to realize that not all Jews were expecting a Messiah, but some were," says Rabbi Joshua Garroway, associate professor of early Christian history at Hebrew Union College. "The kind of Messiah that those Jews were expecting ranges across a broad spectrum. Some Jews were expecting simply a human leader that would collect all of the Jews from around the world, or . . . simply challenge Roman hegemony in the land of Israel and reestablish a Davidic kingdom with its capital at Jerusalem. Other people were expecting a Messiah who would be a great prophet or a great teacher, or work miracles. Perhaps even bring about the end of the world as we know it, through some kind of judgment."

There were certainly more than a few candidates from which to choose. Josephus, our most reliable source on first-century Judaism, mentions a number of prophets and pseudo-messiahs. One of them, called Theudas, rallied hundreds of followers to the Jordan River with promises of miracles and then sent them against a squadron of cavalry, who of course cut them down. Theudas also had his head cut off—shades of John's fate—and paraded in Jerusalem. Theudas and his fate are also mentioned in the Acts of the Apostles in the New Testament. (That book, which historians generally see as an extension of the Gospel of Luke, and by the same writer, recounts the founding of the early Church and its initial growth throughout the Roman Empire.)

The Book of Acts also has the tribune who arrests the apostle Paul in Jerusalem, asking if Paul is "the Egyptian who recently stirred up a revolt and led the four thousand assassins out into the wilderness." This is a reference to a messianic figure from Egypt, whom Josephus calls a "false prophet," who gathered thousands (or, more likely, hundreds) of followers near Jerusalem and promised to bring the city walls down at his command. That didn't happen, but the Roman forces did kill and capture most of those gathered, though the unnamed prophet from Egypt escaped into the wilderness, never to be heard from again.

When it comes to the religious diversity of Judaism in that era, Josephus knows whereof he speaks. During his years of youthful exploration he aligned himself alternately with the Sadducees and the Pharisees and also with the Essenes, a quasi-monastic community of mainly celibate men who lived out in the desert, perhaps by the settlement at Qumran, near where the Dead Sea Scrolls were discovered in the 1940s and '50s.

There is much debate over whether the Essenes authored the scrolls and whether they lived at Qumran, but their existence and influence are in no doubt. They were an ascetic community focused on living simple lives marked by chastity, poverty, and religious study. They "cultivate seriousness," Josephus writes with obvious admiration, "shun the pleasures as vice" and "consider self-control and not succumbing to the passions virtue."

At the age of sixteen, Josephus writes, he joined the Essenes for three years: "I consigned myself to hardship, and underwent great difficulties, and went through them all. Nor did I content myself with the trying of these three only, for when I was informed that one whose name was Bannus lived in the desert, and used no other clothing than what grew upon trees, and had no other food than what grew of its own accord, and bathed himself in cold water frequently, both night and day, to purify himself, I imitated him in those things, and continued with him three years."

Little wonder that Josephus writes about John the Baptist with sympathy, or that many have argued that John, who appears to be so similar to Bannus, must have been an Essene. Yet Meier argues that "the Qumran connection, especially the romantic picture of John being raised in a prep school in the Judean desert, can be overdone." And Ben Witherington, a New Testament scholar at Asbury Theological Seminary, notes that "what's different about [John] is that he comes out of that community and he becomes a lone soul figure, calling other people to repentance, ordinary people to repentance."

In fact, several traits mark John off from the Essenes, and from other Jewish variants of the time. These include his focus on a one-time baptism, his outreach to all of Judaism, and his relative disregard for the niceties of Jewish laws and customs.

True, the practice of baptizing was not wholly unfamiliar. "Indeed, immersion in water was one of the primary ways in which Jews could cleanse themselves through ritual purity in order to qualify themselves for participation in the Temple," says Garroway. "But in Jewish circles, there was also the notion that some kind of cleansing with water could also remove the stain of moral sin. This actually goes all the way back to the prophets Isaiah, Jeremiah, and Ezekiel, who use immersion in water as a metaphor for transforming oneself morally and returning to God. So I suspect that John understood his baptism along the lines of some kind of moral transformation that would prepare Jews for the end times judgment which he considered to be imminent."

Yet John's style of baptizing might be better described more actively: as "dunking" rather than traditional self-immersion in a pool, said Liz Carmichael of St. John's College at Oxford, in a 2011 conference on the Baptist. "In doing the dunking, immersing other people in the water of the Jordan or of a spring, John seems to have introduced something new." In addition, no one else at the time was known by the name Baptist or Baptizer, as John was.

Third, it became obvious that John was bigger than Jesus—at least at first. "I think it's very clear that during their lifetimes, John the Baptist was much more successful than Jesus," says Candida Moss, a professor of early Christianity and ancient Judaism at Notre Dame. "It might seem to us today obvious that Jesus is more important, but at the time, if we'd been alive in first-century Palestine, we would know the name of John the Baptist but we might not know the name of Jesus."

Jesus, following the custom of the day, apparently sought out a religious community—maybe the Essenes, as Josephus later would—and a mentor in John. Yet that context would later prove embarrassing as Jesus's followers tried to explain his uniqueness. That's also why the gospel passages on the Baptist seem to indicate a clear progression. In Mark, as Joan Taylor says, "Jesus is just kind of swept up in this great avalanche of people going to the River Jordan, so that's the reason he's there." Then, in Matthew, John the Baptist protests that, no, Jesus should be baptizing *him*. Luke then links the Baptist by blood to Jesus, by giving the story of the cousins meeting in the womb, so to speak, and by doing so, embeds the Baptist into Jesus's story.

The Gospel of John, more than that of Matthew, Luke, or Mark, finally elevates Jesus as the Christ and has John the Baptist stressing once again, in case there is any doubt, that he is not the Messiah but that Jesus is. In John's gospel, says Mark Goodacre, professor of New Testament and Christian origins at Duke University, the Baptist "is not the prophet, he is not Elijah. He is simply someone who prepares the way for Jesus."

"The Gospels are trying in different ways to decrease the role of John," Goodacre says. "We know that John was hugely popular. We know that many people must have thought of him as a prophet. And one of the things the Gospel writers are trying to do is really a kind of a damage-limitation exercise, to make him solely Jesus's forerunner, and not give him any independent identity of his own." Paul had to do much the same, as recorded in Acts, when he went to Ephesus and found disciples who had not been baptized in the name of Jesus but "into John's baptism" only. Paul quickly sets this aright, informing them that John was only a herald of the Son of God, providing a baptism of repentance, while Jesus offered a baptism of the Holy Spirit—which Paul then administers.

No matter how much the Gospel writers or others try to diminish John's role or contextualize it in the larger Jesus story, however, it still begs a central question: why did Jesus need to be baptized? "If anything, shouldn't the Son of God be doing the baptizing?" says Fr. James Martin, a Jesuit priest and author of *Jesus: A Pilgrimage*.

In the Gospel of Matthew, John asks Jesus the same question, and Jesus provides an answer: "Let it be so now; for it is proper for us in this way to fulfill all righteousness." Then John agrees to baptize him.

What does Jesus's response mean? As Martin says, "It is an obscure answer that may have confused both John the Baptist and the early readers of Matthew's gospel."

The great Protestant theologian Karl Barth posited that because Jesus came to take on the sins of the world, no one was in greater need of baptism. Martin speculates that Jesus felt it was important that he go through what the others had, and to identify himself with the "good fruit" of John's preaching. Perhaps Jesus knew he needed to take some ritual, public step to launch his ministry, which is what came next.

Martin also points to a more compelling reason: "Jesus decided to enter even more deeply into the human condition." It is not that the sinless Jesus *needed* baptism, but it was "an act of solidarity, a human act from the Son of God, who casts his lot with the people of his time." At his baptism at the Jordan River, Jesus symbolically, and physically, waited his turn with his people.

As Martin puts it, "God stood in line."

The central dogma of Christianity is the Incarnation, the belief that God became man, and suffered and died with, and for, all people, good, bad, or indifferent. It is perhaps the most affecting claim Christianity makes, but it is also a belief that has caused great consternation and opposition. Some would see John the Baptist's position as a kind of elder brother and mentor to Jesus as undermining belief in what Jesus's followers believed about him. Yet perhaps Jesus's submission and immersion into the community, and into the River Jordan, were further evidence of his identification with humanity.

WHY THE JESUS MOVEMENT SUCCEEDED AND THE BAPTIST'S DID NOT

Yet, as John the Baptist prophesied, he himself would decrease while Jesus would increase. That prediction certainly came true. Still, why was the movement Jesus started successful—apart from his divinely ordained role—while John's withered? There are four main reasons:

One, Jesus rose from the dead; John did not.

"It's the Resurrection that really singles out Jesus as something completely different," says Taylor. John "always wanted to be a reformer within Judaism, he wanted to call Jews to a righteous path in anticipation of this transformation." He made no claims about himself as anything more than a prophet. "Following John's death, a lot of his followers may have migrated over to the Jesus movement because, unlike Jesus, when John died, he stayed dead," says Geoffrey Smith, a professor of early Christianity at the University of Texas at Austin. "They might also have perceived a connection between the two movements."

Two, as Ben Witherington puts it, "Jesus performs miracles. John performs baptisms. Two different kinds of ministry." Both were important. The gospels note that Judas was presumably among the disciples whom Jesus sent out healing the sick and casting out demons. The early Church Fathers also noted, as Augustine did, that "even wicked men can perform some miracles that the saints cannot," and that one's way of life is the key test.

Three, the miracles surely helped convey Jesus's message, and he used miracles to accomplish another goal that differentiated him from the Baptist: he created a community around him, and for others to share in. In fact, when Jesus heard the news that John had been killed, he was clearly upset—whether out of grief or foreboding over his own fate, or both—and sought to withdraw "to a deserted place by himself," as the Gospel of Matthew records it.

Yet the crowds who had gathered around him insisted on following him, and Jesus "had compassion for them and cured their sick." Later that evening, seeing them hungry and without food, he performed the miracle of the feeding of the five thousand, multiplying a few loaves and fishes to feed the crowds.

John the Baptist, on the other hand, was more of a loner who did not seem interested in establishing a following. "Rather, the Baptist's main concern was to direct a call to all Israel to repent and share in his baptism," says Meier. "The vast majority of those baptized seemed to have returned to their homes." A few hung around with the Baptist, Meier says, but they seemed to come and go as they liked, and his greatest devotees migrated to the Jesus movement after John was killed. The Baptist was more of a classic prophet, Bible scholar Ben Meyer once observed, preaching conversion first and community second. "The daring of Jesus' initiative," Meyer writes, "lay in its reversal of this structure: communion first, conversion second."

One of the most intriguing recruits to the Jesus camp may have been a woman named Joanna, who was later named by Luke as one of the women Jesus healed and who, along with Mary Magdalene, was one of several women who supported the early Jesus movement "out of their own means." Joanna is also mentioned as the wife of Chuza, who managed Herod's royal household. Hence she likely had the inside scoop on the lifestyle Herod led, and on the events surrounding the Baptist's execution. This may explain why the gospel accounts have more details about John's death than Josephus provides.

The fourth and final reason the movement Jesus started was successful and John's was not was that Jesus—or at least his followers—set out to evangelize the whole world. Whether it was the result a divine command or a savvy marketing strategy or a bit of both, it worked.

The bottom line is that John's was different from the other movements in Judaism at that time, and Jesus was different from John. If the Jesus movement was more successful in terms of growth, John had an afterlife of sorts that Jesus could not rival. His relics, pieces of his body venerated by believers, were dispersed throughout Christendom as the reverence for the martyrs grew into the cult of the saints.

"THE VERY SPECIAL DEAD"

"Of all religions, Christianity is the one most concerned with dead bodies," Robert Bartlett writes at the start of his engrossing survey of sainthood, *Why Can the Dead Do Such Great Things?* The title is a line from St. Augustine of Hippo, a fourth-century bishop from North Africa and one of the Church's foundational writers and thinkers. It was Augustine who summed up the divergent views of "the very special dead," as author Peter Brown has called the saints: "We pray *for* our dead but *to* the martyrs," Augustine wrote.

In both cases, the attitude of holy reverence of saints and martyrs would be mirrored by a decidedly different treatment of their bodies, a treatment that by the year 200 CE set Christians apart from Jews, from the Greek and Roman pagans, and, later, from Muslims. Like their Jewish forebears, the early Christians believed the corpse should be treated with respect. This is evident from the gospels themselves, as the followers of John the Baptist took care to recover and bury his body, just as Jesus's disciples would later do with his corpse. As per the customs of the Abrahamic tradition, immediate burial was preferred, cemeteries were sacred ground, and the tombs of holy men were treated as pilgrimage sites. Yet Christians changed the equation when they incorporated the dead, and pieces of their bodies, into their daily lives and living spaces, constructing churches over tombs or decreeing that a saint's body or some physical relic had to be embedded in an altar.

"Moving the remains of the dead into the city churches broke the ancient taboo demarcating the places of the living and the dead, and disregarded deeply felt legal and moral prohibitions on both the disturbance of human remains and on the presence of the dead in the city," Bartlett writes. "It was a development that marked off Christianity sharply from pagan and Jewish religions, which knew the difference between a place of worship and a cemetery, and regarded the cult of corporeal relics as ghoulish."

One of the earliest examples of the Christian devotion to the body of a holy person was the account of the martyrdom of Polycarp, the aged bishop of Smyrna, in modern-day Turkey, which took place sometime after the year 150 CE. Polycarp was burned at the stake in a Roman arena for refusing to light incense to the emperor. Afterward, the Christians in his flock took care to collect his ashes and remains "to have a share in his holy flesh."

What really distinguished Christians from Jews and Muslims was how Christians broke up corpses willy-nilly and moved the pieces here and there—and often fought among themselves over who had the rights to a relic. The earliest recording of this devotion dates to the year 300 CE in the account of a wealthy woman in Carthage who used to kiss the bone of a martyr before receiving the Eucharist. The woman, Lucilla, was in fact rebuked by the local deacon. The Roman authorities were not enamored of the growing practice, either. An imperial law of 386 CE ruled that "no one should divide up or trade in a martyr."

Yet there was no stopping the devotion. Early medieval accounts are full of tales of thefts of bits and bones of the saints. St. Nicholas of Bari, who would later be revered in a more secular fashion as St. Nick, or Santa Claus, had his ribs, arms, and teeth pilfered in the eleventh century by zealous monks. Bishop Hugh of Lincoln, offered a chance to venerate the arm of Mary Magdalene at a French monastery, cut away the silk sheath encasing the treasured relic and, to the horror of the monks looking on, tried to cut off a piece for himself. He then set to work on the Magdalene's index finger with his teeth, "first with the incisors and finally with the molars," gnawing away until he successfully broke off two bits.

Indeed, as the eminent Cambridge University church historian Eamon Duffy has written, by the early Middle Ages, "relics and relic fragments were distributed by monasteries, bishops, and popes as marks of favor or tokens of esteem, missionaries carried them with them into pagan territory to protect and overawe, soldiers bore them into battle as an army of heavenly auxiliaries. Church, monasteries, and cities gained power, wealth, and prestige from the possession of notable relics, and fairs and markets to mark the saints' feast days became crucial to the prosperity of whole regions."

Relics were increasingly associated with miracles, and if holy men and women had worked no wonders in their earthly lives—as John the Baptist apparently did not—that didn't stop people from believing that their remains produced miraculous healings, visions, and the like.

To be sure, the early centuries of Christianity certainly offered up plenty of martyrs, and hence relics, given the imperial persecutions that continued off and on until the emperor Constantine effectively legalized the faith in 313 CE with the Edict of Milan. (It wasn't until 380 CE that Constantine's successors made Christianity the official state religion, a stunning triumph for what was once considered an inconsequential sect, but an altar-and-throne alliance that in many ways would haunt the faith in later centuries.)

Still, there were never enough very special dead to populate the rapidly expanding number of churches, and the trade in sacred body parts (or their facsimiles) began in earnest early on. Around 401 CE, St. Augustine criticized monks who "offer for sale pieces of the martyrs," yet the black market trade grew along with the veneration of saints and their relics. An occasional voice of protest arose, such as that of the brave French monk Guibert de Nogent, who in the twelfth century wrote a treatise on relics in which he related examples of bones and bodies passed off as the relics of saints—for a price, of course.

"I can recall so many like deeds in all parts that I lack time and strength to tell them here," Guibert writes. "For fraudulent bargains are made, not so much in whole bodies as in limbs or portions of limbs, common bones being sold as relics of the saints. The men who do this are plainly such of whom Saint Paul speaks, that they suppose gain to be godliness; for they make into a mere excrement of their money-bags the things which (if they but knew it) would tend to the salvation of their souls."

In *The Canterbury Tales*, Geoffrey Chaucer's fourteenth-century send-up of English society and the Church of the day, the pilgrims on a journey to Canterbury encounter the Pardoner, an unscrupulous seller of church pardons who also claims to have a bunch of holy relics (some of which are pig bones), which he tries to foist on the pilgrims. Such stories were apparently not too far from the truth, and helped fuel the zeal of the Protestant reformers who would try to put an end to much of the cult of relics over the next few centuries. They weren't entirely successful, and in his 1869 book, *The Innocents Abroad*, about a trip through Europe and the Holy Land, American humorist Mark Twain found in the various relics much fodder for his characteristically tart observances. In a chapel in Genoa, coming upon another set of the Baptist's relics (his ashes and the chain that purportedly held him in Herod's prison), Twain feigns confusion: "We did not desire to disbelieve these statements, and yet we could not feel certain that they were correct—partly because we could have broken that chain, and so could St. John, and partly because we had seen St. John's ashes before, in another church. We could not bring ourselves to think St. John had two sets of ashes."

A SAINT FOR OUR TIMES?

Indeed, John the Baptist proved to be especially fertile in terms of relics, and enduring as far as devotion. Part of this could be chalked up to the fact that he was beheaded. "Of all the body parts, the human head has the most complex significance," writes Bartlett, "as the locus of all five senses, the most easily identifiable marker of personal identity." So it was no surprise that head relics were highly prized, but also the source of great scandal.

The earliest mention of John the Baptist's head appears in writings near the end of the fourth century, when Christians believed they had located his tomb at Sebaste, near modern-day Nablus in the West Bank. The ancient writers say that the monastery where the saint's remains were housed was attacked in 361 CE by pagans during a revival of the old religion—remember, Christianity was newly regnant—and the Baptist's relics were damaged in the fire. The remnants, apparently including his head, were gathered by the monks and sent to Egypt and other places for safekeeping. In 391, as Georges Kazan wrote in a 2011 paper on the Baptist, the emperor Theodosius had the head relic taken to Constantinople, where it was enclosed in a small casket or urn, wrapped in a cloak of imperial purple, and transported to the Hebdomon, just outside Constantinople, where Theodosius built a large church to hold it. The description of the small casket, interestingly, closely tracks the reliquary that was unearthed more than sixteen hundred years later, on the Black Sea island of Sveti Ivan.

Then again, there was the so-called Second Finding of the Baptist's Head in the year 453. The Baptist himself is said to have revealed the location of the relic in a dream to monks during their visit to Jerusalem. "They discovered the head, still wrapped in a cloth sack, within what is described as the former palace of King Herod the Great," Kazan wrote. That was only the start of the picaresque tale: "As they journeyed into Syria on their way home, a potter who had been travelling with them, made off with the head to his home city of Emesa"—modern-day Homs, in Syria—"also under the instructions of the Baptist, who had appeared to him in a dream. The relic was still concealed within its bag, and the potter is said not to have known what this contained. Eventually, before he died, he placed it in a sealed urn and left it to his sister, who had no knowledge of what it was."

A priest finally obtained it and, on his expulsion from the city for heresy, left it buried in a cave that later came to be used by other monks, who discovered it, thanks to another vision, in 453. During the subsequent Arab invasions, this head was also taken to Constantinople, where it supplanted the head recovered by Theodosius as the true one in the hearts of the faithful. The Western crusaders who sacked the city in 1204 also found the head still in place.

Not to be outdone, a French pretender emerged in the tenth century with a claim that the Baptist's head was in fact in a monastery in Saint-Jean-d'Angély, near Bordeaux. That claim prompted the monk Guibert to protest that, no, "there were not two John the Baptists, nor one with two heads!" That didn't stop the French from cherishing their head of the Baptist, or the Baptist's head and other remains from multiplying on their journeys across the centuries.

Numerous churches and shrines and mosques claim to have various arms—important because they were used to baptize Jesus—and various fingers are housed in various places, including one in the Nelson-Atkins Museum of Art in Kansas City, Missouri.

A church in Rome claims to have the head of the Baptist, and Islamic tradition holds that John's head is in the Umayyad Mosque in Damascus, the site of a former church. A cathedral was built in Amiens, in northern France, around 1200 to house the Baptist's head, which was reportedly brought by a crusader returning from the sack of Constantinople. Also, churches in Munich, in Germany, and Mount Athos, in Greece, also claim to have parts of the Baptist's skull, while another piece of the head remains in Istanbul, and still another in a church in Egypt.

The town of Halifax in West Yorkshire, in Great Britain, even has the Baptist's head on the official coat of arms, thanks to a legend from the sixteenth century that says the first religious settlers to the area brought with them the "holy face" of John the Baptist— *holy* rendered *halig* in Old English, and *face* as *fax*, hence Halifax.

The only place that seems oddly bereft of a relic of the Baptist is Florence, where John is revered as the city's patron saint. In 1411 it was rumored that Pope John XXIII—who would be deposed and denounced as a false claimant to the Throne of St. Peter during the Great Western Schism—had a skull of the Baptist that he was offering for sale for the enormous price of fifty thousand florins. Negotiations failed to bring the price down, and the buyer had to settle for a finger. A plot to steal the head also failed, and the Florentines were especially upset when Pope Pius II later donated an entire arm of the Baptist to Siena, his hometown and Florence's bitter Tuscan rival.

Little wonder that an 1881 article in the *New York Times* that sniffed at "the silly worship of relics" recounted the story of two rival French monasteries that each claimed to have a head of the Baptist. They explained this away by saying that the first skull belonged to John as a man and the smaller skull was from "when he was a boy." Alas, Kazan said this story is apocryphal and appears to come from a footnote to a translation of John Calvin's *A Treatise on Relics.* (Calvin was not in favor of them.) It shows how easily claims about the Baptist's relics could proliferate, even among skeptics.

The problem with all this colorful history is that, however entertaining, it can understandably prompt a mockery of the importance, and power, of relics, for believers and nonbelievers. John the Baptist's bones provide a window onto a crucial chapter in history, and into a legacy shared by Jews, Christians, and Muslims.

In fact, what is often obscured by our fascination with the Baptist's relics, or his relationship to Jesus, is his own unique role: John is a Christian saint, but he is also pre-Christian. He died before Jesus sacrificed himself on the cross, and later theologians argued that because of that timing, John went down to hell, not straight to heaven, as one would assume. The third-century Church Father Origen, among others, sought to mitigate John's fate by preaching that the Baptist's role in the netherworld was the same as it was here on earth: to announce the coming of Jesus. So when Jesus descended to hell, as the gospels say he did, between the Crucifixion on Good Friday and the Resurrection on Easter Sunday, he rescued for eternity all the righteous who had died since the beginning of the world—including John the Baptist.

This border-straddling role makes John the Baptist something of a bridge among traditions, and across the ages. Eastern Orthodox Christianity views John as the last of the Old Testament prophets as well as a Christian saint, a man of the Jewish world and of the Christian Church. Muslims, as we saw, revere John the Baptists as a prophet, and so do those of the Baha'i faith. The small community of Mandaeans, which formed in the first centuries after Jesus in what we now call Iraq, even view John the Baptist, not Jesus, as the true Messiah. His appeal as a prophet is as old as the Baptist himself, and endures to the present day.

John the Baptist was known as John the Precursor, John the

Forerunner, John the Immerser. Just as important, though, he was John the Truth-Teller. In eleventh-century England, two churchmen debated whether Christians revered as saints should be considered martyrs if they were killed trying to protect their people during an invasion. In the Christian tradition, a martyr is one who is killed for defending the faith, for refusing to deny Christ. One of these churchmen, Anselm, a future archbishop of Canterbury, replied to his correspondent that, yes, those saints were martyrs because if they were willing to die rather than fail to shield the people, then they would certainly have died rather than deny Christ, seen as a much more serious sin.

To make his point, Anselm noted that John the Baptist was killed not for refusing to deny Christ but for denouncing Herod's sinfulness. "What distinction is there between dying for justice and dying for truth? Moreover, since by the witness of holy writ . . . Christ is truth and justice, he who dies for truth and justice dies for Christ."

That is why John the Baptist can be invoked as a forerunner of latter-day martyrs to the truth, such as the Lutheran pastor and Nazi resister Dietrich Bonhoeffer, Mahatma Gandhi, Martin Luther King Jr., and Salvadorean archbishop Óscar Romero. There is a universal quality to John, "the voice of one crying out in the wilderness," that commands respect in every day and age. John's model is perhaps especially powerful, and poignant, today, as stories and videos from the land where he preached tell of so many who suffer the same grisly fate he did—which is why he may be the perfect saint for today.

TWO

THE JAMES OSSUARY

The Hand of God or the Crime of the Century?

The James Ossuary is a two-thousand-year-old burial box that—so its inscription reports—held the bones of Jesus's brother James. But is that engraving a forgery? *(Getty Images)*

It was billed as the Trial of the Century, and when the verdict was delivered in a Jerusalem court in March 2012, the wide world of biblical antiquities, and those who police them, held its collective breath: the State of Israel had accused Israeli antiquities collector Oded Golan and several of his associates of forging biblical artifacts, prime among them the James Ossuary, a first-century CE burial box whose Aramaic inscription identified it as the tomb of "James, son of Joseph, brother of Jesus." To many, this was not the trial of a forger, but of humanity's desire to find evidence that faith was based in reality, with the James Ossuary the most direct physical connection to Jesus of Nazareth the world had ever seen.

In December 2004, Oded Golan and four others were charged with eighteen separate counts of forgery, fraud, and obtaining money through fraud, and were accused of forging, among hundreds of items, the James Ossuary and a stone tablet recording repairs by King Jehoash to Solomon's Temple in Jerusalem. The trial opened in the Jerusalem District Court of Judge Aharon Farkash in the autumn of 2005 and lasted a biblical seven years, partly due to the mechanics of the Israeli judicial system, which adjudicates by judge alone, and as a result, spreads both judges and lawyers thin, and partly because of the case's staggering complexity. In 116 sessions, the court heard a parade of 133 expert witnesses; looked at 200 exhibits, many of them arcane works of biblical scholarship; and compiled nearly 12,000 pages of witness testimony. The prosecution's summation of the case against Golan alone ran 653 pages.

When Judge Farkash retired in October 2010 to consider his verdict, many scholars agreed with the assessment of Professor Aldo Shemesh, an isotope expert at Israel's Weizmann Institute of Science, who had appeared for the defense. "Scientific debates should be discussed and resolved in peer-reviewed literature and scientific conferences, not in court," he said.

Yet the James Ossuary *had* wound up in criminal court—the first time an Israeli criminal court had been asked to rule on a case of antiquities forgery. Now that the trial was over, the world could only wait for the verdict: would the James Ossuary disintegrate in the wake of guilt or take on tantalizing new life in the halo of an acquittal? Either way, the stakes were extraordinarily high.

Could this ancient stone box really provide our first physical link with Jesus and his family? Or could it be one of the most sophisticated forgeries of our time? At the heart of the matter, one question remained constant: who was James? What did he do, aside from being the brother of Jesus, to merit an inscription on an ossuary that still captivates the world?

"JAMES, SON OF JOSEPH, BROTHER OF JESUS"

The New Testament tells us that Jesus had brothers and sisters. The Gospels of both Mark and Matthew detail the names of James, Joseph (or Joses), Judas, and Simon, along with unnamed sisters. Yet how were these siblings related to Jesus?

"The relationship between James and Jesus is very complicated," says Fr. James Martin, S.J, author of *Jesus: A Pilgrimage*. "He's called clearly the brother of the Lord, and the Greek uses the common word for brother. Catholics believe in Mary's perpetual virginity, so the way I've always looked at it, which I think is very reasonable, is that James and the other brothers were Joseph's children from a prior marriage. Joseph would have been older and Mary was younger, so I see them in a sense as stepbrothers."

Scholars and theologians have wrestled with how the doctrine of perpetual virginity can allow for Mary to have had other children, and as with so many facets of Christianity, they've come up with different answers. The Eastern Orthodox Church believes that the brothers and sisters were born to Joseph from a previous marriage and are therefore Jesus's stepsiblings, Protestants think that Mary gave birth to the siblings after she bore Jesus, and Roman Catholicism cites them as cousins of Jesus or stepsiblings, born before Jesus to another mother, which would preserve Mary's virginity.

"There are two big problems about Jesus having siblings, for Roman Catholics, for Eastern Orthodox Christians," says Notre Dame's Candida Moss. "Mary's supposed to be a perpetual virgin, so if Mary is having other children that aren't the sons of God, then suddenly that's out of the window. And it was really that idea, that Mary was a perpetual virgin, that really kicked Jesus's siblings off stage in the history of Christianity."

Kicked off the stage in Christian history, perhaps, but not out of the gospels. Matthew and Mark both recount how Jesus returns to his hometown of Nazareth, a tiny hamlet around ninety miles north of Jerusalem, and provokes the locals with his dazzle:

On the sabbath he began to teach in the synagogue, and many who heard him were astounded. They said, "Where did this man get all this? What is this wisdom that has been given to him? What deeds of power are being done by his hands! Is not this the carpenter, the son of Mary and brother of James and Joses and Judas and Simon, and are not his sisters here with us?" And they took offense at him. Then Jesus said to them, "Prophets are not without honor, except in their home-town, and among their own kin, and in their own house."

The house into which Jesus was born was humble: his father, Joseph, was a carpenter, likely working to repair the mud huts, lintels, and tables within the subsistence economy that was Nazareth, work supplemented by the various construction projects in the nearby Roman garrison town of Sepphoris; his mother, Mary, was keeping a Jewish household and raising a devout Jewish family of at least seven children.

The only biblical story we have of Jesus as a youth comes from the Gospel of Luke, when Joseph and Mary take the twelve-year-old Jesus to Jerusalem for Passover, and then forget about him when they and their fellow travelers depart for home. When Mary and Joseph return to fetch Jesus, they find him sitting in the Temple conversing with the rabbis at a level of sophistication such that "all who heard him were amazed at his understanding and his answers."

When his parents saw him they were astonished; and his mother said to him, "Child, why have you treated us like this? Look, your father and I have been searching for you in great anxiety." He said to them, "Why were you searching for me? Did you not know that I must be in my Father's house?" But they did not understand what he said to them. Then he went down with them and came to Nazareth, and was obedient to them. His mother treasured all these things in her heart.

This astonishing parental neglect can be seen as a reverse biblical *Home Alone* moment that proves Jesus was the baby of the family, remaining an afterthought in the hurly-burly of departure for home from teeming Jerusalem at Passover. Ben Witherington, however, thinks that it proves the opposite. "There is no mention of other brothers and sisters going up to Jerusalem to the festival with them, which surely they would have done if they were older than Jesus . . . Since the New Testament gives no contrary evidence . . . James was Jesus's younger brother and grew up in the same home with him."

There may be no other evidence in the New Testament about the young fraternal lives of Jesus and James, but there certainly is in the "Infancy Gospels," a series of parables imagining what Jesus's young life was like that surfaced in the second century CE. The faithful of the growing religion yearned for stories of the early life of Jesus, while they awaited his return to establish his kingdom. The Protoevangelium (or "pre-Gospel") of James, purportedly written by Jesus's brother James, chronicles the birth and upbringing of Mary, and establishes that Joseph already had sons when he took the Virgin as his betrothed. It is the oldest source describing Mary's perpetual virginity and, as a result, places James in the family hierarchy as the older brother of Jesus.

The Infancy Gospel of Thomas also places James ahead of Jesus, but it is the younger brother who comes to miraculous aid of the older: "And while they were gathering the sticks, an abominable snake bit James on his hand. And as he sprawled out on the ground and lay dying, the boy Jesus ran to James and did nothing but blow on the bite and immediately the bite was healed. And the snake was destroyed."

This union of James and Jesus, with the younger brother saving the elder and smiting the image of Satan at the same time, creates a special relationship between the two, one that will be reflected in both the early Christian Church, and the James Ossuary.

"By bringing James into the story, what occurs is that James, who is known to have been an important leader, is put there with Jesus from the very beginning," says Rev. Bruce Chilton, Bernard

Iddings Bell professor of religion at Bard College, "so that we see an organic connection between them, not only in terms of their relationship but also in terms of their common experience."

Despite this early Christian emphasis on James, his story, to most Christians, remained obscure until, almost two thousand years after his death, the discovery of his burial box lit him up on the world stage. Yet could the Ossuary discovered and presented to the world by Oded Golan actually belong to the blood brother of Jesus? And just how had Oded Golan, a secular Israeli, come to possess it?

"I DIDN'T SEE ANYTHING SPECIAL in this ossuary and frankly I didn't even know that Jesus Christ had brothers or sisters," says Oded Golan, who was born to a prominent and affluent Israeli family in Tel Aviv in 1951.

Golan showed archaeological curiosity and a keen eye at a young age, discovering a crucial piece of Jewish history as a ten-year-old. The State of Israel was only three years older than he when his parents took him and his brother on an excursion to the Sea of Galilee to visit Tel Hazor. In the second millennium BCE, Hazor was the biggest city in what would become Israel, but by 1961 it had returned to the earth—and the earth gave back.

While walking with his parents, Golan found a small clay fragment with inscriptions on it that he recognized as cuneiform, one of humanity's earliest forms of writing, characterized by wedge shapes etched onto clay tablets or pots. Golan wrote a postcard describing his find to Yigael Yadin, an archaeologist who attained heroic stature in Israel not just for his service in the Jewish paramilitary force Haganah during the War of Independence against the British, but as the man who had discovered King Solomon's Gate at Megiddo (the site of Armageddon), about fifteen miles southwest of Nazareth, as well as the hilltop fortress of Masada, where, according to the Jewish-Roman historian Josephus, nearly a thousand Jewish rebels and their families committed mass suicide rather than surrender to the besieging Romans after the destruction of the Temple in Jerusalem in 70 CE.

To the astonishment of Golan's parents, the great Yadin showed up at their Tel Aviv home asking for "Mr. Golan." When he learned that Golan was just a child, Yadin was undeterred. After examining the fragment, he declared that it was part of a dictionary, one housed at the palace of Yavin, king of Hazor, who is mentioned in the Book of Joshua.

Golan was unable to remember exactly where he found the fragment, but imagined where he would put his palace if he were king of Hazor. He pointed to a place on Yadin's photograph of the site, and mirabile dictu, years later discovered that Hebrew University was digging at that very spot, and found the palace.

Oded Golan claims it's less an issue of memory than of ignorance when trying to establish the bona fides of the James Ossuary, whose provenance has been one of its problems. He bought the ossuary when he was studying industrial engineering at the Technion, a technical university in Haifa, in the 1970s.

"I was told by the dealer who sold me—it's quite a long time ago—that it was found near Silwan, a village which is very near to the Temple Mount in Jerusalem," Golan recalls. "I asked, 'Did you find it together with some bottles or some oil lamps or something like that?' and the dealer said, 'No, that's all what I got,' and that's what I bought. So it came by itself and that's what I know about it, not much more."

As an antiquities collector of international standing, whose collection is substantial—"I have actually the biggest private collection of ossuaries in Israel, probably in the world," he says—Golan is certainly aware of the Antiquities Law of the State of Israel of 1978, which effectively nationalized the country's antiquities in an effort to staunch their illegal flow.

Although anyone convicted of breaking the law can go to prison for two years and pay a hefty fine, the law can easily be avoided due to the fact that any artifact unearthed, sold, or bequeathed before 1978 can be legally sold so long as it is registered with the state. Antiquities dealers simply give a false registration numbers to looted goods, and anyone with the desire and the discretionary cash can pick up an ossuary in the maze of antiquities shops in the Old City of Jerusalem.

Ossuaries like the one that might have contained the bones of James were common in the first century CE for practical reasons. King Herod, the puppet ruler installed by the Romans, undertook extensive construction of Jerusalem, with his renovation of the Second Temple being the centerpiece—not only of Jewish religious life, but of the city itself, its great gilded roof glittering in the Mediterranean sunlight as a beacon to the faithful who would find the Temple a place of awe, both literally and spiritually.

The city of Jerusalem was small, an area of about one and a quarter square miles, divided by the Temple into the wealthy Upper City and the humbler Lower City and surrounded by a thick stone wall.

"We have data that in about 20 BCE, in the Herodian period, there were about thirty-eight thousand people in Jerusalem," says Camil Fuchs, head of the Department of Statistics at Tel Aviv University's School of Mathematical Sciences, who not only studies ancient demographics, but also does political polls for the Israeli newspaper *Haaretz*. "At the destruction of the Temple, at 70 CE, there were about eighty-two thousand people. Based on those data, we could assess how many, what was the growth rate and how many people died in this time, that could be interred."

As the population of Jerusalem expanded, space for burial plots shrank, and in the first century CE, the ossuary offered the perfect solution to the problem. "According to Jewish custom, the dead are to be buried outside the perimeter of human habitation, so you don't bury the dead in the same place where people are living. That ring of tombs around the ancient city of Jerusalem was a product of this belief," says Byron McCane, an archaeologist and professor of religion at Wofford College, in Spartanburg, South Carolina. McCane, an "Indiana Jones–esque" seeker of truth in the ancient world, has spent his career examining the Bible through the lens of science.

"A Jewish funeral at the time of Jesus actually lasted a full year," McCane continues. "Having placed the body in the tomb, the family waits until there's nothing left but the bones. And typically we read that on the first anniversary of the death, members of the family—and only members of the family, there's no procession—come back to the tomb and they gather the bones of their deceased loved ones. Those bones are placed in an ossuary, the ossuary is marked with the name of the deceased and then placed somewhere in the tomb. Perhaps in a loculus niche, perhaps on a shelf. And at that point the process of burial had ended."

An ossuary is a stone box hollowed out of the limestone common to the land surrounding Jerusalem. About the size of a toilet cistern, the ossuary had to be large enough to house the femur, the skull, and the pelvis, the largest bones of the human body. Oded Golan believed he had bought one of the thousands of ossuaries that have been excavated from tombs, legally and otherwise, and saw nothing extraordinary about the one that would catapult him first onto the global stage and then into an Israeli courtroom.

"I couldn't decipher the inscription, so I couldn't even understand the meaning of the inscription Ya'akov—James—the brother of Jesus," says Golan, "but even if I noticed it I wouldn't even think that Jesus Christ had siblings. I didn't see anything special in this ossuary."

In April 2002, Golan invited André Lemaire, a professor of Semitic writing at the Sorbonne, to drop by his Tel Aviv apartment and have a look at some antiquities. Lemaire recalled that Golan showed him photos of several ossuaries, but one in particular caught his eye, an ossuary engraved in clear cursive Aramaic, the language that Jesus and his fellow Jews spoke. It read, "Ya'akov, bar-Yosef, akhui di Yeshua"—or "James, son of Joseph, brother of Jesus."

While Golan wasn't aware that Jesus had a brother, Lemaire, as both a scholar and a former Jesuit priest, certainly knew. All his academic life he'd been looking to strike the "big one," and maybe this was it. If the inscription on the side of Golan's ossuary referred to the brother of Jesus, then it would be a cataclysmic moment in Christian history: the first physical evidence of the historical Jesus.

Though the inscription was clear, the first part, "James, son of Joseph," seemed to have been inscribed by a different hand than the "brother of Jesus." The latter inscription could have been written by a different scribe, coming on to the late shift, as it were. Or it could have been added by a forger much later. Now that the ossuary could well be the most important Christian find since the Empress Helena allegedly found the True Cross in the fourth century CE, Golan and Lemaire decided more tests were in order. Indeed, the ossuary needed the test of time, so Golan took it to the Geological Survey of Israel.

Dr. Shimon Ilani was one of the scientists working at the GSI tasked with examining the inscription on the ossuary to see if its patina (the accretion of grit on ancient objects, or more poetically, the accretion of time itself) was consistent with the first century.

Ilani and his team took tiny samples of patina from the ossuary and studied them under a powerful scanning electron microscope (SEM) whose resolution is one nanometer, or one-billionth of a meter.

"We didn't find any clue that this is a modern forgery," says Ilani, "because the patina was very clean—only calcium carbonate, CaCO3." Calcium carbonate is found in many rocks, but especially in limestone. "And we found that the patina is covering the ossuary as well as infiltrated to the letters. And this is very important that you have to know because if the real patina filled the letters means that the letters are from the antiquity."

Ilani and his colleagues also studied the scratches on the ossuary, caused by wear and tear of two millennia in a stone tomb. If the scratches inside the letters had no patina, then forgery would be the reason, but the SEM microscope showed the scientists that even the scratches inside the letters had ancient patina.

Another question now arose. If the ossuary and its inscription were truly as old as Golan believed, what was the possibility that the inscription referred to James the brother of Jesus and not some other James who died at the same time?

Oded Golan went to see the statistical wizard Camil Fuchs and asked him to do some number-crunching time travel: just what was the likelihood that this constellation of names, Joseph, James, and Jesus, would be connected on a first-century CE ossuary?

Fuchs had to take several variables into account in order to calculate the probability: the population of Jerusalem between Jesus's likely birth, in 6 BCE, and the destruction of the Temple in 70 CE; the fact that the names Joseph, James, and Jesus would not be repeated in the same formation within a family as time passed; and the fact that in order to be buried in a tomb, with an inscribed ossuary, the deceased would have to have been affluent and literate or held in such high esteem that his death expenses were paid for by a wealthy admirer.

"My calculations gave the number of 1.71, which is the number of people—their name was James, they had a brother called Jesus, and they had a father called Joseph—who could have been interred in the ossuaries," says Fuchs. "That means that our estimate is about two people that have been with those characteristics or one person who had been with those characteristics. So the combination is quite rare. Could that be these persons that we are talking about? Yes, it could be." Of course, all that under the assumption that the inscription is genuine.

Enter Hershel Shanks, a lawyer with an amateur interest in biblical archaeology so keen that he created the populist magazine *Biblical Archaeology Review*, which has become both a must-read and a bugbear to the world of serious scholarship—Shanks will publish pieces that other, more academically rigorous journals shun. At a news conference in Washington on October 21, 2002, Shanks announced, with his customary flair, that this ossuary was quite possibly connected to Jesus: "This is the first archaeological attestation of Jesus, plus also of Joseph and James, which is kind of mind-boggling," he said.

Oded Golan, a secular Jew still maintaining anonymity, whom Shanks said had bought the ossuary from an Arab dealer for between two hundred and seven hundred dollars, now found himself in possession of an artifact too great—and too valuable—to keep tastefully lit on a shelf in his apartment. Meanwhile, 350 miles northwest, in Canada, lay the perfect stage on which to bring James, brother of Jesus, back into the light of the world.

"THINGS WERE GETTING OUT OF CONTROL WITH JESUS . . ."

When Jesus began his public ministry in around 27 CE, he would have caused turbulence at home, especially if his father, Joseph, was no longer alive, as some scholars believe. "Jesus would have left them, basically in the lurch, to run the family business," says Ben Witherington, "to be artisans on behalf of the family, to work whatever fields they may have had, and this cannot have been a comfortable situation. The village itself was a small village, so tongues would wag about Jesus going off and doing some kind of ministry and leaving his family to take care of business."

Jesus's rabbinical preaching and healing across the Roman-occupied countryside was not unusual in itself, as Roman-ruled Israel was no stranger to messianic Jews, with exorcism, healing, and visions of the divine being part of an occupied people waiting for their deliverance. Jesus, however, was pushing the boundaries of Judaism in shocking ways, and earning negative attention not just from the Romans. The Gospel of Mark relates the story of how Jesus set out to cure the withered hand of a man—and on the Sabbath, no less. This was a great transgression according to his own religion, for the Sabbath was the day of rest, not a day for making magic. So his was an act that directly provoked the religious establishment.

"They watched him to see whether he would cure him on the Sabbath, so that they might accuse him," recounts the Gospel of Mark.

And he said to the man who had the withered hand, "Come forward." Then he said to them, "Is it lawful to do good or to do harm on the Sabbath, to save life or to kill?" But they were silent. He looked around at them with anger; he was grieved at their hardness of heart and said to the man, "Stretch out your hand." He stretched it out, and his hand was restored. The Pharisees went out and immediately conspired with the Herodians against him, how to destroy him.

Jesus's ministry was also negatively affecting his family. "I think there was great concern on the part of Mary and probably the brothers and sisters that things were getting out of control with Jesus," says Witherington. "If Jesus really was not merely an itinerate teacher or preacher or prophet but also a performer of miracles, and if he was healing on the Sabbath, which is a no-no unless it's an emergency, if he was performing exorcisms, then I think when the family heard about Jesus doing these kinds of things, they thought he was 15 degrees shy of plumb."

Indeed, one of the most remarkable Jesus family stories in the gospels comes when Jesus returns to the house where he is staying after he has appointed his twelve apostles. A crowd so large follows him that Jesus and his apostles can't even eat; news of his increasing celebrity reaches his family home, causing alarm. "When his family heard it, they went out to restrain him, for people were saying, 'He has gone out of his mind.'"

When Mary and Jesus's brothers and sisters—James among them, presumably, though not named in the Gospel of Mark—arrive to rescue him, Jesus gives them a chilling rebuff:

> A crowd was sitting around him; and they said to him, "Your mother and your brothers and sisters are outside, asking for you." And he replied, "Who are my mother and my brothers?" And looking at those who sat around him, he said, "Here are my mother and my brothers! Whoever does the will of God is my brother and sister and mother."

Jesus's dismissal of his family would suggest that he had left his brother James behind in his union with a larger spiritual world. "That's a strong statement of how it is that humanity at large all belong to a single family with God, his Father," says Bruce Chilton. "But it's also a rebuke of Jesus's own family; it's a way of saying that that line of connection is no longer determinative for him."

Jesus was now launched on the journey that would lead him in triumph to Jerusalem and, a week later, to a brutal death on the cross. Even though Jesus had rejected his brothers and sisters, it was his brother James who would follow Jesus to Jerusalem—follow him both in ministry and in death.

"THE OSSUARY IS REAL, BUT THE INSCRIPTION IS FAKE . . ."

On November 15, 2002, the James Ossuary made its public debut on the grand stage of the Royal Ontario Museum in Toronto, much to the relief of the museum's organizers, who feared that the exhibition would have to be delayed due to an astonishing reality: the shipping company entrusted by Oded Golan to transport the world's first possible connection to the historical Jesus chose to do so not by encasing it in a stabilized container, but rather, by swathing it in bubble wrap and putting it in a cardboard box. When the ROM curatorial staff opened the ossuary's packing crate, they were alarmed to discover "a latticework of cracks, some of which were new and some of which were extensions of preexisting ones." The cracks were on chunks of the ossuary, which had broken into five pieces.

"I think all of us are very saddened," said ROM director William Thorsell. "A piece like this is a tremendously important piece. I think he [the owner] is going to have to be speaking to the people who packed and shipped it."

Golan's more pressing problem was to speak to his insurers in London to allow the ROM to make repairs before the ossuary, which he had insured for a million dollars, went on display. For five tense days, both the museum and Golan tried to persuade the insurance company to send an adjuster to Toronto, or better still, to use one of the many adjusters who lived in the city. Finally, the insurers dispatched an adjuster from New York, who signed off on the proposed restoration, so the ROM's Ewa Dziadowiec, an expert stone restorer, could repair the damage.

The ROM had collected even the tiniest stone fragments that had fallen from the ossuary in transport and placed them in plastic bags. Dziadowiec set to work fitting the pieces together and gluing them back to the ossuary, using a very strong but water-soluble (and thus reversible) polyvinyl acetate in resin. To fill in areas where pieces of the ossuary had fallen off, she used calcium carbonate, which is the main chemical component of limestone; dry pigments to match the ossuary's color; and polyvinyl alcohol.

The ossuary had an existing crack that had widened during transport, and as it was part of "history," Dziadowiec couldn't contaminate its patina by filling it with glue. So she inserted tiny epoxy pegs to keep the crack from widening further. Once the repairs were done, the ossuary, ironically, was more stable than it had been before its shipping misadventure.

The exhibition at the ROM was such a success in its seven-week run, with crowds lining the chilly winter streets of Toronto to get a glimpse of Jesus history, that Golan applied to the Israel Antiquities Authority, the state's official antiquities bureau, for an extension of his export license, to continue fulfilling humanity's longing to connect with a limestone box possibly connected to Jesus.

The IAA, which had rubber-stamped Golan's original export papers, now said no. The IAA initially thought that Golan's was just another ossuary, and like Golan, it had no knowledge of James, brother of Jesus. Now that it had caught up with the worldwide phenomenon of the limestone burial box, it smelled something "too good to be true," which is the thing every archaeologist yearns, and fears, to find. The IAA, responsible for the import and export of all artifacts from Israel, and the zealous guardian of the country's fourteen thousand archaeological sites, wanted to have a closer look.

"The Antiquities Authority said, well, 'in his application he didn't actually say what it was so we didn't realize it was such an important item that he wanted to send abroad,'" says Matthew Kalman, a British journalist based in Jerusalem who followed the story closely from the beginning and was the only reporter to cover the entire trial of Oded Golan. "And so, when it comes back, we'd like to take a look at it, please, because, if it's so important, then, you know, it'd be nice to have a look at it. They were a bit embarrassed that they didn't know anything about it."

At the time, the IAA was investigating another blockbuster antiquity: the Jehoash Tablet, which contains a long inscription from Jehoash, son of King Ahaziah of Judah, about the repairs to the Temple of Solomon, and which corresponds to the Book of Kings 2, chapter 12.

"The way it got started was that the [Israeli] education minister, Limor Livnat, saw a news item about the tablet from Solomon's Temple published in the newspaper, and she immediately instructed the Israel Antiquities Authority to go and find it," says Kalman. "Because as far as she was concerned, this was the most important Jewish archaeological item ever discovered, and she wanted to know why it wasn't in the hands of the government, why it appeared to be in the hands of a private dealer. And it was during the research into the tablet from the Temple of Solomon that they started querying whether the inscription on the ossuary might not also be a fake."

On May 31, 2003, the IAA held a press conference in Jerusalem to announce the findings of its scientific committee on the James Ossuary. "The ossuary is real, but the inscription is fake," said Shuka Dorfman, a former IDF brigadier general who was then director general of the IAA. "What this means is that somebody took a real box and forged the writing on it, probably to give it a religious significance." Gideon Avni, one of the archaeologists who investigated the ossuary, said that he believed "this forgery was done sometime in the last decades, maybe in the last years."

Oded Golan was not surprised by the result, as he believed the IAA was out to get him, not only for his vast collection of indeterminate provenance, but also for having embarrassed the organization by exporting such a potentially important artifact without revealing its significance.

"It's only the IAA officials, who are sometimes not even archaeologists, who decided to claim that we are talking about a forgery," says Golan. "But if you read the conclusions of each one of the individuals [on the IAA's examining committee], you see very clearly that most of them are standing behind the conclusion that this is authentic, or at least that there is no reason to think that it's not authentic."

Golan believes that the IAA had decided months before it declared its result that the ossuary was a partial forgery—even before it assembled its team of investigators. "In an interview before nominating the committee, in *Maariv* in January 2003," Golan says, referring to an Israeli newspaper, "the heads of the IAA claimed in writing that they think it's a forgery. So the committee was nominated after this claim."

The IAA's suspicions about Oded Golan grew, to the point that it had its agents staking out his apartment and tailing his movements. They wanted to get their hands on the mysterious Jehoash Tablet, which was still eluding them, and which they suspected Golan was hiding. But they wanted the James Ossuary, too.

On July 31, 2003, two IAA agents who were staking out Golan's apartment walked up to his third-floor residence, saw that he was out, and then made their way to the roof of his building to get relief from the summer heat. On the roof the agents saw a structure that looked like an unused laundry room. The lock on the door was loose enough for them to peek inside, and to their astonishment, they saw a room stacked with antiquities.

The Tel Aviv police quickly located Golan and brought him back home, and in the presence of two defense lawyers, the IAA searched his apartment. They found chemicals, wax, books of Hebrew, sketches of letters on bullae and ostraca (shards of pottery that scribes used to convey messages), but no Jehoash Tablet or James Ossuary.

Then they went up on the roof. Golan didn't have the key to the storage room, so the IAA picked the lock, and when they pulled open the door they found blank ossuaries; they found partially in-scribed ossuaries without patina; they found dentist's tools and diamond-cutting drills; and they found the James Ossuary—sitting on top of a toilet. To the IAA it was ocular proof that the James Ossuary was a fake.

To Oded Golan, however, the humble storage unit on his roof was clever security.

"The IAA published my address in the *Haaretz* newspaper," he says. "So I was really scared for the safety of the ossuary and I moved it to the roof, to a small room which was closed for more than forty years at that time, and it was the safest place in the building. And when they came to look at my apartment, I took them, by myself, to this small room." Golan had wrapped the James Ossuary in bubble wrap, "so no one, even if somebody entered by mistake to the room, he couldn't actually know what is inside."

As for the tools the IAA found and suspected of being part of the mastermind forger's arsenal, Golan dismissed them as further delusion on the part of zealous antiquities cops. "This is just ridic-ulous. All what I had in a small box are very old tools that are used by almost any collector to store and to repair antiquities. So we are not talking about any laboratory or not about any special tools and in order to forge, by the way, an inscription, you don't need any laboratory, you only need a hammer and the chisel."

It didn't matter. The IAA arrested Oded Golan that afternoon and charged him with forgery. What would become a nine-year trial of Golan and the James Ossuary had now been put in motion.

THE JAMES OSSUARY was not the first to claim an archaeological connection to the Bible. In 1990, construction workers building a water park in Jerusalem's Peace Forest discovered a burial tomb from the first century CE. They called in the IAA, which saw that but for one burial shaft, the tomb had already been looted. Yet inside that lone shaft were twelve highly decorated ossuaries. Inside one of the burial boxes, archaeologists found the bones of a sixty-year-old man. His ossuary was inscribed "Joseph, son of Caiaphas." There was no question of provenance here: the ossuaries had been unearthed from the tomb not by shady looters but by the IAA itself. Could this ossuary be connected to the man who, according to the gospels, pronounced a death sentence on Jesus?

The Gospel of Matthew gives the most dramatic account of the trial of Jesus before Caiaphas, the high priest and leader of the council of Sanhedrin, the elders who governed Jewish life within the constraints of Roman occupation. Matthew tells us that Jesus is arrested and taken to the house of Caiaphas, where he is interrogated by the high priest and an assembly of scribes and elders.

> Then the high priest said to him, "I put you under oath before the living God, tell us if you are the Messiah, the Son of God." Jesus said to him, "You have said so. But I tell you, from now on you will see the Son of Man seated at the right hand of Power and coming on the clouds of heaven." Then the high priest tore his clothes and said, "He has blasphemed! Why do we still need witnesses? You have now heard his blasphemy. What is your verdict?" They answered, "He deserves death."

The discovery of Caiaphas's Ossuary, as it became known, created the kind of climate that archaeologists, collectors, believers, and forgers all love: the landscape of possibility that the next ossuary connected to the Bible could lie just under the next hill.

Golan's trial began in December 2004. He and four other men were charged with being part of an international forgery ring specializing in biblical artifacts. "The Israeli police indicted Oded Golan on more than forty charges of faking and dealing with forged items, and dealing in stolen antiquities," says Matthew Kalman. "And they said that this forgery ring was faking the historical record by forging such important items as the burial box of James, the brother of Jesus."

Over the course of the next seven years, more than one hundred twenty expert witnesses took the stand to shed light on the charges through the powerful lenses of their expertise, from archaeology to ancient languages to geology to geochemistry. As the trial wore on, the James Ossuary's inscription took the most scrutiny, and the pendulum of guilt and innocence swung back and forth.

Scholarly skirmishing over the ossuary's legitimacy had focused on the inscription from the beginning of the ossuary's public life, an inscription that seemed to be in two scribal hands—"James, son of Joseph" in one and "brother of Jesus" in the other, leading to a direct charge by the Israeli police that Oded Golan had forged the second half of the inscription shortly before the ossuary met the world in 2002.

The IAA's case was bolstered by the discovery that Golan had an accomplice, an Egyptian named Samech Marco Shokri Ghattes, who lived in Golan's apartment on and off and whose health was compromised by the chemicals he had to use to make forged antiquities for Golan, earning between two hundred and two thousand dollars per "antiquity." The Egyptian, a Coptic Christian, went back to Cairo to recover. It was there that Maj. Jonathan Pagis, an Israeli policeman who had studied archaeology in college and was fluent in Arabic, heard Ghattes's story.

"He was the one who made the forgeries on behalf of Oded Golan," says Pagis. "He was the person—a very talented person—who made all the engravings and polishing the artifacts and doing everything to make them look genuine. We took his testimony, and he told us himself that he made the Jehoash Tablet and other artifacts, so there was no question about it; Oded Golan was responsible for the forgeries."

What seemed like a major breakthrough was dashed by the Egyptian's refusal to come to Israel to testify in court, reasonably fearful of what charges might land on him. "According to Israel law, we cannot claim that we have the forger of the Ossuary without him being present in court and testifying," says Pagis. "So we could not say that this Egyptian person forged the Ossuary and not have him go on stand, so without the main collaborator, without the testimony of the person who made the forgeries, the case is quite weak."

Golan's team countered with ocular proof that the Egyptian was lying. "During the trial," says Matthew Kalman, Golan "was able to produce a photograph that showed a corner of the ossuary on a bookshelf in his bedroom at his parent's apartment, together with telephone directories and books from his university courses in the mid-1970s." The inscription was visible in the photograph. "And he was also able to produce a girlfriend who said she remembered seeing it there at that time. And so he was able to prove that he'd been in possession of the ossuary at least since the mid-1970s. He even brought in an FBI expert to prove that that photograph hadn't been faked. And that completely swept away the charge in the indictment that it had been recently faked."

The prosecution then turned to the question of the patina in the inscriptions, the layers of grit that had accumulated on the ossuary over the centuries. Seven samples were taken from the inscription, to be compared by IAA scientists with other areas of the ossuary.

They discovered the presence of tap water in the patina samples, clear evidence of forgery.

Oded Golan had an answer for that, too. He had stored the James Ossuary in his parents' apartment and said that perhaps his mother, who was a professor of microbiology—or a maid, or Golan himself—had cleaned it with soap and water. When the scientists tested this explanation, "they found it fits, one hundred percent, cleaning materials that were used to clean the James Ossuary during the years," says Golan. "So it was a big mess and a big misunderstanding. The expert they chose for this mission had no experience whatsoever in patina. He doesn't understand anything in patina; he compared it to something which is completely wrong."

On the witness stand, the IAA scientists were cross-examined about their findings, and had to admit that the sample taken from the topmost coating of the Aramaic word for Jesus—allegedly a forged addition—indeed contained ancient patina. The prosecution of Oded Golan and his ossuary was back at square one.

"NO MATTER WHERE YOU ARE, YOU ARE TO GO TO JAMES THE JUST"

With all the heat and light around the science of the James Ossuary, it was easy to lose sight of why the ossuary was important: its spiritual connection to the birth of Christianity through its literal connection to James, the brother of Jesus. But just who was James? And what was his role in the survival of this new religion once his brother was dead?

"As early as the gospel of Thomas—which is a noncanonical gospel from at least the early second century or so—we hear James spoken about as the person who will succeed Jesus," says Mark

Goodacre, of Duke University. "The disciples come up to Jesus and say, 'What shall we do when you've gone?'"

The Gospel of Thomas clearly tells us what Jesus wanted. "Jesus said to them, 'No matter where you are, you are to go to James the Just, for whose sake heaven and earth came into being.'" Not only is James considered pious, with the appellation "Just," but he's also clearly named as the successor to Jesus, and divinely ordained as such. Despite this, there is no mention in the New Testament of James being present at the Crucifixion of Jesus, or text in any way conveying that the mantle of messianic destiny now fell upon him. With the Romans on the hunt for anyone who followed the crucified Jesus and his mission, James and the other apostles lie low in Jerusalem. Though the gospels make no mention of the resurrected Jesus appearing to James, it is Paul who notes the event in a letter to the Corinthians: "Then he appeared to more than five hundred brothers and sisters at one time, most of whom are still alive, though some have died. Then he appeared to James, then to all the apostles. Last of all, as to one untimely born, he appeared also to me."

"The appearance to James is a life-changing experience for James," says Mark Goodacre. "He has probably found the whole business of Jesus being crucified about as traumatic, about as life-changing, as you can imagine. This is a member of your family—a close member of your family—who's gone through a gruesome, horrific, shameful execution, and at the same time seems to have been someone adored by crowds of people, and the Resurrection is the moment where James comes to believe that Jesus really is something special. It's the moment where everything changes for James."

This reunion marked the beginning of James's leadership role in the early Christian church in Jerusalem. The apostle Peter and the convert Paul are seen as the driving forces behind the new religion, but it is the Christian community that James establishes in Jerusalem that becomes the core of the new religion.

Indeed, some scholars believe that the New Testament's "Epistle of James" was written by the brother of Jesus. The letter, addressed to the "Twelve Tribes of the Dispersion," speaks of faith and perseverance during the turbulence of following this new and revolutionary strand of Judaism.

"The degree to which this letter echoes the teaching of Jesus supports the writer identifying himself as a servant of the master teacher, Jesus," says Ben Witherington. "Also, a later Christian writer would have called James 'the brother of Jesus,' or 'James the Just of Jerusalem.'" The fact that this epistle, the oldest copy of which dates from the third century CE, even refers to James is, for Witherington, evidence that its author is the brother of Jesus.

While Paul and Peter are spreading and adapting the message of Jesus around the Diaspora to embrace all who hear it, James holds tight to the purity of that message. It's an issue that threatens the new faith. "The apostle Paul provides a problem for people like James, because James thinks that the most important thing about Jesus is that he's the Jewish Messiah," says Mark Goodacre. "He's somebody who fulfills everything that the Scriptures have looked forward to. He's the person who's come to redeem Israel, and there's big worry when the apostle Paul is getting all these gentile converts who are not getting circumcised and who are not keeping the law—is there a chance that that's going to bring the movement into disrepute?"

The conflict between the ministry of Jesus and James as opposed to that of Paul is the question of just who gets to join this new religion. James believed that Jesus was remaking Judaism for Jews, and that anyone who wanted to join would first have to become a Jew—with circumcision for adult males being a necessary action. Paul, on the other hand, had never met Jesus, and was expanding his ministry with the momentum of his own genius. The matter came to a head in Jerusalem twenty years after the death of Jesus, circa 50 CE, at the Council of Jerusalem.

"Paul brings Titus, an uncircumcised Greek, with him to the Jerusalem Council as a kind of provocative act," says Goodacre. "He wants to say 'Look, you must acknowledge that this person is indeed a Jesus follower in spite of the fact that he's uncircumcised.'"

In the end, James agreed with Paul, though life after the council was not so straightforward, and a split developed between James and Paul over the commingling at the dining table of the Jews for whom Jesus was the Messiah and the Gentiles who had joined the new faith. Paul and Peter would continue their missionary work in the Diaspora, while James would stay in Jerusalem, remaining faithful to the ministry of his brother, in the city where he died.

In the decade after the Jerusalem Council, the political climate in Jerusalem roiled with turbulence. Various Jewish factions all laid claim to their interpretation of the sanctity of the Temple, with James proclaiming that Jesus himself was the Temple, and through belief in him as the Son of God, worship in the Temple was worship of Jesus. Just as his brother had done, James threatened the establishment, itself increasingly corrupt and fractious. The high priest Ananus, the grandson of the man who condemned Jesus to die, took advantage of the fact that there was no Roman governor in office in Judea since the death of the comparatively just procurator Porcius Festus in 62 CE, and he took a great judicial liberty: he charged James with blasphemy.

The New Testament is silent on the matter, but the historian Josephus, himself from a priestly Jewish family, wrote of what happened to the brother of Jesus within a generation after the event: "[Ananus] assembled the Sanhedrin of judges, and brought before them the brother of Jesus, who was called Christ, whose name was James, and some others [or, some of his companions]; and when he had formed an accusation against them as breakers of the law, he delivered them to be stoned."

Less than a thousand feet from where his brother was executed thirty years earlier, James, too, was put to death for his faith. Hegesippus, a second-century CE chronicler of the Christian Church, who himself was a Jewish convert, dramatically described the event: "The aforesaid scribes and Pharisees accordingly set James on the summit of the temple, and cried aloud to him, and said: 'O just one, whom we are all bound to obey, forasmuch as the people is in error, and follows Jesus the crucified, do thou tell us what is the door of Jesus, the crucified.' And he answered with a loud voice: 'Why ask ye me concerning Jesus the Son of man? He Himself sitteth in heaven, at the right hand of the Great Power, and shall come on the clouds of heaven.'"

Hegesippus relates that many in attendance were convinced by James's response, which only inflamed his accusers. "Thus they fulfilled the Scripture written in Isaiah: 'Let us away with the just man, because he is troublesome to us: therefore shall they eat the fruit of their doings.' So they went up and threw down the just man, and said to one another: 'Let us stone James the Just.' And they began to stone him: for he was not killed by the fall; but he turned, and kneeled down, and said: 'I beseech Thee, Lord God our Father, forgive them; for they know not what they do.'"

In less than a decade, the Temple would be a ruin, the final catastrophic casualty in the Jewish war with Rome.

"BEYOND ALL REASONABLE DOUBT"

On March 14, 2012, Judge Aharon Farkash delivered his 475-page verdict and came down on the side of Golan: "The prosecution failed to prove beyond all reasonable doubt what was stated in the indictment: that the ossuary is a forgery and that Mr. Golan or someone acting on his behalf forged it."

Oded Golan was acquitted of all but three minor charges of illegal antiquities dealing, and fined the equivalent of eight thousand dollars. The authenticity of the James Ossuary had not been demolished in a court of law (though it had come close to being so a few times in its tumultuous decade), but neither had it been completely reprieved.

"This is not to say that the inscription on the ossuary is true and authentic and was written 2,000 years ago," the judge said. "We can expect this matter to continue to be researched in the archaeological and scientific worlds and only the future will tell. Moreover, it has not been proved in any way that the words 'brother of Jesus' definitely refer to the Jesus who appears in Christian writings."

Once again the world was back where it started, faced with evidence that had survived an Israeli court, but whose provenance, divine or otherwise, was still in doubt. "The judge was very specific in his ruling to say that the acquittal verdict did not prove anything as regards the authenticity or the non-authenticity of the objects themselves, because that wasn't what was on trial," says Matthew Kalman, who was present when the verdict was delivered. "What was on trial was whether or not Oded Golan was proved to have faked them. And the prosecution failed to prove that Oded Golan faked them. And the judge said, 'that's not a ruling on the authenticity or not of the objects themselves.'"

After Golan's acquittal, the prosecution tried to convince the judge that the artifacts should remain the property of the state, equating their return to Golan, says Kalman, to "giving a drug dealer who'd got off on a technicality all his drugs back."

For the antiquities cop Jonathan Pagis, Golan's acquittal was devastating. "I was very disappointed. We had a very strong case, in my opinion, but apparently the judge was not convinced about this and he let him go. I think it's a shame that Oded Golan is a free person today."

In the end, Golan had to fight the state for the return of his property. When he received the James Ossuary, a reddish stain was streaked across the word *Jesus*, created by the sloppy science of his accusers. "The forensic department of the Israeli Police poured red silicone into the inscription," says Golan. "And when they took out the silicone when it was dry, they took with it most of the natural patina."

Now it's impossible to prove if this was indeed the burial box of Jesus's brother. Which brings the story back to where it started, one based on faith. "I know it sounds disappointing to think that we'll never know if this item's really genuine or really associated with the brother of Jesus, but the fact is that if you speak to any archaeologist, they'll tell you that that's all we ever knew anyway," says Kalman. "Because you can never say, in archaeology, that a particular item is definitely associated with a particular figure from the Bible. It's almost impossible to do that."

Even so, the James Ossuary connected much of the world with a story it didn't know, or had neglected, and for scholars, that's more important than declaring it true.

"The controversy about the ossuary has caused people to become more aware of James," says Rev. Bruce Chilton. "However you look at it from the point of view of authenticity, it always makes a difference when you can show a picture of something obviously ancient; it makes people take more seriously the idea that that figure might have existed. So I don't think that the ossuary is a case where we can say with any certainty that it is authentic, but it has done some good in any case."

Oded Golan agrees. Now that he has the James Ossuary back in his possession, he wants to show it to the world once again. "I think that the real place for it is not in my storehouse," Golan says. "It should be exhibited to people who have emotion and who have interest in early Christianity, and I hope that it will travel among these places during next years and it will be shown to the public. And of course, whoever wants to, to study it, will be able to get any assistance in this way."

St. Jude Children's
Research Hospital

ALSAC · Danny Thomas, Founder

Finding cures. Saving children.

stjude.org

THREE

MARY MAGDALENE

Prostitute, Apostle, Saint—or Jesus's Wife?

This is a section of "The Gospel of Mary," a papyrus text that may date to the second century CE. Discovered in Egypt in the nineteenth century, the gospel only became publicly known after the 1950s. This is the only early Christian text to be named after a woman—apparently Mary Magdalene—and she has a central role that at least one of the male disciples defends against criticism from the others: "For if the Savior made her worthy, who are you then for your part to reject her?" argues Levi. "Assuredly the Savior's knowledge of her is completely reliable. That is why he loved her more than us." *(Courtesy of the Egypt Exploration Society)*

One of the greatest revelations in Christian history came not from the lips of an angel or the pages of the Bible, but from the daily newspapers on a September day in the Year of Our Lord 2012. The stories were based on a few lines of faded Coptic script clumsily scrawled on a slip of yellowed papyrus no bigger than a business card, yet apparently as old as the Scriptures themselves.

The Gospel of Jesus's Wife, this new ancient text was called—a title that says it all yet doesn't begin to convey the import of what it would mean if Jesus had been married. The implications of the discovery were matched by something equally new, and just as threatening: the speed with which the Internet was able to disseminate this new gospel. The news quickly rocked the world's traditional believers, inspired its more female-friendly adherents, and entertained critics who had always viewed the Church as a bastion of patriarchy, obsessed with controlling sexuality, and based on a pack of myths that only became dogma thanks to the passage of time and the machinations of a hidebound hierarchy. Here was proof that they were right.

Other early Christian texts and so-called gospels had come to light in previous years, some of them with startling messages, a few hinting at a much larger role for women in the early Church. Some suggested there was something more than a platonic relationship between the Savior and his most famous female follower, Mary Magdalene. The most significant and historic find was the discovery in 1945, by an Egyptian peasant digging in the steep hills around the Nile town of Nag Hammadi, in Upper Egypt, of a trove of more than fifty old papyrus texts bound in leather. Most of the texts were associated with an early Christian movement known as Gnosticism, whose name derives from its followers' emphasis on divine revelations and secret knowledge—*gnosis*, in Greek—as the one true way to salvation.

Yet it took decades for the papyrus codices to make their perilous journey through the global antiquities market and into the hands of scholars, who in turn took their time translating and fighting over what the papyrus texts said, and what they meant. Only in 1979, with the publication of Princeton scholar Elaine Pagels's bestselling book *The Gnostic Gospels* did these sacred texts and their novel teachings begin to enter the public consciousness. They forced many to rethink who Jesus really was, and what his teachings really mean.

Over the ensuing decades, popular culture appropriated the suggestive passages and ideas in the ancient texts, ran them through its dream-making machine, and manufactured various products related, if only tangentially, to the Nag Hammadi codices. Most notable among these was *The Da Vinci Code*, the surprising 2003 blockbuster novel (and later a hit Tom Hanks movie), which used what author Dan Brown said were historical facts to underpin a page-turning potboiler about the marriage of Jesus and Mary Magdalene and their line of descendants extending to the present day—a secret maintained by a bloody, two-thousand-year-old plot concocted by the Catholic Church.

Of course that was fiction, even if millions believed Brown's version. There had been nothing like the Gospel of Jesus's Wife, an actual patch of Christian text from the ancient world that seemed like a real-life prequel to Brown's twenty-first century fantasy.

What did this "gospel" say? In eight lines it appears to recount the middle of a conversation between Jesus and the apostles, the twelve men he chose to serve as the foundation of his ministry and, tradition says, of the church that they would go on to build after his Crucifixion. Yet the piece of papyrus is so small—a bit more than three inches wide by an inch and a half high—that it reads more like a transcript of a cell phone call that cuts in and out:

"... not [to] me. My mother gave to me li[fe] ..."
"... The disciples said to Jesus ..."
"... deny. Mary is [not?] worthy of it ..."
"... Jesus said to them, 'My wife ...'"
"... she is able to be my disciple ..."
"... Let wicked people swell up ..."
"... As for me, I dwell with her in order to ..."
"... an image ..."

Despite the fragmentary text, the papyrus directly addresses several issues that have fascinated both believers and nonbelievers alike: Was Jesus married and did he have sex? And could women be priests (and bishops) on an equal footing with men?

It's hard to overstate how much was at stake. For Catholics, a celibate Jesus was key to a celibate priesthood: "The fact that Christ himself, the eternal Priest, lived his mission right up to his Sacrifice on the Cross in the state of virginity is the point of reference to understand the tradition of the Latin Church on this subject," Pope Benedict XVI wrote in 2007. Yet it didn't stop there: "Celibacy is really a special way of conforming oneself to Christ's own way of life." In other words, not having sex is the way to be most like Jesus.

This wasn't a special claim by Catholics. There is a broad ecumenical agreement that Jesus was not married. Protestants may disagree with Catholics on whether Jesus's mother, Mary, remained a virgin. Yet if Jesus had sex, then God himself had sex. That's something Zeus and those horny pagan Olympians did. The one true God? That would be heresy.

Now Karen King, a highly regarded scholar of early Christian texts at Harvard Divinity School, was about to upset all that. An anonymous collector had given King the papyrus for verification, and she determined that it was legitimate. As she told reporters, while this wasn't proof that Jesus was married, it was the earliest-known statement from antiquity referring to Jesus having a wife. King and experts she consulted said the papyrus itself was written in Coptic, probably in the fourth century, but copied from an even earlier gospel, perhaps from the second century, about a hundred years after the Crucifixion and around the time the canon of Christian Scriptures, the New Testament, was being collected.

"This fragment suggests that some early Christians had a tradition that Jesus was married," King told the *New York Times*. Adding even more sizzle to the story, King said the "Mary" in the text probably refers to Mary Magdalene, the famously sensuous early follower of Jesus universally known as a prostitute, who changed her ways under the influence of the Messiah.

That news in itself would have been enough to rattle the foundations of the Church, but King and the Harvard Divinity School, working with the Smithsonian Channel, which had exclusive rights to the fragment for a documentary to air later in September, rolled out the discovery for maximum impact: not only was there coordinated coverage in major U.S. dailies, but that day, King announced the discovery in Rome, at a Catholic college across the street from the Vatican, where the world's leading Coptic scholars were gathered for a major conference held every four years.

King called the text the Gospel of Jesus's Wife, a title that left little doubt as to its central claim or its authority—only the gospels of Matthew, Mark, Luke, and John had made it into the New Testament as the definitive "good news" (from the word *evangelion*, in the common Greek of the earliest Christian texts) brought by the Son of God. As much as earlier discoveries did, this new gospel called those assumptions into question, said Roger Bagnall, director of the Institute for the Study of the Ancient World and professor of ancient history at New York University, who helped King authenticate the papyrus. It "helps to remind us that practically everything that later generations told about Jesus was put together and edited by somebody well after his death, and represents the view of Jesus that they were trying to get across," Bagnall told the *Boston Globe*.

In other words, *gospel truth* is a relative term, and nothing about the New Testament was as it seemed. Much was at stake, not only for the faith of billions of believers, but also for King and the world of biblical archeology.

King had learned about the Gospel of Jesus's Wife in that round-about, serendipitous way that is business as usual in the antiquities trade, a netherworld market that recognizes few rules or national boundaries, and flouts even the most minimal conventions of academic rigor and scientific method. Artifacts of all kinds are routinely looted from secret sites in Egypt—most certainly where the Gospel of Jesus's Wife would have originated. They pass through many hands on their way to a museum or collector, and are often cut up or broken apart in order for the seller to have more bits to sell and thus more money to make. The chain of evidence to ascertain the provenance and legitimacy of such items is often guesswork, and sometimes a murky tale of a relic's origin is told simply to camouflage the fact that it is a fake designed to earn the seller a big payday or generate fifteen minutes of fame.

"In this field, we keep having these things appear," King said. "So I think it's almost a reflex to be suspicious." In her case, a stranger's e-mail from out of the blue in 2010 alerted her to the existence of the papyrus. The owner had a collection of Greek, Coptic, and Arabic papyri, and he told King he had acquired this fragment, along with several others, in 1999, from an unidentified German collector. Accompanying the papyrus fragment was a handwritten note in German, from the 1980s, that cited a professor of Egyptology in Berlin, who had since died, as saying the fragment was "the sole example" of a text in which Jesus claims a wife.

The owner, whose identity, and even nationality, King agreed to keep secret, sent King a photo of the so-called gospel. The Coptic words for *Jesus* and *my wife* jumped out at her, but she didn't know what to make of the text. "I didn't believe it was authentic and told him I wasn't interested," King said later. She moved on to other projects and put the papyrus aside, despite its explosive suggestions. In the summer of 2011, the owner e-mailed King again to ask her to give it a second look. This time she noticed some similarities to phrases from other early, noncanonical texts, such as the Gospel of Thomas and the Gospel of Mary, both of which were written around the same time, about a century after Jesus lived.

King now needed to see the Gospel of Jesus's Wife up close. In December 2011 the owner brought the fragment to the Divinity School. King examined it more closely, and sent photos of it to Bagnall, who showed it to a small group of other papyrologists. As Bagnall told the *Globe*, "We put it up on the screen, and we all sort of said, 'Eeew.' We thought it was ugly. And it is ugly. The handwriting is not nice—thick, badly controlled strokes made by somebody who didn't have a very good pen."

In March 2012, King slipped the papyrus into her red leather handbag and went to New York to meet Bagnall and AnneMarie Luijendijk, a papyrologist and religion professor at Princeton University. For several hours they sat around a table in Bagnall's office, examining the fragment under different lights and magnifications.

The papyrus looked real, and old. Yet since ancient papyrus can be bought on the black market, determining whether the ink was just as old (rather than applied in recent times) was key. It appeared that it was: the ragged edges of the papyrus showed traces of ink that had been used before the material was damaged. Moreover, the language was in Sahidic Coptic, an ancient dialect from southern Egypt.

"It's hard to construct a scenario that is at all plausible in which somebody fakes something like this. The world is not really crawling with crooked papyrologists," Bagnall told the *New York Times*.

King worried that news of the fragment would leak, and in ways that might distort its meaning and significance. She had not put the papyrus through the crucial carbon-14 dating tests that could determine its true age; nor had she tested the ink to see if it could be a later addition. Yet the papyrus seemed to be authentic; several scholars reviewed it, though one was very critical. Still, King decided to unveil it at the conference in Rome, accompanied by a big media rollout.

"This is not a career maker," King told the *Boston Globe*. "If it's a forgery, it's a career breaker."

Those words had barely been printed before powerful objections to the authenticity of the papyrus were raised, and serious doubts began creeping in.

"HOW TO DATE JESUS' WIFE"

"I would say it's a forgery," said Alin Suciu, a papyrologist at the University of Hamburg, after King presented her fifty-two-page paper at the Rome conference. One of the very elements that had convinced Bagnall and others of the papyrus's authenticity, the unusual amateurish writing, made Suciu and others suspicious. "The script doesn't look authentic" when compared to other samples of Coptic papyrus script dating to the fourth century, he told the Associated Press.

Others, such as noted Coptic expert Wolf-Peter Funk, said that without any context it was impossible to tell what the papyrus meant, even if it was real, which he doubted. "There are thousands of scraps of papyrus where you find crazy things," said Funk, codirector of a project editing the Nag Hammadi Coptic library (a collection of Gnostic texts) at Laval University in Quebec. "It can be anything."

"There are all sorts of really dodgy things about this," agreed David Gill, professor of archaeological heritage at University Campus Suffolk and author of the blog *Looting Matters*, which tracks the illicit trade in antiquities. "This looks to me as if any sensible, responsible academic would keep their distance from it."

The Vatican's semiofficial newspaper, *L'Osservatore Romano*, weighed in a few days later with two stories, one a punchy column by the editor arguing that King's interpretation of the fragment's content is "wholly implausible" and bends the facts to suit "a contemporary ideology which has nothing to do with ancient Christian history, or with the figure of Jesus."

Of course the Vatican *would* say that, responded defenders of the new gospel. Yet critics noted a number of shortcomings in King's interpretation: for example, even though King acknowledged that Jesus could have been speaking metaphorically—invoking a common analogy in the early Church as "the bride of Christ"—she was still reading the text too literally. Early Christian texts often used references to kisses and embraces to denote a "spiritual intimacy" between Christ and his disciples rather than an actual sexual or marital state.

Others pointed out that two of the three anonymous scholars the *Harvard Theological Review* asked to review King's paper raised doubts about the fragment's authenticity and its grammar, and the way it had been translated and interpreted. To many, this was, as one writer put it, "less a full-fledged gospel than an ancient crossword puzzle"—and some were too eager to fill in the blanks with their own answers.

There is an adage in the field of biblical archeology that says that if something seems too good to be true, it probably is. Increasingly, this appeared to be one such case. Here you had a slip of papyrus with just eight fragmentary lines of text that raised all the hot-button concerns for contemporary Christianity—whether Jesus was married, and to Mary Magdalene, and whether women could be priests just like men. Sex and gender, power and authority—all in one scrap of text that, as a bonus, would unmask one of the greatest conspiracies of all time.

Before the month of September was out, the doubts caught up with the early claims. King's scholarly article on the gospel, set to run in the January 2013 edition of the *Harvard Theological Review*, was put on hold, and a Smithsonian Channel documentary about the papyrus was shelved until King could supply more corroborating information.

Then, crickets. Testing on the papyrus was supposed to take a few weeks, maybe months. Yet a year passed and—nothing. Harvard put off repeated requests for information about the status of the testing, and wouldn't say who was conducting the tests or when they might be completed. Scholars and bloggers filled the silence with debates about the gospel's authenticity based on what was already known. You could find an argument, often quite valid, for almost any viewpoint, though the lengthening silence contributed to a sense that something was seriously amiss with the Gospel of Jesus's Wife.

Finally, in April 2014, just before Easter and a year and a half after King first shocked the world with her announcement, she revealed that testing had shown that the papyrus was ancient and not a modern forgery. King understandably felt vindicated. "I'm hoping now that we can turn away from the question of forgery and talk much, much more about the historical significance of the fragment and precisely how it fit into the history of Christianity and questions about family and marriage and sexuality and Jesus," King told reporters.

Her hope would be short-lived. Critics immediately noted a glaring discrepancy with King's original claims—namely, the testing showed that the papyrus dated to 741 CE and as late as the year 859 CE, more than five centuries later than King had first said. This result came after the first effort to carbon-date the papyrus returned a date of four hundred to two hundred years *before* Jesus was born. Moreover, the ink itself could not be directly tested because this would have necessitated destroying a piece of an already small fragment. Also, spectroscopic tests showed that it was a type used between 400 BCE and as late as 800 CE, a huge window of twelve centuries. As one wag tweeted: "BREAKING: 'Jesus' wife' fragment could date to 400 years before he was born." An article in *Christianity Today* was cleverly titled "How to Date Jesus' Wife."

Scholars were just as scathing. Leo Depuydt, an Egyptologist at Brown University, wrote in a rebuttal included in the *Harvard Theological Review* that the papyrus "seems ripe for a Monty Python sketch." More concretely, he said that the papyrus contained serious grammatical errors and appeared to lift lines directly from the Gospel of Thomas. He noted that other scholars found that it even included a typo that is in the Thomas gospel. What were the chances? "I don't buy the argument that this is sophisticated. I think it could be done in an afternoon by an undergraduate student," Depuydt told the *Boston Globe*.

King, Bagnall, and the defenders parried these objections, saying that Depuydt was misreading the Coptic. Besides, they said, many ancient Christian texts lifted passages from each other. The scholarly article was published, and the Smithsonian documentary was broadcast—and the controversy died down. The only remaining questions seemed to be: why was this gospel suppressed and why was the early Church (and the current patriarchy) so worried about anything that indicated that Jesus was married or had sex, or that women could exercise as much authority as men—especially a "fallen woman" such as Mary Magdalene?

Within a month, however, this strange saga took another and perhaps final twist.

JESUS GETS A DIVORCE

When King was presenting her blockbuster discovery at the Coptic conference in Rome in September 2012, a young American scholar named Christian Askeland stood at a lectern in an adjacent room presenting a paper on a Coptic version of the Book of Revelation, an important appearance for any academic starting a career. Of course, King's paper was the focus of everyone's attention, but after Askeland returned to Germany, where he is an assistant research professor at Protestant University Wuppertal, he began examining the images of King's gospel more closely.

It was only in April 2014, however, when the *Harvard Theological Review* posted the testing results and all the relevant documentation online, that Askeland could really get a good look at the gospel. What he found would make a bigger splash than any academic paper.

First, he found among the images posted by the *Review* a photo of another small, tattered piece of papyrus that appeared to be a fragment of a Coptic manuscript known as the Gospel of John. That papyrus scrap had been given to King by the same collector who'd supplied the Gospel of Jesus's Wife. It turns out that Askeland had written his doctoral thesis on Coptic versions of the Gospel of John, and he now compared the version King had been given to an authentic early papyrus version of the Gospel of John in Coptic that had been discovered in a jar in an Egyptian grave in 1923.

The similarities "defied coincidence," as he said. The Gospel of John fragment that King had been given copied every other line from the authentic 1923 version, and the line breaks were identical—something that would never have happened, given that in the ancient world, pieces of papyrus were of varying size and every scribe had a different writing style. Moreover, the style of writing in the two fragments King had been given was in the same hand; it was highly improbable that the same scribe had written both texts. The Gospel of John fragment had to be fake, then, and it came from the same collector who supplied the Gospel of Jesus's Wife.

Askeland theorized that a contemporary forger had copied the Gospel of John fragment off a version found on the Internet. If that fragment was a fake, so, too, was the Jesus's Wife gospel. "To me, the odds that I'm going to be hit by lightning twice in the same day means [this fragment] is moving into the realm of the absurd," Askeland told the *Washington Post*. "It gets worse and worse from there."

Indeed, Askeland also noted that the real Gospel of John was written in the Lycopolitan dialect, which experts say died out around the fifth century. The fragment of the Gospel of John given to King dated to the same range as the Jesus's Wife Gospel (the seventh to ninth centuries), meaning the language used in the newly discovered Gospel of John fragment, written in the same hand as the Jesus's Wife Gospel, died out at least two hundred years before the text was written.

"Simply put: If one is a forgery, they're both forgeries," scholars Joel S. Baden, an associate professor of Old Testament at Yale Divinity School, and Candida Moss, a professor of New Testament at Notre Dame, put it in a CNN article. "Like steroids in sports, it's safe to assume that the best bad guys are always one step ahead of the science." Added Mark Goodacre, "Given the massive similarities, it does suggest that we are dealing with a forgery."

Some tried to defend the gospel as best they could. A blog post titled "Jesus Had an Ugly Sister-in-Law" (a reference to the Gospel of John fragment's relationship to the Gospel of Jesus's Wife fragment) accused Askeland of sexism. A column at the Religion Dispatches website also suggested that as an evangelical Christian associated with the Green Collection, a compilation of ancient biblical texts and artifacts funded by Steve Green, president of Hobby Lobby and himself a conservative evangelical, Askeland must have an agenda. "It's always exciting to find something new, but I take no joy in messing things up for Karen King," Askeland told the *Washington Post*. "I'm very frustrated at whoever did this hoax, but I'm convinced it is a hoax."

King herself seemed to take a deep breath and consider the worst. "This is substantive, it's worth taking seriously, and it may point in the direction of forgery," she told the *New York Times*. "This is one option that should receive serious consideration." But, she added hopefully, "I don't think it's a done deal."

She was right about that. Even if evidence showed conclusively that the papyrus had been fabricated by some academic trying to show up his or her gullible peers in the guild of biblical archeologists, or by a crooked collector looking to make a quick buck, the arguments would never end (and the suspicion never disappear). How could they? Questions about sex and Jesus and women and authority have always fueled debates in Christianity, and the focus of those debates always comes back to one person: Mary Magdalene.

"Since the early Christian era, Mary Magdalene has functioned as a figure who elicits questions about the nature of feminine religious authority, the relationship of spirituality and sexuality, and the social and political positions of women in institutional religions," Theresa Coletti writes in her book *Mary Magdalene and the Drama of Saints*. What's remarkable is how much this single woman has been asked to bear, given how little the New Testament actually says about her.

"MARY MAGDALENE WAS THE CHURCH IN HERSELF"

Before the events of Holy Week, the final act and dramatic high point of the story of Jesus's life on earth, Mary Magdalene is mentioned just once, in the Gospel of Luke. In chapter 8, the evangelist is describing Jesus's travels around the Galilee, preaching and performing miracles, and writes:

> *The twelve were with him, as well as some women who had been cured of evil spirits and infirmities: Mary, called Magdalene, from whom seven demons had gone out, and Joanna, the wife of Herod's steward Chuza, and Susanna, and many others, who provided for them out of their resources.*

This passing reference provides a few details about Mary Magdalene that would contribute to some of the myths and confusions that grew up around her, but also information that, as we will see later, would eventually help illuminate who the Magdalene actually was.

Mary Magdalene really emerges fully and powerfully only when Jesus goes to Jerusalem for Passover and the events that would culminate in his death and Resurrection.

Though she appears just a few times, she is there in all four gospels. It's important to remember that those episodes are also the most historically credible simply because they took place at the end of Jesus's life, when he had a significant following. In addition, most of the Holy Week events of the Passion were public ones. Jesus's entry into Jerusalem on Palm Sunday, his trial and flogging, his Crucifixion and burial were all witnessed by untold numbers of people, and they made such an impression on Jesus's immediate followers that they were later willing to die rather than deny them, and to ensure that someone committed the stories to a written text.

Jesus himself left no written record, and some believe that he may not even have known how to write. It was left to others to tell his story, which has largely come down to us in the four gospels of the New Testament. As we discussed in a previous chapter, three of those gospels—Matthew, Mark, and Luke—are so close in form and content that they are called the synoptics, from the Greek word meaning "looked at from the same point of view." The fourth gospel, the Gospel of John, was written later, perhaps as late as 100 CE, and has a markedly different style.

Mary Magdalene enters the Passion drama in Mark, the earliest written gospel, named as one of the women who stayed at Calvary when Jesus died. By then the men who once declared their devotion to him have fled—or, in the case of Judas, betrayed the Messiah. The faithfulness of the women who followed Jesus has always set them apart from the men, the twelve apostles, to the former's credit. On the other hand, as Candida Moss notes, women "wouldn't have been seen as political threats in the same way that the twelve might have been. So we can imagine that it's more dangerous for the twelve [to stay at the cross] than it is for Mary and the other women, because they can fly under the radar."

In his description of the Crucifixion, the author of Mark's gospel also notes that Mary Magdalene and these women at the cross "had followed [Jesus] when he was in Galilee and ministered to him." Mary Magdalene, the author writes, and another woman named Mary, kept watch over the tomb after the body was taken down that Friday afternoon.

Mark then recounts how Mary Magdalene and another Mary, the mother of James, and Salome went to the tomb very early on Sunday morning, the first day of the week, to anoint Jesus's body with spices in preparation for burial. At the time, this was a task for women, and they could not do it the day before, Saturday, because that was the Sabbath. On their way to the tomb, the women worry about whether they will be able to roll back the huge stone covering the entrance, but when they arrive, they find that the stone has already been pushed aside. They enter the tomb and see that Jesus's body is gone; instead, a young man is seated there, clothed in a white robe. He tells the women that Christ has been raised from the dead and that they should go tell Peter and the other disciples.

The women are afraid and bewildered, however, and say nothing. Then, in a passage that may be a later addition, Jesus appears to Mary Magdalene alone, and she then goes to alert the others. Yet the men do not believe her, and understand only when Jesus himself appears to the eleven remaining male apostles, rebuking them for their faithlessness.

In Matthew's version, too, the Magdalene remains at the scene of the Crucifixion while others flee, and she watches over the sepulcher. Then, on Sunday morning, she and the other Mary go to the tomb, which is still sealed. In Matthew's version there is an earthquake, and rather than a young man in white, as in Mark, an angel in white descends, rolls back the stone, and sits down. The guards put there by the Romans, to keep anyone from stealing the body (and faking a resurrection), faint dead away in fright. The angel tells the two Marys not to be afraid, that Jesus has risen from the dead. Running back to tell the others, they meet Jesus himself, and fall to embrace his feet. He also tells them to go tell the others the news.

Luke's gospel says that all the women who followed Jesus from

Galilee—presumably including the Magdalene—stayed at the cross and checked the tomb. Mary Magdalene is mentioned by name only when Luke recounts how the women returned Sunday morning to anoint Jesus's body with spices. Mary Magdalene and the unnamed other women find the stone rolled away, and no body. Two men "in dazzling garments" appear and tell them Jesus has risen from the dead, but when they rush back to tell the others, again their story is dismissed. "Their story seemed like nonsense" to the men. Once again, it is only when Jesus himself appears to the men that the story is believed.

The most moving, and memorable, version of these Easter morning events is found in the Gospel of John, the odd man out among the evangelists.

In John's gospel, Mary Magdalene goes to the tomb alone, so early in the morning that it is still dark. She sees the stone rolled away and the body gone and runs to tell Peter and the others. Peter and another disciple who shows up at the tomb see that what she has said is true, but they do not understand what has happened and they leave.

The Magdalene, steadfast as always, remains at the tomb crying:

As she wept, she bent over to look into the tomb; and she saw two angels in white, sitting where the body of Jesus had been lying, one at the head and the other at the feet. They said to her, "Woman, why are you weeping?" She said to them, "They have taken away my Lord, and I do not know where they have laid him." When she had said this, she turned around and saw Jesus standing there, but she did not know that it was Jesus.

Jesus said to her, "Woman, why are you weeping? Whom are you looking for?" Supposing him to be the gardener, she said to him, "Sir, if you have carried him away, tell me where you have laid him, and I will take him away." Jesus said to her, "Mary!" She turned and said to him in Hebrew, "Rabbouni!" which means Teacher.

Jesus said to her, "Do not hold on to me, because I have not yet ascended to the Father. But go to my brothers and say to them, 'I am ascending to my Father and your Father, to my God and your God.'" Mary Magdalene went and announced to the disciples, "I have seen the Lord"; and she told them that he had said these things to her.

This rendering of the discovery and meeting with Jesus is so dramatic, so intimate, and so powerful and full of meaning that it would inspire artists and dramatists for centuries to come. It would also plant the seed of suspicion that Jesus was closer to the Magdalene than he was to any of his other followers, and perhaps closer than the canonical texts wanted to let on.

What's important to remember here is that all four gospels recount the primary role of Mary Magdalene in the discovery of the empty tomb, the first appearance of the risen Jesus, and the injunction to go tell the others the amazing news. That is a remarkably consistent record across the texts and it attests to the Magdalene's central role and her historic importance.

"Mary Magdalene is the first one to whom the risen Christ appears and so she is of immense importance to Christianity," says the Jesuit author the Rev. James Martin. "But more important than that, I think, is that in the time between [when] Mary Magdalene sees Jesus at the tomb and runs and tells the disciples the good news and shares with the community the good news, Mary Magdalene was the Church. For that hour or two, Mary Magdalene was the only one who knew about the Resurrection, and so Mary Magdalene was the Church in herself."

Fortunately, from these few clues, historians of the Bible can make some other educated guesses about what sort of person Mary Magdalene might have been and what role she may have played.

MR. AND MRS. JESUS?

The first point to make is that Mary Magdalene was almost certainly a real person who existed in that time and place in history and who probably played a role in the Jesus story much along the lines of that described in the New Testament.

As we noted in the discussion of John the Baptist, Bible scholars (notably John Meier) cite the "criterion of embarrassment" as evidence that something related in the gospels is probably true. In the case of John the Baptist, his role as a mentor to Jesus, and his baptizer, proved embarrassing to later Christians, and the fact that they kept the Baptist and his role in all four gospels bolsters the authenticity of his story. Same with Mary Magdalene: her loyal presence at the Crucifixion while the men fled, and the fact that she was the one who discovered the empty tomb and first met the risen Christ—and was told to spread the news, even though the testimony of women in those days had little standing—would have been embarrassing to the men who would write the gospels and go on to lead the Church. So if early Church leaders were recasting history with an agenda in mind, as conspiracy-minded types believe, Mary Magdalene would have been the first to go. But she stayed.

So who was she?

One fact that seems indisputable—even as it contributed to the later sexual speculation surrounding Mary and Jesus—is that the Magdalene's name shows that she comes from the town of Magdala, or Migdal, on the northeast corner of the Sea of Galilee (a lake, really, thirteen miles long and also known as Lake Tiberias or Lake Kinneret). Migdal in Hebrew means "tower" or "fortress," and the Aramaic version, Magdala, adds the connotation of "elevated" or "magnificent"—all terms that the early Church leaders liked to apply to the Magdalene.

The Galilee region around Magdala is the area where Jesus was raised and where he conducted most of his public ministry, preaching the Sermon on the Mount on a hill next to the lake, walking on its stormy waters, and calming its dangerous waves. Jesus called fishermen such as Peter to be his "fishers of men," and on the banks of the lake, after the Resurrection, he prepared a breakfast of grilled fish over an open charcoal fire for his disciples.

Fish was a critical supply of protein for the region's inhabitants, and Magdala became a prosperous city thanks to the fishing industry. That prosperity may also have contributed to Magdala's reputation as the Sin City of the Galilee, and in fact Magdala was destroyed in 75 CE in part because of its "its infamy and the licentious behavior of its inhabitants," as Susan Haskins writes in her landmark study, *Mary Magdalene: Myth and Metaphor*. While there is no evidence that Mary of Magdala was herself licentious, her hometown's reputation did not burnish hers. Its prosperity, however, may have provided her the kind of income that allowed her to support Jesus's ministry.

For centuries it was assumed that Mary Magdalene and the other women followers did pretty much as most Jewish women of the day: leading lives marked out largely by domestic duties such as grinding flour, baking bread, washing clothes, and weaving wool. Yet more recent research is changing that perception of the women who followed Jesus. "Mary and the other women played a very important role in the early Jesus movement. They were there to finance and to support this movement of itinerant men who had given up their jobs to go out and preach the gospel," says Professor Geoffrey Smith. "It's also likely," Smith adds, "that Mary's role as a financier of the early Jesus movement would have given her some sort of influence over that movement." This was unusual, given the conventions of the day.

"Mary Magdalene seems atypical for a Jewish woman of her time," agrees Rabbi Garroway of Hebrew Union College. "Most Jewish women in the Galilee would have been in some kind of a domestic setting, either as a daughter or a mother or a wife, but to be out in the wilderness with an itinerant preacher, with a name that does not link her to any man, is unusual."

That name, the Magdalene, is another important clue—and another contributing factor to her later reputation. Following on the conventions of the day, married women were generally identified by the name of their husband. At that time, a woman's husband provided her a name and identity as well as sustenance. Yet like Jesus of Nazareth, Mary of Magdala evidently was not married, or was perhaps widowed, so is identified by her hometown. "It is therefore as an *independent* woman that she is presented," Haskins says. "This implies that she must also have been of some means, to have been able to choose to follow and support Christ."

So, no Mrs. Jesus? It's not likely. Leaving aside the theological objections, the historical record just doesn't support the idea that either Jesus or Mary Magdalene was married, and certainly not to each other.

At several points in the gospels, for example, the crowds around Jesus note that he is surrounded by his mother and his brothers and sisters, a catalogue of relations. Yet a wife is not mentioned, neither then nor when Jesus is crucified and buried, nor after the Resurrection. If he had a wife, it's hard to imagine that she would not have been named.

Some make the "argument from silence"—that precisely because no wife is ever mentioned, Jesus's wife must have been edited out. "Why is it that only the literature that said he was celibate survived?" as Karen King put it in defending the Gospel of Jesus's Wife. "And all of the texts that showed he had an intimate relationship with [Mary] Magdalene or is married didn't survive? Is that 100 percent happenstance? Or is it because of the fact that celibacy becomes the ideal for Christianity?"

Yes, celibacy did become the Christian ideal and, in the view of many, came to be overemphasized. Indeed, even the leader of the Roman Catholic Church today, Pope Francis, has noted that mandatory celibacy for priests is a Church law dating only to the twelfth century and could be altered to address today's realities.

Yet the argument from silence is a very weak one, and in this case it is based on a number of presumptions about men, and Jewish men in particular. As the hero of *The Da Vinci Code*, "symbologist" Robert Langdon, says, "The social decorum during that time virtually forbid a Jewish man to be unmarried. According to Jewish custom, celibacy was condemned." Indeed, Dan Brown's protagonist says bachelorhood was "unnatural" and would have been explained by the gospel writers if Jesus had been single.

Well, not really. A celibate man such as Jesus may not have been the norm, but he would hardly have been unusual. Indeed, in the first century there were communities of Jewish men living quasi-monastic lives in the desert around the Dead Sea. As we saw earlier, John the Baptist may have belonged to one, the Essenes, and Jesus may well have, too. Philo, the famous Jewish philosopher from Alexandria, in Egypt, and a contemporary of Jesus, spoke highly of the Essenes and their celibate commitments: "This now is the enviable system of life of these Essenes," Philo wrote, "so that not only private individuals but even mighty kings, admiring the men, venerate their sect, and increase their dignity and majesty in a still higher degree by their approbation and by the honors which they confer on them."

Remember also that Jesus spoke (in the Gospel of Matthew) about "eunuchs who have made themselves eunuchs for the sake of

the kingdom of heaven." He added: "Let the one who is able to receive this receive it." The apostle Paul—sometimes called the "second founder of Christianity," given his influential role as an evangelist
and the number of his writings that made it into the New
Testament—amplified this view, most clearly in his First Letter to
the Corinthians. In that epistle, Paul recommends celibacy as
the better way, and wishes "all men were even as I myself." (Also
echoing Jesus, he adds that those who cannot stay celibate should
marry, because "it is better to marry than to burn.")

That many today remain convinced Jesus must have been married, and to Mary Magdalene, may say more about our own preoccupations with sex than about the realities of life, and faith, for Jews
living in first-century Palestine, and early Christians around the Roman Empire. "There's a lazy, implicit thing that she and Jesus are
a good-looking couple. She's good-looking and roughly his age," says
Candida Moss. "But she might not have been any of those things.
She might have been a very attractive young widow, in her late teens
or early twenties, whose husband died and left her a lot of money,
or she might've been a very successful independent businesswoman
who's maybe in her sixties, who's not attractive, but who's worked
hard and now, in the later years of her life, is focused on spirituality and spiritual growth."

In any case, the New Testament doesn't provide much else to
go on, and after the Resurrection, the Magdalene disappears from
the canonical narrative. The sudden gap is jarring, given her important role.

"One of the great mysteries of early Christianity is what happened to Mary Magdalene, because there she is on the pages of the
gospels, in all the key moments: at the end of his life, at the tomb,
and experiencing the Resurrection," says Mark Goodacre. "And then
we don't hear any more about her, and we just don't know." One
possibility, he says, is that "she was a preacher, she did go out on

mission, but that those male authors never thought to tell us about it, given their sexist perspective on the world."

Or, Goodacre says, "it may also just be that she was quite old and died. It may be that nothing else much happened to her after that. It's entirely possible that if she was a widow, that she died not long afterward and nobody remembered anything much of anything beyond that key moment at the tomb."

Whatever the case, the Magdalene is nowhere in the letters of St. Paul or the other writings that make up the bulk of the New Testament and recount the growing pains of Christianity during its first few decades. Her hometown fared no better: after its destruction by the Romans, Magdala never recovered; there were no shrines to speak of, few pilgrims, no miracles or visions associated with the site. Even in recent years, the town, or what's left of it, has been little more than a weed-choked stretch of hardscrabble ground, marked by a small, battered roadside sign.

Yet even as her roots in history withered, the Magdalene's story, and her reputation, only grew in the minds of the faithful.

"A MUDDLE OF MARYS"

It wasn't just the absence of information about Mary Magdalene in the gospels that encouraged so many to fill in the blanks. It was also the surplus of Marys in the New Testament that helped people to embroider her story so creatively.

From burial records and surviving documents of the era, scholars estimate that as many as half of all women in first-century Palestine were named either Salome or Mary, or some version of that (such as Miriam). Christ's circle of followers was typical: in addition to his mother, Mary of Nazareth, aka the Virgin Mary, he had at least four other female followers named Mary: Mary, the mother of James the Less and Joses; Mary of Bethany, the sister of Martha and of Jesus's friend Lazarus; Mary of Clopas; and of course our own Mary of Magdala.

It's "a muddle of Marys," as the author Marina Warner calls it, and early Church leaders yielded to the temptation to try to clarify things—and explain the inconsistencies in the Easter narratives in the different gospels—by combining many of those Marys into one Magdalene.

The metamorphosis started with the conflation of Mary Magdalene with the Mary who is the sister of Martha as described in the Gospel of Luke. In that story, Jesus and the disciples stop in a village and are welcomed by Martha into her home. As she is busy preparing their meal, her sister Mary—never called the Magdalene—sits at Jesus's feet, hanging on his every word. In an exchange that has resonated through the ages, Martha complains:

> *"Lord, do you not care that my sister has left me to do all the work by myself? Tell her then to help me." But the Lord answered her, "Martha, Martha, you are worried and distracted by many things; there is need of only one thing. Mary has chosen the better part, which will not be taken away from her."*

Nowhere is this Mary identified as Mary Magdalene, but that physical and emotional closeness she shares with Jesus seems to be of a piece with the intimacy that Mary Magdalene and Jesus will later share at the cross and the tomb.

The connection between Jesus and Martha's sister Mary is further solidified in the Gospel of John, which is the only one to tell the story of the raising of Lazarus from the dead. Martha and Mary are identified in the story as Lazarus's sisters, and Jesus as a close friend: "Now Jesus loved Martha and her sister and Lazarus." In one of the most affecting scenes in the gospels, the sisters send word that Lazarus is ill and Jesus must come to heal him. But Jesus tarries, and Lazarus dies. When he arrives at the village, Bethany, Martha greets him, but when he meets Mary she falls at his feet and says, "Lord, if you had been here, my brother would not have died." Her words upset Jesus, and he weeps at the tomb of Lazarus. Then he raises him from the dead.

In this passage, Mary, Martha's sister, is again never called the Magdalene but is described as "the one who had anointed the Lord with perfumed oil and dried his feet with her hair." In the very next chapter, Martha again serves him at dinner while Mary, her sister, "took a liter of costly perfumed oil made from genuine aromatic nard and anointed the feet of Jesus and dried them with her hair."

This touching scene foreshadows the villainy of Judas Iscariot, who complains that the perfume should have been sold and the money given to the poor. (We are told he really wanted to steal the money—Judas was greedy, John is telling us, and that greed will lead to the betrayal a few days later.) "Leave her alone," Jesus says. "Let her keep this for the day of my burial. You always have the poor with you, but you do not always have me."

This Mary, sister of Martha, was early on identified as Mary Magdalene, and once that connection was made, however unfounded, it was a short step to assuming that Mary Magdalene was also the "sinful woman" in Luke, chapter 7, who, on learning that Jesus is dining at the house of a Pharisee, brings an alabaster jar of pricey perfume with which to anoint his feet. The woman, who is never named, wets Jesus's feet with her tears, wipes them with her hair, and finally anoints them with the scented oil. The Pharisee protests that Jesus should not let such a woman do this to him, but Jesus says her great love has redeemed her many sins. "Your faith has saved you," he tells the woman. "Go in peace."

In the very next chapter, Luke introduces Mary Magdalene by name, the first time he mentions her, describing her as the woman "from whom seven demons had gone out." The proximity with the sinful woman in the previous chapter and the clear identification of Mary Magdalene as a woman who had been plagued by demons sealed the Magdalene's fate in the eyes of the world. (The ending of the Gospel of Mark, which was likely added well after the original text was composed, also identifies the Magdalene as the woman "out of whom [Jesus] had driven seven demons.")

Demonic possession was read by some as code for unbridled lust, which was especially disturbing in a woman, and early exegetes (preachers and interpreters of the Scriptures) also began associating Mary Magdalene with the unnamed woman caught in adultery in John's gospel. Some even saw Mary Magdalene as the Samaritan woman at the well in the fourth chapter of John, whom Jesus pegs as having had several husbands while living in sin with another man who is not her husband.

It seemed that nothing could save Mary Magdalene's reputation.

Her fate as a repentant debauchee was sealed on September 21 in the year 591, when Pope Gregory the Great preached a homily in the Basilica of San Clemente in Rome on Luke's story of the sinful woman anointing Jesus's feet with her tears and with ointment from an alabaster jar.

"We believe that this woman," Pope Gregory declared, "whom Luke calls a female sinner, whom John calls Mary, is that Mary from whom Mark says seven demons were cast out." Those seven demons, of course, symbolized the seven deadly sins, the worst of which, as always, was lust:

> It is clear, brothers, that the woman previously used the unguent to perfume her flesh in forbidden acts. What she therefore displayed more scandalously, she was now offering to God in a more praiseworthy manner. She had coveted with earthly eyes, but now through penitence these are consumed with tears. She

displayed her hair to set off her face, but now her hair dries her tears. She had spoken proud things with her mouth, but in kissing the Lord's feet, she now planted her mouth on the Redeemer's feet. For every delight, therefore, she had had in herself, she now immolated herself. She turned the mass of her crimes to virtues, in order to serve God entirely in penance.

As the saying goes, *Roma locuta est, causa finita est.* "When Rome speaks, the argument is over." From then on, Mary Magdalene was the lascivious vixen who repented, and would be forever depicted with long, flowing hair (and often nothing else) and a jar of ointment.

Not that Gregory's sermon dented the Magdalene's popularity with the faithful. On the contrary, everyone wanted a piece of her—Magdalene relics proliferated throughout Europe in the Middle Ages, and there were plenty of versions of the Magdalene's story to keep everyone happy.

According to one tradition, Mary Magdalene accompanied John the Evangelist—the gospel writer who gave her such a dramatic and detailed role in the Easter morning discovery—to Ephesus, on the coast of modern-day Turkey. She was accompanied by the Virgin Mary, according to this version, and both ended their earthly lives there. Mary Magdalene's body was eventually enshrined at Constantinople, in 886 CE, laid next to the body of her brother, Lazarus.

Another story says that Mary Magdalene made a side trip to Rome and met the emperor Tiberius, proclaiming the news of Christ's resurrection and showing the emperor a plain egg as a symbol of that new life. Tiberias reportedly laughed and said that rising from the dead was as likely as the egg in her hand turning red, and before the words were out of his imperial mouth, the egg turned red. Hence, one explanation for our modern tradition of coloring eggs at Easter.

The most popular Magdalene story, however, is also the most entertaining: in this version, following the execution of Jesus's brother James, leader of the Church in Jerusalem, Mary Magdalene sets out in a boat without oars, rudder, or sails, along with Lazarus and his sisters, all under the guidance of a disciple named Maximin. The group eventually, and miraculously, lands in the South of France and establishes a church there, led by Maximin. Mary Magdalene wins many converts preaching to the pagans around Marseilles, it is said, before retiring to a cave in the hills outside town—La Sainte-Baume, which means "holy cave" in the local dialect—where she spends her final years subsisting in the wilderness like a hermit.

(That version of the Magdalene story, the so-called *vita eremetica*, is actually a conflation with the story of St. Mary of Egypt, a prostitute from Alexandria who repented her sinful ways and went off to live in the desert for the rest of her days, the most ascetic of penitents, subsisting on whatever she could scrounge, nearly naked and barely recognizable as a human being.)

According to tradition, as Mary Magdalene lay dying in her holy cave, angels carried her to Aix-en-Provence, where Maximin lived. When she died, Maximin embalmed her body and built a chapel for her, St. Maximinus at Villa Lata, where she was laid to rest—but not forever: In 771, reportedly out of fear of Muslim invaders in the South of France, the Magdalene's relics were transported to a new Benedictine abbey founded in the hill town of Vézelay, in Burgundy. An enormous basilica, one of the glories of Romanesque architecture, was built on the site and became a major pilgrimage center in medieval Europe (though local peasants were taxed so heavily to pay for it that, at one point, they rose up and killed the abbot in retaliation).

In 1279, Charles II of Anjou, King of Naples, ordered an excavation at Saint-Maximin-la-Sainte-Baume in Provence. He looked into the sarcophagus there and found most of the Magdalene's body intact, as well as the skull, minus the lower jaw, which was venerated at a basilica in Rome. These were the Magdalene's real relics, he proclaimed. A Dominican convent was erected at the site, and in the competition to exalt their respective Magdalenes, the Dominicans won out. (It may have helped that King Charles exempted the townspeople of Provence from taxes to fund the construction.) Mary's lower jaw was reunited with the rest of her head in 1295, and today the blackened skull stares out at pilgrims from an ornate golden bust that echoes the Magdalene's reputed beauty in life.

If all these traditions and transpositions, myths and mash-ups, were an insult to the historical reality of the woman from Magdala, and to her earthly remains, they also represented an exaltation that brought her, and Christian women in general, closer to wielding genuine authority in the Church, to a degree not seen since its earliest years.

"SHE WAS EQUAL TO JOHN THE BAPTIST"

From the distance of centuries, and through the fogged-up lens of today's hot-and-heavy conspiracy theories about the suppression of the "real" Mary Magdalene, it can be hard to recognize just how popular this saint once was.

If the Virgin Mary was the Queen of Heaven, the mother of us all and the first recourse of rosary-reciting supplicants seeking special access to Jesus, then Mary Magdalene was "the people's saint." She was one of us, a depraved sinner—forget the real story—who cleaned up her act and earned a special place among the followers of Jesus, if not the *best* place, there at the Resurrection. She is the Lost Sheep rescued by the Shepherd, and as Jesus said, "there will be more rejoicing in heaven over one sinner who repents than over ninety-nine righteous persons who do not need to repent." Mary Magdalene is better the way she is, and we can be, too.

Mary Magdalene was also tailor-made for the "rediscovery of the individual" that blossomed in the twelfth century. In that era, tales of great heroes and great saints became enormously popular, and Europeans hung on every word about Mary Magdalene—and authors made sure to give them every word about her they could find, or invent. Especially successful was the book known as *The Golden Legend*, a dense collection of biographies of dozens of saints and miracle stories cobbled together from various traditions by a Dominican bishop named Jacobus de Voragine in about 1260. By the fifteenth century, the volume by de Voragine was the most printed book in Europe, and some nine hundred manuscripts of it survive, a remarkable number.

Yet more than just storytelling and mythmaking elevated the Magdalene above the others. Instead, it was the recovery of her original role in announcing the Resurrection that gave her at least the aura of authority.

Starting in the 800s and peaking in the 1200s, the greatest preachers of the age began referring to Mary Magdalene by the title by which she would become widely known, *Apostola Apostolorum*, the "Apostle to the Apostles," because it was she who announced the Resurrection to the other apostles. Augustine first applied the title to her in the fourth century, but now Abbott Geoffrey of Vendôme specifically referred to the Magdalene's words as preaching—at a time, as often remains the case today, when women were barred from preaching. The Magdalene, Abbott Geoffrey said, was a *praedicatrix* who "preached what Peter denied," that is, the Resurrection. Psalters and hymnals and other illuminated texts also began to depict Mary Magdalene as the "Apostle to the Apostles," showing her wagging a finger as she lectures doubtful male apostles about the truth of Christ's teachings.

This was revolutionary. The Jewish world that the historical Mary of Magdala grew up in wasn't exactly what a modern-day observer would consider egalitarian. Women of the time were barred from divorcing their husbands, though a husband could divorce his wife for any number of violations, including leaving her hair unbound, as the Magdalene would be shown doing in later depictions. Divorce could also be a devastating fate: it often left a woman with no support and few opportunities in a dangerous world; if accused of adultery, she could be threatened with stoning.

In the synagogues, women sat apart from men in a small gallery, and were considered "unclean" during menstruation. While they could read the Torah, they were not allowed to preach on the text or perform any liturgical functions. "Rather should the words of the Torah be burned than entrusted to a woman!" said the first-century rabbi Eliezer. "Whoever teaches his daughter the Torah is like one who teaches her lasciviousness."

Jesus set a different example, welcoming prostitutes as well as tax collectors, lepers, and beggars—all society's outcasts. "Jesus appears to have preached a very radical ethics, which emphasized that the high and mighty and powerful people in society would give way to some of the lower elements in society: the sick, the poor, the infirm, and many women may have been inspired by this message because they, too, were at the bottom of the societal totem pole," says Garroway.

Yet if Jesus was unusually inclusive, he didn't leave any statements that would have explicitly endorsed women as wielding authority on a par with men in Judaism, or in a future church. So whatever Jesus thought of the role of women, his later followers reverted to the cultural norm, reinforcing, and at times amplifying into outright misogyny, the existing barriers to women's participation.

Like Jesus, the apostle Paul initially promoted a new role for women. In letters to his fellow believers, he emphasized that there is "neither male nor female, for you are all one in Christ Jesus," and Paul frequently referred to the crucial role that women, especially widows and wealthy benefactors, played in hosting fledgling congregations in house churches. He called one female colleague, Junia, an apostle, and another, Phoebe, a deacon—an office held by both men and women in the early Church.

Yet in other places, Paul also writes about the secondary role women should play, holding their tongues and submitting meekly to men, who have a God-given authority over them. In his first letter to the church at Corinth, for example, Paul writes that if women "want to learn anything, they should ask their husbands at home. For it is improper for a woman to speak in the church." And in his First Letter to Timothy, he repeats that refrain: "Let a woman learn quietly with all submissiveness. I do not permit a woman to teach or to exercise authority over a man; rather, she is to remain quiet."

Despite this, scholars ranging from Jerome Murphy-O'Connor to Elaine Pagels believe that these assertions are so out of character for Paul that they were later additions by editors trying to limit or eliminate positions for women in the Church. "A hundred years after Paul, women were no longer allowed to have positions in the churches that were prominent," Pagels says. "They weren't allowed to speak, they weren't allowed to lead congregations and so forth. And this probably has to do with the movement of Christian groups into upper-class Roman culture, in which women didn't have these roles and men had all of the prominent roles. So what you see is the Christian movement taking on the cultural shape of its neighbors, naturally. And with that, women are excluded from positions of leadership."

The restorationists, who wanted to reassert patriarchal authority, were successful. As the decades and centuries passed, women were increasingly barred from active participation, while the Church Fathers who shaped the faith trafficked in a hair-raising degree of outright misogyny.

For Clement of Alexandria, for example, "the very consciousness of women's own nature must evoke feelings of shame," and the third-century theologian Origen (who may have castrated himself to spur his devotion to purely spiritual matters) called women "the devil's gateway" for introducing sin and death into the world. St. John Chrysostom was terrified of women, describing their beautiful bodies as "a whitened sepulcher," a death trap for men seeking holiness. His fourth-century contemporary St. Augustine was similarly disposed, viewing women as essentially inferior and arguing that if a woman "wishes to serve Christ more than the world, then she will cease to be a woman, and will be called man."

Even Mary Magdalene, the Apostle to the Apostles, was enlisted in the campaign against women. St. Ambrose, the archbishop of Milan in the fourth century and one of the most influential churchmen of the era, interpreted Christ's tender words to her on Easter morning, "Do not cling to me" (the famous Latin phrase *Noli me tangere*) as meaning that women were forbidden to teach in Church— and this from a passage about a woman announcing the Resurrection itself!

By the twelfth century, the prohibition had expanded to mean that women could not preach or administer the sacraments, and a series of decrees over the next century ensured that women were explicitly forbidden from touching sacred objects, carrying the consecrated host to the sick, or even entering the sanctuary, which became a male-only arena.

Mary Magdalene, on the other hand, represented a popular and seemingly irrefutable witness against these decrees. "She showed she was equal to John the Baptist in being more than a prophet . . . Her deeds are equal to his," wrote a Cistercian monk in an early twelfth-century account. This language marks a turning point in the conception of Mary Magdalene. Yes, she was still the repentant sinner and all those other historically unsupported yet profoundly moving conflations, but now the Magdalene was also the first and greatest preacher of the Word as well.

Indeed, when Charles of Anjou had the Magdalene's original sarcophagus at Saint-Maximin-la-Baume opened in 1279, his officials reported finding a green palm shoot growing from the saint's tongue. What better proof that she had a special role in preaching the message of new life?

Yet preachers—the men, at least—were nothing if not inventive, and just as they had done a thousand years before, they gradually explained away the Magdalene's privileged role. Yes, she was a preacher, some conceded, but only by a special divine dispensation because the Church had so few preachers at the time of Jesus. (Perhaps because all the men had fled?) Others argued the Magdalene had to bring the message of the Resurrection to the world to balance out the fact that Eve, the first woman, had brought death to the world by her sin in the Garden of Eden. Some even taught that Jesus first appeared to Mary Magdalene because he knew women couldn't keep quiet about anything and therefore a woman would be the best vehicle for spreading the news fastest. "Foolish preachers," fumed the thirteenth-century author and poet (and woman) Christine de Pisan.

As usual, however, the most common explanation for Mary Magdalene's special role returned to her great sinfulness: Christ revealed himself to such a depraved soul to reinforce the message that he had come not for the righteous but for the sinners.

For almost five hundred years the image of Mary Magdalene as the Apostle to the Apostles inspired the faithful and encouraged women. Yet Church leaders would have their way, and increasing devotion did not translate to women wielding authority.

THE "LAST TEMPTATION"

The Magdalene fared no better when the secular world began adopting her as its own. This first started happening in earnest as vainglorious Renaissance royal courts and minor aristocrats began supplanting bishops and monasteries as the primary patrons of the arts. In adapting sacred topics to their secular ends, they found the Magdalene every bit as attractive and malleable as the faithful did. Suddenly, on canvases in drawing rooms across Europe, Mary Magdalene's "penitential guise now adorned the flesh of kings' mistresses, duchesses, other aristocrats, and the 'lighter ladies' of the court, as well as artists' wives, mistresses and daughters," Haskins writes. The saint's image, she says, was "adopted merely as an irreverent joke or as yet another fancy dress, alongside the shepherdesses, goddesses, virtues and other allegorical figures as whom these predominantly upper-class women chose to have themselves portrayed." Somehow a saint who had been a reproach to vanity and luxury now became the embodiment of indulgence.

In a similar fashion, but with a completely different goal, eighteenth-century reformers in England began appropriating the Magdalene as justification for purging society of prostitutes and wayward ladies, establishing asylums for these lost souls that they dubbed "Magdalene houses." Yet instead of producing newly minted saints like their namesake, these reformatories, often run for the state by both the Protestant and Catholic Churches, became more like prisoner-of-war camps. The saint who had been an icon of consolation was now a cudgel to use against young women.

Eventually, the churches grew more enlightened than the secular world. Unlike the Catholics and even most Protestant traditions that emerged from the Reformation, the Eastern Orthodox churches had never bought into the Magdalene-as-prostitute mash-up, and always venerated her as a disciple first, with some even arguing that she, like Jesus's mother, was a virgin. In the 1960s, the Vatican finally caught up to reality, officially declaring what everyone knew was the historical truth: that Mary Magdalene was not the sinful woman or any of those other mislabeled Marys in the gospels, but was first and foremost "the first person to whom Christ appeared after his Resurrection."

Ironically, just as the Christian world was rehabilitating Mary Magdalene, popular culture picked up where European aristocrats had left off, ensuring that the Magdalene, as Haskins writes, "remained locked in her mythical persona." The advent of film proved especially tantalizing for directors who couldn't resist the siren call of a lascivious vixen who becomes enchanted with the one man she can't have. Cecil B. DeMille's 1927 silent epic *The King of Kings* even expands the sexual tension, setting up a love triangle with Jesus and Judas and the Magdalene, who is depicted as a lavish courtesan riding out on a zebra-drawn chariot to get Judas back because he is spending too much time with the Messiah.

Subsequent movies and dramas did little to redeem the Magdalene from this stereotype, or from centuries of misrepresentation. In the 1971 musical *Godspell*, Mary Magdalene is the adulteress Jesus saved from stoning, and a year earlier, in the rock opera *Jesus Christ, Superstar*, she is a woman of ill repute who falls for Jesus but can't figure out how she can relate to him without having sex with him. "I don't know how to love him," she sings in one of the sound track's signature songs. (The love triangle also emerges here, as Judas grows increasingly jealous of the Magdalene, which fuels his eventual betrayal.)

In Franco Zeffirelli's 1977 TV miniseries, *Jesus of Nazareth*, Anne Bancroft likewise portrays Mary Magdalene as a prostitute, and Mel Gibson's *Passion of the Christ* (2004), while focusing only on the days leading up to the Crucifixion, manages to wedge in a flashback of Mary Magdalene as the woman taken in adultery. The movie climaxes on an evocative shot of the Resurrection, but with no reference to the Magdalene. Her most important role was left on the cutting-room floor.

The most explicit and controversial movie Magdalene was Barbara Hershey's Mary in the 1988 Martin Scorsese version of *The Last Temptation of Christ*. Scorsese's Magdalene is a composite of nearly every sinful woman mentioned in the gospels. She becomes a prostitute when Jesus refuses to marry her, and he later saves her from stoning when she is accused of having sex with Romans on the sabbath. The "last temptation" is, in fact, Jesus's fantasy, as he hangs on the cross, of marrying the Magdalene, who then becomes pregnant with their child. But she dies shortly thereafter, and Jesus marries both Martha and her sister Mary, enjoying children and a long life. This is, however—spoiler alert!—a dream sequence planted by Satan. In the end, Jesus rejects that option and returns to die on the cross and fulfill his mission. Again, there is no Resurrection, and no female Apostle to the Apostles announcing the good news.

Even a Catholic as avowedly orthodox as Fox News' Bill O'Reilly, in his best-selling 2013 book on the gospels, *Killing Jesus*, presents the young Mary Magdalene as a wayfaring girl whose parents are destitute. Her innocence, O'Reilly writes, "will inevitably be shattered in the shabby confines of that outlaw village" and she will "grow up to be a prostitute."

The pervasive representation of the Magdalene as a repentant bad girl has endured despite simultaneous efforts of Bible scholars to recover the real Magdalene of history, a far more interesting and challenging figure than the siren shown on film. Yet it seemed to have no effect, and more than a few scholars have used historical research to undergird speculations about the sex lives of the Magdalene and Jesus. In 1970, for example, Presbyterian theologian Wil-

The life of Jesus was dramatically reconstructed in the CNN series *Finding Jesus*

Joseph hoists his son Jesus, with brother James and sister waiting their turn.

As a boy, Jesus helps his mother, Mary, with daily household chores. As a man, he would leave that home for a dangerous mission.

> "And everyone who has left houses or brothers or sisters or father or mother or children or fields, for my name's sake, will receive a hundredfold, and will inherit eternal life."
> —Matthew 19:29

Jesus, as a youth, learned carpentry, to follow in his father Joseph's footsteps.

The tools of a first-century carpenter.

Jesus, flanked by Judas and Mary Magdalene, traveled the length and breadth of Judea and Samaria, proclaiming his divine vision.

"Soon afterwards he went on through cities and villages, proclaiming and bringing the good news of the kingdom of God. The twelve were with him, as well as some women who had been cured of evil spirits and infirmities: Mary, called Magdalene, from whom seven demons had gone out . . ."
—Luke 8:1–3

Judas, with the thirty pieces of silver he received for betraying Jesus. The Gospel of Matthew states that after Jesus died, Judas returned the money and hanged himself out of guilt.

"Then one of the twelve, who was called Judas Iscariot, went to the chief priests and said, 'What will you give me if I betray him to you?' They paid him thirty pieces of silver. And from that moment he began to look for an opportunity to betray him."
—Matthew 26:14–16

Mary Magdalene came from the fishing village of Magdala, and she supported Jesus and his ministry with her own funds, says the Gospel of Luke. She is thought to be the second most important woman in his life, after his mother.

"The Savior loved you more than all other women."
—The Gospel of Mary Magdalene

Jesus enters Jerusalem in triumph before the feast of Passover, with the crowds cheering him as their savior. A few days later, he would be dead.

"When he entered Jerusalem, the whole city was in turmoil, asking, 'Who is this?' The crowds were saying, 'This is the prophet Jesus from Nazareth in Galilee.'"
—Matthew 21:10–11

James (left) with his brother, Jesus. After Jesus died, James became the leader of this new strand of Judaism in Jerusalem. He would die for his faith, too.

"... but I did not see any other apostle except James the Lord's brother." —Paul, Letter to the Galatians 1:19

Roman soldiers fashioned a crown of thorns and placed it on Jesus's head to mock him as "King of the Jews."

"... and after twisting some thorns into a crown, they put it on his head. They put a reed in his right hand and knelt before him and mocked him, saying, 'Hail, King of the Jews!'" —Matthew 27:29

The tools of a Roman crucifixion squad. Tens of thousands of people were killed by crucifixion during Jesus's lifetime.

"Therefore I send you prophets, sages, and scribes, some of whom you will kill and crucify ..." —Matthew 23:34

A Roman soldier pierced Jesus's body with a spear to make sure that he was dead.

"... one of the soldiers pierced his side with a spear, and at once blood
and water came out. . . . These things occurred so that the scripture
might be fulfilled, 'None of his bones shall be broken.'"

—John 19:34–36

Pharisees watch Jesus's entry into Jerusalem. His message is a direct threat to
their authority.

"Then the scribes and the Pharisees began to question, 'Who is this who is
speaking blasphemies? Who can forgive sins but God alone?'" —Luke 5:21

Mary, mother of Jesus, and Mary Magdalene witness Jesus's crucifixion. Jesus's disciples have fled.

"There were also women looking on from a distance; among them were Mary Magdalene, and Mary the mother of James the younger and of Joses, and Salome. They used to follow him and provided for him when he was in Galilee."   —Mark 15:40–41

A Roman soldier prepares to hammer a nail through Jesus's wrist.

Simon of Cyrene helps the bloodied and beaten Jesus carry his cross to Golgotha.

"As they went out, they came upon a man from Cyrene named Simon; they compelled this man to carry his cross."
—Matthew 27:32

The Romans placed a mocking "titulus" on Jesus's cross, reading "INRI"—in Latin, "Iesus Naza-renus Rex Iudeaorum."

"Over his head they put the charge against him, which read, 'This is Jesus, the King of the Jews.'"
—Matthew 27:37

"Then Jesus, crying with a loud voice, said, 'Father, into your hands I com-mend my spirit.' Having said this, he breathed his last."   —Luke 23:41

liam Phipps suggested that Jesus married Mary Magdalene, and that she was unfaithful—though of course Jesus forgave her. In 1992, Australian Bible scholar Barbara Thiering doubled down on that thesis, and the "last temptation" narrative, in her book *Jesus the Man*, in which she argues that Jesus survived the Crucifixion and later married—twice.

The most influential of these theories, and the most bizarre elaboration of Magdalene myths since Jacobus de Voragine in the thirteenth century, is the 1982 book *Holy Blood, Holy Grail*, by Michael Baigent, Richard Leigh, and Henry Lincoln. In this "scholarly" investigation, the authors determine that the Crucifixion was faked, and Jesus was smuggled onto that boat with Mary Magdalene and her brother, Lazarus, bound for the South of France. Once there, Jesus and Mary settled down and had kids, children of the Messiah's "holy blood," or "royal blood"—or in the French dialect, *sang réel*. Of course, if you say the words real fast, they sound like *saint graal*, or—voilà!—"Holy Grail." Thus the Holy Grail is not the cup from the Last Supper, as we have thought, but the bloodline of Jesus, borne by Mary Magdalene, herself a sacred vessel. In this theory, the progeny of that bloodline goes on to marry into the Merovingian dynasty of French aristocrats, with designs on ruling a reunited Christendom. All this is conspiratorially protected by a shadowy group known as the Priory of Sion, a legacy of the Knights Templar.

In the end, the Magdalene's modern devotees seem to have done her no favors. Or were they onto something? Startling discoveries from the sands of Egypt indicate that some of the earliest Christians were also debating the relationship between Jesus and Mary Magdalene, and the role of women in the Church.

Can these discoveries tell us anything about who the Magdalene really was—and what she means for believers today?

"EVERY FEMALE WHO MAKES HERSELF MALE WILL ENTER KINGDOM'S HEAVEN"

When an Egyptian farmer named Muhammed al-Samman came upon twelve leather-bound codices while digging in the hills near the Nile village of Nag Hammadi in Upper Egypt in 1945, he almost single-handedly changed how historians and the public would view Christianity.

The corpus of fifty-two texts were almost all from the school of what we call Gnosticism, a diverse array of Christian communities that flourished in the decades after the canonical gospels were written (that is, after about 90 CE) and died out—or were crushed, depending on which version of history you prefer—within a few centuries. They take their name from the Greek word for knowledge, *gnosis*, and in their case it is a very particular, and secret, knowledge. Salvation in this theology came not as much through belief in Jesus and the sacrifice on the cross as through a type of learning that could be attained by the select few who had the divine spark within and were thus privileged with a secret revelation. For Gnostics, this special knowledge was more than power. It was salvation itself.

Gnostic doctrines were often wildly divergent, but they tended to share beliefs that the present world and all that is in it is "evil through and through" and that human beings, because they consist of matter and exist in this corrupted time and space, are also inherently bad. That's why the goal of wise people is to escape this wicked, material world and "outward human existence."

Also, the Gnostics believed, with traditional Christians and Jews, that this world of ours was created by the God of the Old Testament—except, for the Gnostics, that God was not the real, true God, or even a good god. Rather, this creator-god was a lesser deity, a foolish and malevolent being who formed this cruel world and everything in it, often in cahoots with a number of other dodgy deities.

In the Gnostic doctrine, you were saved not by worshiping the God who created this present world, but by escaping the world he created to reach a higher existence and spiritual union with the pure, holy, and true divinity. Needless to say, this dualistic theology (which includes innumerable other pantheons and deities), with its rejection of the body and the material world and the God of Abraham, was heresy to the orthodox version of Christianity that was fighting to maintain its beliefs and predominance in the fast-growing early Church.

Yet until the Nag Hammadi finds, almost all we knew about the Gnostics came from their enemies—through polemics such as the second-century treatise *Against Heresies*, by Irenaeus, Bishop of Lyons, in France. Irenaeus and his allies eventually won out, and for nearly two millennia the Gnostics were a ghost from Christianity's dim past. Even after the discovery of the Nag Hammadi codices, it took decades for the texts to make their way through the antiquities market and into the hands of scholars, and only in 1979, with the publication of *The Gnostic Gospels*, by Princeton University's Elaine Pagels, did Gnosticism enter the public consciousness. And did it ever. Amazingly, a book about these esoteric texts nearly two thousand years old captured the imagination, and the book became a best seller, and sparked an ongoing fascination with what really happened in the early days of Christianity, and whether the Church has been hiding the truth all these centuries.

At times, this conspiratorial view has gotten out of hand, and the Gnostic texts have often been simplified, sanitized, and hitched to various modern hobbyhorses, to the detriment of the historical record. In fact, Gnostic beliefs were so diverse and downright bizarre in their cosmology that many of their proponents have begun asking whether the term *Gnosticism*—which was coined by modern scholars—really has any value.

Leaving all these debates aside, one aspect that emerged early on after the popularization of the Gnostic gospels, and the one view about Gnosticism that has persisted, is that is it a far more female-friendly version of the faith than anything that survived in orthodox Christianity. As Esther de Boer, a leading scholar of Gnosticism, has put it, the range of female characters and images in the Gnostic library is "impressive." Sophia is a goddess, Norea is a savior, the soul is decidedly feminine, and women disciples play a major role, none more than Mary Magdalene. For example, one major Nag Hammadi text is the Pistis Sophia, or "Faith Wisdom," a long, and often uninspiring, series of gnostic reflections presented as Jesus's answers to questions from his disciples. Of the sixty-four questions in the Pistis Sophia, thirty-nine are asked by a woman who is referred to as Mary, or more explicitly, as Mary Magdalene.

At one point Jesus even says of Mary: "Mary, thou blessed one, whom I will perfect in all mysteries of those of the height, discourse in openness, thou, whose heart is raised to the kingdom of heaven more than all thy brethren."

More tantalizing to modern sensibilities accustomed to a chaste Jesus is that the Gnostic texts seem to depict the Magdalene not only as a leader but as an intimate of Jesus. To take one well-known example: the papyrus text of the Gospel of Philip, part of the Nag Hammadi library, has many holes and missing words, but one passage can be reconstructed as reading:

The companion of the [Savior] is Mary Magdalene. The [Savior loved] her more than [all] the disciples, [and he] kissed her often on her [mouth]. The other [disciples] . . . said to him, "Why do you love her more than all of us?" The savior answered and said to them, "Why do I not love you like her? If a blind person and one who can see are both in darkness, they are the same. When the light comes, one who can see will see the light, and the blind person will stay in darkness."

Jesus kissing Mary? On her—well, it must be her mouth, even though there's a frustrating gap in the text at that point. Yet readers of these texts were quick to fill in the blanks, and a new conventional wisdom soon emerged: that key parts of the Jesus story had been suppressed, especially when it came to sex, specifically between Jesus and the Magdalene, and that Gnosticism was the lost feminist version of Christianity.

Yet even the most die-hard champions of the Gnostics caution against reading too much egalitarianism, or hanky-panky, into these texts. For one, thing, they note that these "gospels" are not gospels in the way that we think of Matthew, Mark, Luke, and John. Not just because they did not make the official, "orthodox" canon of sacred scripture, but because they do not purport to be actual versions of Jesus's life and ministry. They were written decades, even centuries, after the gospels of the New Testament, and they are often rambling disquisitions on an arcane theology, or—as in the case of the Gnostic "Gospel of Thomas"—a collection of sayings that can seem impenetrable because they have so little context.

As for Jesus and Mary Magdalene as a couple, scholars say that the Gnostics, like many early Christians, were often intimate in nonsexual ways. There was always a great deal of hugging and kissing by way of greeting. In the Gospel of Philip, for instance, Christians greet each other with kisses to convey the sense that they are a spiritual family. Yes, there does seem to be a particular fascination in some Gnostic texts with the idea that Jesus had a close—too close—physical relationship with women. Yet that tension is also resolved through a characteristically Gnostic solution: Mary becomes, as in the Pistis Sophia, an "entirely pure spirit." She leaves the corrupt body and her gender behind.

"The Gospel of Philip is a mystical text," says Pagels. "It speaks of Mary as the Holy Spirit, as the Church, which is the Bride of Christ, as Divine Wisdom. So Mary here represents these spiritual qualities in the Gospel of Philip . . . She's extrapolated to speak about the spiritual, feminine companion of Jesus."

This points to another serious reservation about seeing the Gnostics as especially female-friendly: the Gnostic texts view the male sex as superior, and women as women are no more valued than they are in orthodox Christianity. For example, the Gospel of Thomas records Simon Peter telling Jesus that Mary [Magdalene] "should leave us, for females are not worthy of life." Jesus does not rebuke Peter but instead says: "Look, I shall guide her to make her male, so that she too may become a living spirit resembling you males. For every female who makes herself male will enter kingdom's heaven."

Studies have shown that throughout the Gnostic texts, in fact, for every episode in which a woman plays a central role, there are two in which the man is dominant. Also, in some of the episodes in the canonical gospels that feature women prominently, women have been scrubbed from the scene in the Gnostic version. The Magdalene in the Gnostic texts is in fact highly regarded, but "precisely because she has transcended her inferior femaleness," as de Boer writes. (De Boer died at fifty-one in 2010.) The Magdalene was not transformed into a penitent prostitute the way she was by the Church Fathers, but neither was she the strong female character who played an important role in the early Church, as so many women clearly did. She had moved beyond her gender. "Why can't a woman be more like a man?" wonders an exasperated Henry Higgins in *My Fair Lady*. The Gnostics, like many in the ancient world, wondered the same thing. "It is far too simple to conclude that orthodox Christianity would have given Mary Magdalene little credit while Gnostic Christianity would have had high esteem for her," de Boer says.

Yet there is one thread running through these Gnostic texts that does underscore a debate that was going on in all streams of Christianity in its infancy, just as it is today, two millennia later: women are trying to speak up, to assert themselves, and that really infuriates the men. "My master," Peter says to Jesus in the Pistis Sophia text, "we cannot endure this woman [Mary Magdalene] who gets in our way and does not let any of us speak, though she talks all the time." Mary confides to Jesus that "I am afraid of Peter, because he threatens me and hates our gender."

This conflict is set out most clearly, and with perhaps the greatest relevance for today, in the Gospel of Mary—the only such text from early Christianity to be named after a woman.

BACK TO THE GOSPELS . . . BACK TO THE FUTURE?

The Gospel of Mary was not part of the Nag Hammadi discoveries in 1945 but was instead excavated somewhere near the village of Akhmim, in Upper Egypt, a half century earlier. It first turns up in the official records when it was purchased in Cairo in 1896 by a German scholar, Carl Reinhardt, and then taken to Berlin. The Gospel of Mary was found together in a codex with two other important Gnostic papyri, the Apocryphon of John and the Sophia of Jesus Christ. They were probably copied and bound in the late fourth or early fifth century and are Coptic translations from Greek texts that scholars such as Karen King date to the second century. Together they are known as the Berlin Gnostic Codex.

While the Gospel of Mary was discovered decades before the Nag Hammadi finds, it wasn't published until 1955, due to a series of misfortunes: A burst water pipe at a German publishing house in 1912 destroyed the entire edition as it was set to go to press. Then World War I erupted. Then the scholar trying to get out a definitive edition died in 1938, right on the eve of another global war that would devastate Europe and delay publication. Scholarly wheels grind slowly as well, and it wasn't until 1955 that the Gospel of Mary was finally published. It took the renewed interest in Mary Magdalene and Christian feminism two decades later, and Elaine Pagels's work on *The Gnostic Gospels*, to give this gospel the attention it deserves.

Yet for all its importance, the document has also suffered the vicissitudes of the centuries and contemporary antiquities wranglers. The text is missing pages 1 to 6 and pages 11 to 14, so we are left with chapters 4 and 5, and then chapters 8 and 9, where the gospel seems to end. It is a total of eight pages, about half the original.

Even with these gaps, the Gospel of Mary is one of the most important texts to emerge from the sands of Egypt, given the central role it gives to "Mary," who is presumed by most experts to be Mary Magdalene (though some contend that this Mary could be Jesus's mother). It is a thrilling document to see up close, with the clarity of the writing on the page. And it has such a provocative title: Mary Magdalene's version of her relationship to the Savior.

The Gospel of Mary is simple to summarize: It picks up with a dialogue between Jesus and his disciples, with the Savior delivering his wisdom about the fate of the material world and sin, and then exhorting them to "go then and preach the gospel of the Kingdom," and not to be legalistic about it. Then Jesus leaves. Yet the disciples are confused about what he has told them, and fearful that they will be persecuted. It is Mary Magdalene who bucks them up. "Do not weep and do not grieve nor be irresolute, for His grace will be entirely with you and will protect you." Peter concedes that "the Savior loved you more than all other women" and asks that she share any private revelations Jesus gave to her.

She agrees, and begins teaching them, many of the teachings contained in the missing pages. At the start of chapter 9, Mary concludes and falls silent. The apostle Andrew pipes up first, challenging her: "I do not believe that the savior said these things, for indeed these teachings are strange ideas." Peter then weighs in (as he often does in Gnostic texts, the counterpoint to the woman), fretting over why Jesus would share such teachings with a woman. "Are we to turn around and listen to her?" he says to the others. "Did he choose her over us?"

This brings Mary to tears, and Levi speaks up in her defense, telling Peter he has always been hotheaded (as he is in the canonical New Testament) and he should accept what Mary says:

> *For if the Savior made her worthy, who are you then for your part to reject her? Assuredly the Savior's knowledge of her is completely reliable. That is why he loved her more than us. Rather we should be ashamed. We should clothe ourselves with the perfect Human, acquire it for ourselves as he commanded us, and announce the good news, not laying down any other rule or law that differs from what the Savior said.*

This seems to calm Peter and the others, and after Levi speaks, they go out to teach and preach, and the Gospel of Mary comes to a close.

Scholarly, and popular, opinions vary on what all this means and how much weight to give the Gospel of Mary. For Karen King, the gospel "presents the most straightforward and convincing argument in any early Christian writing for the legitimacy of women's leadership," and it "asks us to rethink the basis for church authority." Some believe this gospel may even have been written by a woman. Esther de Boer argues that the Gospel of Mary is only superficially Gnostic, and ought to be categorized as closer to the traditional,

Judeo-Christian theology emerging in the century after Jesus. Others tend to downplay the gospel as another esoteric Gnostic text, a late addition to the debate among early Christians, and one whose acolytes faded away along with the ink on the papyri of their sacred texts.

In the end, no text, and no single woman, can bear the weight of so many expectations for what Christianity ought to be, and what role women should play in the faith. The Gnostic gospels of the second century certainly cannot stand up to such scrutiny, and neither can the medieval legends of Jacobus de Voragine or modern-day incarnations of such myth makers as Dan Brown. Also, hoping for some "lost gospel" to emerge from the Egyptian sands, or a forger's studio, to definitively show that Jesus and Mary Magdalene were married (or not) is more likely to lead us down a rabbit hole than to enlightenment.

Today's believers will instead have to work out for themselves, just as their brothers and sisters in the early Church did, what the role of women in the Church ought to be, and where they can find inspiration and justification for their views. For some, the Virgin Mary, or Mary of Nazareth, will be the principal model. For others, it will be Martha, or one of the other Marys in the New Testament, or one of the women who helped the apostle Paul evangelize the Mediterranean world. Others will be drawn for many reasons to the woman caught in adultery, or to the Samaritan woman at the well.

At the center of it all, though, as from the beginning, will be the "tower" of strength and faith from Magdala, the woman who supported the early Church out of her own means and delivered the news of the Resurrection as the Apostle to the Apostles. Neither repentant prostitute nor Mrs. Jesus, the Mary Magdalene of the New Testament stands on her own.

FOUR

The Gospel of Judas

Christianity's Ultimate Whodunit

The Gospel of Judas tells a different story about history's greatest betrayal—that Judas was acting on the instructions of Jesus himself. Or does it? *(Getty Images)*

Better an honest slap in the face than an insincere kiss.
—YIDDISH PROVERB

I f believers and skeptics alike know one thing about the New
Testament—apart from Jesus's birth in a manger (Christmas) and
death on the cross (Easter)—it's that Judas is the apostle who betrayed Christ and consigned him to a brutal death by crucifixion.

That's a notable exception to the widely remarked phenomenon
of "biblical illiteracy" that frustrates Church leaders. Yes, surveys
show that nine out of ten Americans own a copy of the Good Book,
and many of them cite chapter and verse to support their position
on any number of contentious issues. Yet the polls also consistently
show that owning a Bible isn't the same as knowing the Bible: only
half of all Americans can name a single gospel, and most Americans can't name half the Ten Commandments, even though the
Decalogue has become a focal point in the culture wars. Fifty percent of high school seniors think Sodom and Gomorrah were a married couple, rather than Old Testament cities associated with sexual
libertinism.

Research shows, however, that there is one biblical figure whom
a large majority of people recognize: Judas Iscariot. In one poll, up-
ward of 70 percent pegged him as the man who betrayed Jesus and
set in motion the events that led to the Crucifixion.

This finding should come as no surprise. Judas's crime is hei-
nous, and more easily recalled because it is so repulsive. Also, all

four Gospels tell the story, with varying details, recounting how Judas took thirty pieces of silver as the price for turning Jesus over to the authorities after the Last Supper. He then betrayed him with a kiss in the Garden of Gethsemane to seal his infamy, and went out and hanged himself in remorse, an acknowledgment of the guilt that would never be erased. "Woe to that man by whom the Son of Man is betrayed!" Jesus tells the disciples, including Judas, one of the original twelve, at that final meal, realizing full well what is about to befall him. "It would have been better for that man if he had not been born."

Death was certainly no release for Judas. The great medieval Italian poet Dante Alighieri sticks Judas in the bottom pit of the Inferno, the lowest circle of hell, where Dante consigns the "Traitors to their Benefactors" to an icy eternity of torment. At the center of it all is the monstrous figure of Satan, with three horrible heads and three of history's most notorious sinners dangling from each mouth: Brutus and Cassius, who assassinated Caesar; and in the center, Judas, who, unlike the other two, is being eaten head first, constantly flayed by the gnashing teeth but never killed:

> *"That upper spirit,*
> *Who hath worst punishment," so spake my guide,*
> *"Is Judas, he that hath his head within*
> *And plies the feet without."*

For centuries it continued thus for Judas. The Wednesday of Holy Week was dubbed Spy Wednesday because it was on the eve of Holy Thursday and the Last Supper, tradition holds, that Judas made the fateful decision to double-cross his master. The very name "Judas" was used to tar anyone who turned on his friends, and early on it was attached with especial ferocity to the Jewish people as a whole. As St. Jerome wrote in a sermon around the year 400 CE: "The

Jews take their name not from the Judah [fourth son of the patriarch Jacob] who was a holy man but from the betrayer." And what a price Jews paid for that ghastly slander! Some even argue that Judas was invented out of whole cloth by the gospel writers as a way to shift the blame for Christ's death from the Romans (whose terrible ire those early Christians did not want to provoke) and onto the Jews, a collective scapegoating. "The creators of this character and [of] the traditions related to him knew what it was they were seeking to do, and in this they have succeeded in a manner far beyond anything they might have imagined and that would have astonished even their hate-besotted brains," wrote Robert Eisenman, a professor of Middle East religions and archaeology at California State University–Long Beach and one of the more polemical scholars in biblical studies.

Few give credence to the "Judas-as-myth" theory. He is there from the earliest and most historically reliable accounts of Jesus's life, and in various sources. Moreover, Judas's betrayal is another good example of the "criterion of embarrassment" that indicates something in the Bible is true: "Why the church should have expended so much effort to create a story that it immediately had to struggle to explain away defies all logic," writes Bible scholar John Meier. As the late Bible scholar Raymond Brown notes in his magisterial work on the death of Jesus, early opponents of Christianity pointed to Jesus's choice of an apostle who would betray him as proof that Jesus was not perfect, and therefore was not divine. So there was ample motive for his followers to cut Judas out, but they didn't.

What is also beyond question is that Judas became an easy stand-in for any sort of perfidy. Herdsmen in rural lands refer to the "Judas goat" that leads the sheep to slaughter while the goat itself is spared; and a "Judas window" is the secret peephole by which guards can check on prisoners unobserved. In a more biblically literate time, which is any time before the last century, the usual analogies for an evil person were Pharaoh, whom everyone recognized for his cruelty in keeping God's chosen people in bondage in Egypt; Pontius Pilate, for allowing Jesus to be killed; and Judas, for initiating the homicidal process.

After the horrors of the Holocaust, "Adolf Hitler" supplanted the names all previous bad guys as the shorthand for ultimate evil, but Judas, much more than Pharaoh and Pilate, has endured as an almost universally recognized symbol of evil.

When rock legend Bob Dylan famously abandoned his acoustic guitar to "go electric" at a concert in 1965, at least one concertgoer yelled that he was a "Judas." Decades later, the jab still stung. "Judas, the most hated name in human history!" Dylan told *Rolling Stone* in 2012. "If you think you've been called a bad name, try to work your way out from under that. Yeah, and for what? For playing an electric guitar? As if that is in some kind of way equitable to betraying our Lord and delivering him up to be crucified."

For everyone, from churchgoers to rock fans, Judas was as low as you could go: he made his choice, did the deed, paid the price. End of story. Or so we thought.

Then, at Easter 2006, came an announcement that made headlines around the world: Judas, it turns out, had his own gospel, and in this ancient account the betrayer is in fact the hero, greater than any other apostle. This version of the Christian origin story upended everything we had known about Judas, and Jesus, and it had been lost—or suppressed—for eighteen hundred years.

"THE GOOD NEWS OF THE GOSPEL OF JUDAS"

"This scriptural text could shatter some of the interpretations, even the foundations, of faith throughout the Christian world," Herbert

Krosney wrote in the official account of the discovery of the Gospel of Judas, published by the National Geographic Society, which helped sponsor the restoration of the papyrus in exchange for exclusive rights to promote the stunning find. "It was not a novel," Krosney said. "It was a real gospel straight from the world of early Christianity."

So what was this "gospel," this revolutionary account of the "good news" of Jesus Christ, and what did it say?

The text was written on the front and back of thirteen sheets of crumbling papyrus, each about twelve inches by six inches, and bound in a frayed leather cover. The writing was in ancient Coptic, composed sometime in the third century CE, experts said, and most likely copied from an original Greek text written more than a century earlier, which would have been only a few decades after the canonical gospels of Matthew, Mark, Luke, and John were compiled. It was part of the Gnostic school of early Christian thought, those strange texts that died out—or were suppressed by the early Church—by the third or fourth century. It was mentioned in passing by Irenaeus, but no one knew what the gospel itself said, or that one might have survived all these centuries, until a handful of Gnostic experts were given a sneak peek.

This new gospel was, as it states in the opening lines, "the secret account of the revelation that Jesus spoke in conversation with Judas Iscariot in the days before he celebrated Passover"—that is, a series of dialogues held before the Last Supper and the events leading to the Crucifixion. Those conversations feature several remarkable exchanges between Jesus and his betrayer, who in this version is seen not as a villain but as Jesus's most intimate apostle, "the consummate insider, the one to whom Jesus delivers his secret revelation," said Bart Ehrman, a leading expert on early Christianity and Gnosticism at the University of North Carolina–Chapel Hill. The hero of this story is not John, the beloved disciple; nor Peter, the future pope to whom Jesus gave the keys to the kingdom and the role as corner-stone of the future Church. No, Jesus's most loyal follower is Judas Iscariot. "Judas is the one faithful disciple, the one who understands Jesus, the one who receives salvation," Ehrman said. "The other disciples, and the religion they represent, are rooted in ignorance."

Indeed, those other disciples, those who would go on to be recognized as leaders of the early Church and first in the unbroken line of apostolic succession that continues to this day, grew angry at Jesus "and began blaspheming against him in their hearts." In this gospel, the apostles are the real traitors to the Savior. Only Judas Iscariot is virtuous enough to engage Jesus, and Jesus in turn takes Judas aside to disclose revelations that mark him as the favored one, for all time. "Your star has shone brightly," Jesus tells Judas, and those others will "curse your ascent to the holy (generation)," meaning that Judas will be exalted above all others, not condemned to eternal punishment.

"Look, you have been told everything," Jesus concludes. "Lift up your eyes," he tells Judas, "and look at the cloud and the light within it and the stars surrounding it. The star that leads the way is your star." Then the scribes and high priests approach Judas, "and he received some money and handed him (Jesus) over to them."

Yet, in this version, that's a good thing, as the most earthshaking passage in the new gospel says. In it, Jesus refers to the other disciples and tells Judas, "But you will exceed all of them. For you will sacrifice the man that clothes me." In other words, rather than turning Jesus over to a fate that would cause him terrible agony—"My Father, if it is possible, let this cup pass me by," as Jesus prays in the canonical gospels, sweat pouring down his face like blood—Judas is actually doing Jesus a favor. He is helping kill the body that "clothes" Jesus to enable "the liberation of the spiritual person within."

"Judas could do no less for his friend and soul mate, and he betrays him," said Marvin Meyer, a prominent scholar of Gnosticism from Chapman University. "That is the good news of the Gospel of Judas." And in the twenty-first century, unlike in the first century, it was news that spread like wildfire. National Geographic broadcast a documentary about the Gospel of Judas, gave it cover story treatment in its magazine, and published two books by champions of the gospel. A host of leading scholars of early Christianity also weighed in, with astonishing claims about the import of this gospel. Elaine Pagels, who for decades has led efforts to bring the Gnostic writings to a wider audience, welcomed the Gospel of Judas for "exploding the myth of a monolithic Christianity and showing how diverse and fascinating the early Christian movement really was."

That diversity, Pagels and others contended, included a kind of "spiritual-but-not-religious" form of Christianity that not only dovetails with similar modern sensibilities about faith, but which may in fact represent a truer, purer form of the faith Jesus preached. "The author of the Gospel of Judas is like a sectarian Christian who thinks the whole movement has gone off track," Pagels says. "It is not so different, actually, from what you find even in the Protestant revolution in which Martin Luther and other Protestants protest against Roman Catholic teaching, saying that the Church has moved away from its original mission from the message of Jesus and has actually served the wrong powers. So the Gospel of Judas suggests that Church leadership is mistaken, is more diabolic than divine."

The Jesus of this new version of the faith is a kind of Christian Buddha, "a friendly, benign teacher who radiates wisdom," says Krosney. The Gospel of Judas is a spiritual manifesto in which Jesus tells Judas to "follow his star" to find salvation. Religion is bad, in this version; churches are worse, preaching false beliefs. Indeed, Judas is not only a hero but a victim, his gospel "mercilessly doomed to destruction," according to Rodolphe Kasser, the Swiss scholar who for years worked in secret to restore and translate the gospel.

Yet Judas, it appeared, had the last word. "The betrayer becomes a hero," as Krosney put it, "and Jesus Christ arranges his own execution." The Crucifixion of the Son of God is no longer the fault of Judas or the Jews.

Such shocking claims, popping up so suddenly, and just as billions of Christian were preparing to celebrate Easter and the Resurrection of Jesus, were bound to prompt swift reactions, and these weren't long in coming.

The Gospel of Judas "tells us nothing about the historical Jesus and nothing about the historical Judas," wrote James M. Robinson, the leading American authority on the Gnostic text from Nag Hammadi—and a scholar who had been outmaneuvered in his quest to break the news of the Judas papyrus. "It tells us only what, 100 years later, Gnostics were doing with the story they found in the canonical gospels." The claims about the gospel's significance, Robinson said darkly, were "consciously misleading."

Or, as New Testament scholar Simon Gathercole put it in a somewhat lighter vein, "The Gospel of Judas is certainly an ancient text, but not ancient enough to tell us anything new . . . An analogy would be finding a speech claimed to have been written by Queen Victoria"—who reigned in the nineteenth century—"in which she talked about *The Lord of the Rings* and her CD collection."

Even nonbelievers detected something amiss. The claims for the new gospel "feel uncomfortably hyped," Adam Gopnik wrote in *The New Yorker*. The Gospel of Judas, he said, "appears at a time of a new fashion, not to say rage, for 'alternate' Gospels and revisionist retellings of the Jesus story. These are not the egalitarian, feminist versions of the story that were among the first fruits of the Nag Hammadi discovery. Instead, the new obsession is to introduce, or reintroduce, into Christianity something hidden, strange, and cultic—to reveal a deliberately suppressed story."

So what should we believe? Was everything we knew about Judas wrong? This was no mere academic debate. A central Christian dogma was at stake, as was the credibility of sacred Scripture and the ability of Jesus's followers to be taken seriously in today's world.

Resolving this debate required answering two main questions about the Gospel of Judas: First, was it fake? Second, was it true? That is, if the papyrus text was authentic, what did it really say and what did it really mean?

"FRAYING INTO OBLIVION"

The story of how the Gospel of Judas was discovered, lost again (several times), and recovered after it was nearly destroyed reads like a cross between *The Maltese Falcon* and an Indiana Jones screenplay, with as much skullduggery and betrayal as anything in the traditional account of the Judas story.

The tale begins south of Cairo, in the Jebel Qarara hills of Middle Egypt, sometime in the late 1970s, though, like so much about the Gospel of Judas, many details are murky. Two local farmers, known as *fellahin*, were climbing into the barren foothills that border the Nile. The hills are much drier than the bottomland a few minutes' walk away, a steady climate that has proven amazingly effective at preserving even delicate papyri for centuries and even millennia. The *fellahin* live a hardscrabble existence and are always on the lookout for ways to make some extra money. In the 1970s, the market for antiquities was heating up, and grave robbing was the shortest route to a quick score for an Egyptian peasant. Ever since the stunning discovery of the gilded objects in the 3,300-year-old tomb of King Tutankhamen in 1922, Westerners had been obsessed with anything related to the pharaohs and ancient Egypt. Relics of Tut's tomb went on tour in the 1970s, and ginned that fascination to a fever pitch—and antiquities prices with it.

Yet the *fellahin* also knew that dealers were willing to pay handsomely for items that might have been consigned to the trash heap of history years earlier. Anything and everything could be sold; there were few rules to this trade, and those that did exist were routinely ignored or circumvented.

The two peasants stumbled into a cave hidden among the rocks, and as they ventured inside, they were confronted with the sight of a sarcophagus containing a skeleton. If the occupant was no pharaoh, he was obviously a wealthy man—the tomb was a gallery of sorts, with many square columns carved into the limestone rock so that a visitor could stand upright and walk around easily. The main occupant had been wrapped in a shroud and buried here untold centuries earlier, with many of his relatives entombed along with him. Next to the sarcophagus sat a white limestone box containing the books that he apparently wanted to accompany him into the next life.

The peasants had no idea what the books said—they were illiterate, like most of the inhabitants of the region—but they knew that the books were old and, as Krosney writes in his gripping reconstruction of the events, that "they were winners of one of the great lotteries of Egypt."

Still, the men had to be very careful. If they told the wrong person about their find, or if word got out about its exact location, they could easily be killed and the precious site pillaged. So they confided their secret to Am Samiah, a local garlic famer but one who was known to have contacts with people in the bustling artifacts trade in Cairo. At some point, Am Samiah paid off the *fellahin* and made the three-hour car ride north to Cairo, the invaluable manuscripts wrapped in old newspapers, the way Egyptians transported most anything. Once there, he sold the papyri texts to an antiquities dealer named Hanna Asabil.

Hanna Asabil (a pseudonym to protect his identity) paid Am Samiah the equivalent of a few thousand U.S. dollars and three gold bracelets—trinkets, really—to give to his wife. It made Am Samiah one of the wealthiest men in his village, but it was nowhere near what the manuscripts were worth, or what Hanna Asabil would try to get for them. The dealer was a Coptic Christian, a member of one of the first churches of antiquity, yet even he didn't understand what was written on the folios. He just knew they were worth big bucks, and he set his asking price at three million dollars, a huge sum in 1979.

Alas, the price was too high. Hanna cast about for buyers, mainly in Switzerland, which served much the same purpose to the underground antiquities trade as it did to wealthy people looking to hide assets in secret bank accounts. Anything was possible, but before Hanna could strike a deal, burglars struck his apartment in Cairo and carried off his entire collection of gold pieces, statues, textiles, coins—and ancient manuscripts. It was probably an inside job; just days before, Hanna had shown his collection to a potential buyer, so word was spreading.

Within a couple of years, items from the burglary began showing up on the market, though there was still no sign of the papyrus texts. Agents in this netherworld bazaar knew that Hanna was desperate to recover anything he could, and after a series of communications between Geneva, Athens, and Cairo, a Swiss-based dealer from Greece, Nicolas Koutoulakis, let Hanna know that he had access to the manuscripts. Finally, in 1982, after a tense meeting in a Geneva hotel room, Hanna got the ancient texts back. He immediately put them in a Swiss safe-deposit box, of course, and a few months later, in May 1983, several scholars were given a chance to examine them, again at a closely guarded hotel room in Geneva. It was the first time any experts had looked at the texts, and these were among the best.

The same could not be said for the papyrus. "The material was being stored in three cardboard boxes lined with newspaper," recalled

Stephen Emmel, a young Coptologist who was there as an emissary of James Robinson, the preeminent American expert on Gnostic texts. Using tweezers, Emmel and the others began examining the brittle papyrus and immediately recognized them as Gnostic texts, two of them familiar: one the so-called Letter of Peter to Philip, the other the First Apocalypse of James, both known from the Nag Hammadi cache. The third text was unfamiliar to Emmel and the others, and they were given little time to do a close examination of it. They saw the name Judas but assumed it referred to another disciple, Judas Didymus Thomas, who shows up in the Gnostic Gospel of Thomas.

Still, they knew the texts were of tremendous value, but even pooling funds from their respective institutions, the scholars could come up with just $150,000, not even close to the $3 million Hanna was asking. The deal was off, the scholars went home, and the Gospel of Judas, still unidentified as such, was left to molder.

Then it got worse for Judas. Looking for a big payday, Hanna brought the fraying papyrus to America in 1984, wrapped in newspaper and stored in carry-on luggage that he did not have to declare at customs. Using contacts in the prominent Coptic community around New York, he made several efforts, in meetings featuring Coptic priests and armed bodyguards, to sell his prizes, but everything fell through, even though he had lowered his price to one million dollars.

Desolated by the failure, he found a friend in the Coptic community to drive him and the manuscripts to a Citibank branch in a strip mall in Hicksville, Long Island. There, he rented a safe-deposit box and placed them inside it. The conditions in suburban Long Island are not nearly as ideal for preservation as they are in Middle Egypt, and for the next sixteen years the Gospel of Judas lay there "fraying into oblivion," as Krosney put it.

Then, in 2000, an antiquities dealer based in Switzerland, Frieda

Nussberger Tchacos, who'd first seen the papyri in 1980, dragged Hanna from Cairo to New York intent on making a deal.

"I WAS CHOSEN BY JUDAS TO REHABILITATE HIM"

Tchacos was a remarkable, cosmopolitan figure. She was born in Egypt, was educated in French-speaking Geneva, and held Greek as well as Swiss citizenship. In addition to Arabic, French, and Greek, she spoke English, Italian, and some German. She was also the rare female dealer in the elite ranks of European gallery owners. Tchacos's specialty was artifacts, not papyri, but she was intrigued by the potential of the manuscripts that Hanna first showed her in 1980. The passage of years, during which she had had no word on the fate of the texts, had done nothing to dim her interest, which was rekindled quickly when she was brought into the negotiations once again, almost twenty years after her first encounter with them.

"I had a mission," she said later with the kind of messianic passion that the gospel seems to inspire in its devotees. "Judas was asking me to do something for him. It's more than a mission, now that I think of it. I think I was chosen by Judas to rehabilitate him."

Yet it looked as if it would take divine intervention to save Judas at this point. When Hanna and Tchacos opened the safe-deposit box in Hicksville, they found the sheets crumbling, almost illegible, in worse condition than anyone had expected. The state of deterioration spurred Hanna finally to make a deal, for far less than even the one million he'd been asking. He returned to Cairo with some money for his decades of toil, and Tchacos took the papyrus fragments to the experts at the Beinecke Rare Book and Manuscript Library at Yale University, an hour and a half north of New York City.

A few days later, as Tchacos was preparing to return to Zurich, the manuscript expert examining the sheets called her excitedly. "Frieda, this is fantastic!" Robert Babcock, one of the Beinecke's chief curators, told her. "Judas's name ends this codex. It's a great find. There's nothing like it!"

Tchacos knew nothing about such gospels, Gnostic or otherwise, but she knew this was big. Yet, after several months of deliberation, Yale decided that the provenance of the manuscript was too tainted, and the university's potential legal exposure too great, to take a chance on buying the texts. So Tchacos found another potential buyer, in Akron, Ohio, and set up another deal. Once again, it all went south in a cascade of broken promises, financial shenanigans, and legal proceedings. Meanwhile, as these negotiations were going on, the potential buyer was storing the papyri in his freezer. He thought that was a good idea. It wasn't.

Tchacos eventually retrieved the pages from Ohio, brought them back to Switzerland, and in 2001 finally, finally, found a secure buyer and home for Judas: the Maecenas Foundation for Ancient Art. Now there was money to care for the texts, and expert restorers, the best in their field, were hired to attempt the herculean task of putting Judas back together again.

"If you take a nine- to ten-page typed document and rip it up into tiny pieces, throw away half the pieces, and try to reconstruct the other half, you will see how difficult this process is," said Rodolphe Kasser, the elderly and esteemed Coptic expert chosen by Maecenas to oversee the operation and translation. More than a jigsaw puzzle, the papyrus was so brittle that it crumbled at the slightest touch, and was indecipherable in parts. The case looked hopeless.

Almost miraculously, some 85 percent of the manuscript was recomposed and preserved. Yet its very existence, and its contents, was still known only to a small circle of people who had been sworn to secrecy. By 2004 the National Geographic Society had entered the picture, providing funding for the restoration, in exchange for exclusive rights to film and reproduce the Gospel of Judas. On a cold, gray, windswept December day of that year, it brought three renowned experts to the small studio in the Swiss town of Nyon, on Lake Geneva, where the gospel had been resurrected.

They were A. J. Timothy Jull, director of the National Science Foundation's Accelerator Mass Spectrometer Facility in Tucson, Arizona, and an expert in carbon-14 dating ancient manuscripts, such as the Dead Sea Scrolls; Stephen Emmel, the American Coptologist, now at the University of Münster, who had briefly viewed the papyrus years before; and the UNC scholar Bart Ehrman.

With Kasser, Tchacos, and a National Geographic television crew looking on, the trio examined the papyrus to determine what it said, if it was authentic, and if it was ancient. They quickly identified what the text was about: "There, right on the page in front of our eyes, were the Coptic words for Judas Iscariot," Ehrman recalled. "This was the lost Gospel of Judas." They also knew it was not a forgery. No one could have done this, and anyone who had certainly wouldn't have reduced such a valuable fake to such a perilous condition.

All that remained was to date the sheets. This couldn't be done there; Jull had to take back specimens of the papyrus for C-14 testing. This would necessitate destroying the samples, so five one-quarter-inch-square pieces from different parts of the manuscript were cut and put in tiny nylon bags; Jull then took these back to Tucson to run the tests. It was the final indignity for a text that had suffered so many already, but it was worth it. The results came back a month later, in January 2005: Jull could say with 95 percent confidence that both the papyrus and the leather binding came from sometime between 220 CE and 340 CE, with 280 CE as the best guess.

There was still one more hurdle, however: one of the most critical tests to determine whether the Gospel of Judas was real or forged was not on the papyrus itself, but on the ink of the writing, on the very words that threatened to overturn a central narrative of the New Testament story. That task had been given McCrone Associates, a prestigious lab in Illinois. As the work proceeded in January 2006, with a deadline fast approaching—National Geographic wanted to unveil the Gospel of Judas in time for Easter—Joseph Barabe, who was leading the team of researchers, suddenly spotted a red flag.

Barabe had reason to be leery. He had worked with the FBI on cases that found that paintings being fobbed off as authentic were in fact forgeries, and in 2009, three years after his work on Judas, he produced conclusive evidence that a version of the Gospel of Mark, once thought to have dated to the early Middle Ages, had in reality been manufactured no earlier than 1874. It's not difficult to find a piece of ancient papyrus, and a really crafty forger can then write anything he wants on it.

As Barabe and his team put the Gospel of Judas papyrus under an increasingly sophisticated series of spectroscopic and microscopic examinations, he became suspicious of the mix of chemicals used in the ink. The testing showed that the scribe (or forger) who'd penned the text had used two inks, black and brown, mixed together. The black ink, known as lampblack, was familiar to Barabe because it was the type used in ancient Egyptian writings. The brown ink, however, puzzled the researchers. It was rich in iron but it lacked elements of sulfur usually found in this type of ink, known as iron gall.

"One thing that made this a little bit more dramatic than we would have liked is, we did the sampling in the third week of January of 2006, and the [National Geographic] press conference was already scheduled for the third week in April of that same year," Barabe told Live Science in recalling the episode in 2013. "So we had three months to turn this critter around with a conclusion, and it really put an enormous amount of pressure on us, because we were faced with what was essentially a three-month rush project."

On the plus side for the gospel's authenticity was the fact that the ink had not pooled and collected in between the warped fibers, which is what would have happened if someone had tried to apply new ink to an ancient piece of papyrus. Yet how to explain the ink's odd composition?

Barabe scoured the archives on ancient inks and finally came upon a study of Egyptian marriage certificates and land documents from the Louvre showing that contracts from the mid-third century used the traditional lampblack ink but were officially registered in the traditional Greek style, which used brown iron gall ink. Moreover, the study showed that the metal-based inks of that era contained little sulfur. "What the French study told us is that ink technology was undergoing a transition" in the third century CE, which is when the Gospel of Judas was composed.

That was enough. The Gospel of Judas was real, not a hoax, and a few weeks later the Gospel of Judas, with its explosive new account of the betrayal of Jesus, was revealed to the world.

Yet "real" is not the same as "true," and with the papyrus and text verified as legitimate, questions now arose as to what the Gospel of Judas said about Jesus and Judas and Christianity, and what it meant.

"WAS IT THE JEALOUS JUDAS OR THE COWARDLY PETER WHO LOVED CHRIST?"

A major reason the Gospel of Judas seemed so credible and so appealing is that the canonical gospels, and the accepted teaching and tradition of the Church, provided relatively little information on

Judas, especially given his outsize role in the life and death of Jesus, and the birth of Christianity.

Indeed, after Jesus, Judas is perhaps the most important figure in the gospels, central to the drama of death and resurrection that is at the heart of Christian belief. Yet in many ways his character is far more mysterious. In total, Judas is mentioned twenty-two times in the New Testament, in the gospels of Matthew, Mark, Luke, and John and at the beginning of the Acts of the Apostles, when the remaining eleven followers of Jesus (one of whom is also called Judas, as it was a common name) choose Matthias to take the place of Judas the traitor.

Initially, Judas Iscariot is mentioned only in passing, as one of the original twelve apostles chosen by Jesus, though he is always last in the list of names and his future betrayal is always duly noted. It is only as the gospels move toward their final act, the events of the final days of Jesus's life known as the Passion narrative, that Judas moves front and center.

Judas's main role in the Passion narrative is played out in his negotiations with the high priests over the price for Jesus's head, his presence at the Last Supper, his betrayal of Jesus in the Garden of Gethsemane, and his later remorse and death. Even here, as is often the case (more than many believers want to admit), the gospels provide varying accounts of Judas's actions, and of his fate.

In the Gospel of Mark, Judas goes to the high priests offering to betray Jesus and they offer him an unspecified sum of money in return. In Matthew's version Judas seeks payment for the deed—a deal is struck for the infamous thirty piece of silver. John's gospel, from the passage just cited, also indicates that money is a chief motive, with inducement from the Devil. According to Luke, the motive is mainly demonic—"Satan entered into Judas"—and the bounty paid by the high priests is an afterthought.

At the Last Supper, a short time later, all four gospels recount how Jesus tells the twelve that one of them, eating with him that night at table, will betray him. In Matthew and John, Jesus clearly indicates that he knows the guilty party is Judas, and in John he seems to give Judas license to act, saying, "What you are going to do, do quickly." Because Judas holds the common purse, the others think Jesus is sending him out to buy more food for the feast or give alms to the poor for Passover.

Similarly, all four gospels tell much the same story of the betrayal in the garden, with a torch-bearing mob, led by Judas, arresting Jesus. Only John omits the notorious kiss.

Oddly, Judas's death is recounted in only two places, and they differ on his fate. Matthew says Judas is overcome with remorse at what he has done "in betraying innocent blood," flings the coins into the Temple, and goes and hangs himself. The high priests cannot keep blood money, so they buy a plot of land as a potter's field to bury foreigners, and called it the Field of Blood.

In the Acts of the Apostles, on the other hand, Judas's fate is mentioned when the apostles gather to elect someone to replace him. Peter tells the 120 disciples that Judas "bought a parcel of land with the wages of his iniquity" and at some point, "falling headlong, he burst open in the middle, and all his insides spilled out." That's why the land was called the Field of Blood, Peter said.

Yet given the crucial part he plays, not much else is known about Judas. He sticks out from the rest of the apostles because he is believed to be the only one who comes from Judea, in the rocky, mountainous southern part of Israel, rather than from Galilee, in the north, a relatively lush region from where Jesus and the other apostles hail. Even Judas's name is a matter of debate: one widely held view is that he is called Iscariot because he comes from the region of Kerioth in Judea: *ish* in Hebrew indicates a man, so *Ish-Kerioth* would be "a man from Kerioth," hence Iscariot.

This seems to be the best explanation, though there is no shortage of other theories, most of them implausible. One notion holds that Judas was a member of the Sicarii, an extremist splinter group of the Zealots, who fought to expel the Romans from Israel. The name came from the Latin word *sicarius*, or "dagger wielder," because the Sicarii were known for assassinating their political enemies by pulling a short knife, a *sicae*, from their cloaks to kill up close. Yet as John Meier notes, the Sicarii arose as an identifiable group only a decade or two after Jesus, and if Judas was one of their number, he would have been expected to stab Jesus to death, not turn him over to the very authorities whom the Sicarii hated.

A theory that links the word *Iscariot* to Judas's work as a red dyer or to his red hair or ruddy complexion is one of many fanciful conjectures, yet artists are hardly bound by scholarship. Judas is such a tempting blank canvas that he (and Jews who were denigrated along with him) was long depicted with red hair, to make him stand out as the oddball, the "other," the evil one. A yellow cloak, the mark of a coward, was another, later addition.

That's pretty much all that the Scriptures and history can tell us. Surely there must be more to the story? This wasn't so much a whodunit as a mystery about the motive for the crime—why would a man chosen by Jesus as one of his original twelve apostles, devoted to him, then turn on his master?

Greed and evil, inspired by Satan, are the two simple, and rather simplistic, explanations. As the Jesuit Bible scholar John Donahue says, flat assertions that the Devil made a greedy Judas do it "tell us everything and nothing."

Yet for the first couple of centuries of Christianity, Church leaders pretty much doubled down on those reasons. Much as we moderns have done, early Christian commentators were content to dismiss Judas as the incarnation of evil and the antithesis of Jesus. In fact, before the middle of the second century CE (that is, in the one hundred years after the events of Christ's Passion) the tendency was to inflate Judas's reputation for evil rather than try to explore or explain or understand his actions.

In the early second century, for example, Papias of Hierapolis wrote a particularly vivid description of Judas, who, he contended, survived his attempt at suicide by hanging only to go walking about "as an example of godlessness in this world, having been bloated so much in the flesh that he could not go through where a chariot goes easily, indeed not even his swollen head by itself." The traitor's eyelids were so fat that his eyes could not be seen, and his genitalia oozed pus and worms. Judas's fate, in this exaggerated version, was to be run over by a chariot and to have his impious guts strewn about the street. A later text that circulated among Christians, the Arabic Gospel of the Infancy, shows Judas as a childhood friend of Jesus, but one who becomes possessed by the Devil and hits his playmate—prefiguring a worse fate to come.

By the late second century, as Christianity began to spread like wildfire, along with alternative versions of the faith, interest in Judas grew because of the questions his betrayal raised. "Judas's actions appear to have become a liability for the apostolic Christians. How could you trust a religion whose leader was betrayed by his closest follower?" says April DeConick, a Rice University scholar of early Christianity and a leading expert on the Gospel of Judas. Moreover, if Jesus had to die—"for God so loved the world that he gave his only begotten son," as the famous verse in John reads—wasn't Judas simply playing his part in a role preordained for him and for Jesus?

Three centuries later, St. Augustine said in effect that, yes, God sent his son, indeed, God himself, to die on the cross for the salvation of humanity. Yet Judas, he said, was responsible for consigning Jesus to death for his own selfish motives. St. Jerome and many others argued that Christ was actually offended more by Judas hanging himself than by his act of betrayal. During the Renaissance, the Dutch theologian and Catholic priest Erasmus argued, like a good humanist, that in fact Judas had free will and could have changed his mind—so, too bad for him. The Protestant reformer Martin Luther responded, as was his wont, that, no, Judas's will was that he betray Jesus, and it could not be changed. John Calvin, originator of the idea of predestination, naturally believed that Judas's actions were foreordained.

None of that theologizing, however, satisfied artists and dramatists. As the novelist Graham Greene put it in *The End of the Affair*: "Hatred seems to operate on the same glands as love: it even produces the same actions. If we had not been taught how to interpret the story of the passion, would we have been able to say from their actions whether it was the jealous Judas or the cowardly Peter who loved Christ?"

THE PASSION OF JUDAS

It is a penetrating question with no easy answers. The Argentine short story writer Jorge Luis Borges wrote "Three Versions of Judas" in order to plumb the many possibilities, and in his beautiful oratorio *St. Matthew Passion*, Bach has Judas call himself *der verlorene Sohn*, a reference to the Prodigal Son, who finds his way back to his father and ultimate forgiveness. Fast-forward 250 years and in the 1970 rock opera *Jesus Christ, Superstar*, Andrew Lloyd Weber and Tim Rice depict Judas as a loyal disciple who reluctantly betrays Jesus because he fears a Roman backlash against the Jews.

Others tried to explain the mystery of Judas's betrayal of his beloved master by exonerating him. One of the oldest-known English ballads, dating to the thirteenth century, transfers the main blame to Judas's sister: Jesus gives Judas thirty pieces of silver to buy food for the band of apostles, it says, but on his way to the market, Judas comes upon his sister, who ridicules "the false prophete that tou bilevest upon." Judas protests his love for Jesus, but she induces her brother to take a nap, and steals the money. In despair, Judas sells Jesus to Pilate for that same amount. Once again, if Judas isn't the bad guy, a woman is to blame.

In the nineteenth century, the Irish poet George Russell gave the story a more Freudian slant, casting Judas as an innocent "knit with his doom," almost as Jesus himself was born to die on the cross:

In ancient shadows and twilights
Where childhood had stray'd,
The world's great sorrows were born
And its heroes were made.
In the lost boyhood of Judas
Christ was betray'd.

The problem is that something happened in the small band of Jesus followers during those critical days before Passover two millennia ago. Judas was not a post facto invention, nor was he an outsider, an add-on to the band chosen by Jesus, only to fulfill a role as a traitor. "In order to betray, one must first belong," Kim Philby, the famous British double agent of the Cold War, once said. So, again, the question of "why" continues to press in.

In his provocative drama *The Last Days of Judas Iscariot* (superbly directed by the late Philip Seymour Hoffman), playwright Stephen Adly Guirgis at one point envisions Judas as an innocent boy who was kind to his friends. The dilemma of Judas had dogged Guirgis's imagination since his days in Catholic school, and in *Last Days* he tries to work out the problem by finally getting Judas a hearing (in Purgatory) before a judge and jury.

Sexual tension has been explored as a motive, which is no surprise given its role in so many crimes. Once again, Mary Magdalene—the only other Gospel figure who has inspired as much speculation based on so little information—enters the picture as the vixen who vexes Judas, and sets up a love triangle with Jesus.

Political passions have provided another explanation. Seen through this lens, one that has become understandably more common in our age of guerrilla wars and terrorist insurgencies, Judas wanted Jesus to be a real, powerful King of the Jews, a Messiah who would drive out the Romans and finally free Israel from subjugation. That, indeed, is what many Jews of the day would have wanted, and a few decades later, their effort to overthrow the imperial yoke would lead to the destruction of the Temple, the collective suicide at Masada, and the end of ancient Israel as a nation—a fate that was only reversed, miraculously, in 1948.

The 1961 remake of *The King of Kings* also features that plotline: Judas as a rebel disillusioned by Jesus's insistence on a spiritual, nonviolent revolution—so he turns him in, out of resentment or perhaps hoping that he will force Jesus to declare his earthly kingship. This is also the thrust of Edward Elgar's oratorio *The Apostles*, and of Taylor Caldwell's 1978 novel, *I, Judas*.

Yet it was always the emotional bond between Jesus and Judas that provided the greatest mystery, and fueled the deepest fascination. In popular representation, such as the 1970s musical *Godspell*, the pair joke and dance together, and the relationship between Judas and Jesus is the dramatic spine of *Jesus Christ, Superstar*—told in the film version from the perspective of Judas, as an African American. In the rock opera, Judas rationalizes his decision to betray Jesus, saying that if he doesn't do the deed, the Romans will destroy Israel (which they do anyway). Judas is innocent, or naïve, a tragic figure misunderstood at the time and by history. Again, he is also jealous of Mary Magdalene, who has become Jesus's closest companion now, not Judas. Judas commits suicide, but returns in a vision to taunt Jesus in the title number: "Jesus Christ, / Superstar! / Do you think you're what they say you are?"

Rock musicians seemed to have a genuine weakness for the Judas story. "But I can't think for you," Dylan sang in 1964. "You'll have to decide / whether Judas Iscariot / had God on his side."

In Martin Scorsese's 1988 film, *The Last Temptation of Christ* (based on the 1953 novel by Nikos Kazantzakis), Judas is a Zealot (though the Zealots postdate Jesus in Jewish history), and Jesus is building crosses for the Romans, whom he despises. Yet they are friends, though their differing views cast a shadow of mortal peril that will play out in the final act. As Jesus realizes he must die on the cross to fulfill the Old Testament prophecy, he insists Judas must help him carry out that mission. Jesus even sets up the plot by which Judas will betray him. It is a powerful scene, profoundly controversial—and it sounds much like the dramatic dynamic of the Gospel of Judas that will come to light nearly two decades after Scorsese's movie.

The main difference, of course, is that an early Christian text depicting Judas as a hero would have immeasurably greater weight than a twentieth-century film or rock song. So much weight, in fact, that it could capsize two thousand years of accepted teachings and traditions.

Yet for all the hype and inherent appeal of the Judas gospel, at least two large red flags seriously undermine the claims, and the enduring popular conception, that the Gospel of Judas is somehow just as authoritative as Matthew, Mark, Luke, or John, or that Judas is the real hero of the Passion.

A "HIGHLY CONFUSING AND BIZARRE" THEOLOGY

The first issue is one that was also considered in the discussion of Mary Magdalene—namely, that the Gospel of Judas is part of the corpus of wildly diverse texts that come under the umbrella of Gnosticism.

For the most part, all we knew about the Gnostics comes from their enemies—in texts such as the second-century polemic against heretics by Irenaeus, Bishop of Lyons. Irenaeus represented the orthodox, apostolic Christianity that was still struggling to become the normative faith for the Church. It eventually triumphed, and the Gnostics died out, or were suppressed. Either way, for nearly two millennia they were forgotten. Then, in the last century, they made one of the most surprising comebacks in history when a trove of their texts, most of which had been known only by their titles or from passing ancient references to their contents, came to light after their accidental discovery in rural Egypt.

It was as if scientists had brought a woolly mammoth back to life. Gnosticism became all the rage, depicted as an alternative to the Church-mandated Christianity we know, and maybe even the true faith that Jesus preached, but one that was too radical, too spiritual for his early, authoritarian, patriarchal followers to embrace. As Meyer put it, the Gnostics were "religious mystics who proclaimed gnosis, knowledge, as the way to salvation. To know oneself truly allowed gnostic men and women to know [G]od directly, without any need for mediation of rabbis, priests, bishops, imams, or other religious officials."

In the writings of Meyer (who died in 2012) and other Gnostic scholars, notably Elaine Pagels, "the Gnostics are validated as a direction in which Christianity could have gone and which would have made it warmer and fuzzier, much nicer than this cold orthodoxy stuff," as the NYU classics scholar Roger Bagnall has said.

The Gospel of Judas seemed to fit perfectly into that schema. The "real" story advanced by tradition—that Judas was a bad man who made a bad choice and paid for it—wasn't the case at all. Jesus was a spiritual being who wanted to be freed from this earthly bondage, and he wouldn't have condemned anyone to the sort of fate Judas suffered in orthodox belief. Instead, Judas was doing Jesus a favor, and he in turn would be favored in eternity with a prime spot in the highest heaven.

Yet it wasn't quite that simple.

The "Gnostic" label refers to one school in the range of "lost Christianities," as Bart Ehrman has called them, that emerged in the century or two after mainstream Christianity. Some of them, such as the Marcionism (founded by a wealthy Christian from Asia Minor named Marcion) rejected Judaism entirely and believed that Yahweh, the God of the Hebrew Bible, was not the God of Jesus, and certainly not his Father. Ebionism, on the other hand, was a Jewish form of Christianity whose followers believed that Jesus was just another Jewish prophet, not God, but was speaking for God to help Jews live according to Mosaic Law.

Gnosticism was a particularly complex and multifaceted school, and modern interpreters have often harmonized and synthesized Gnostic beliefs and philosophies in ways that make them more comprehensible, and appealing, to the average reader. Yet a growing number of Gnostic scholars, such as Karen King of Harvard, say that this homogenizing process doesn't reflect the reality of what the Gnostics were. She and others question whether *Gnostic* is even a legitimate label or whether modern scholars are rewriting history to make it fit a contemporary label. (The term *Gnosticism* wasn't even coined until the seventeenth century.)

As the experts note, there was a wide range of so-called Gnostic

Christianities, with varying degrees of influence and vastly differing relationships to what was emerging as mainstream, orthodox Christianity. Some Gnostics rejected orthodox, or apostolic, Christianity altogether, while others embraced some Gnostic beliefs and some orthodox beliefs. Some of those whom we might call Gnostics worshipped with apostolic Christians in churches on Sundays, but at other times met in lodges or seminaries with like-minded Gnostics to pursue their more esoteric teachings.

Valentinianism was one of the major schools of Gnosticism whose followers associated closely with mainstream Christians. They took their name after a leading theologian, Valentinus. They apparently believed in the traditional sacraments but thought that these had esoteric purposes that were unknowable by ordinary Christians without special, further instruction and initiation, which may have involved another baptism.

Basilidianism (after Basilides, a renowned Christian philosopher) was another significant stream of Gnosticism. Basilidians worshipped separately from orthodox, apostolic Christians and had a very complex cosmology—they believed there was a different heaven for each of the 365 days of the year, for example. Among the many deities and angels that initiates had to learn was the chief one, Abrasas, whose name in Greek has the numerical value of 365. Basilides sounded like an early version of John Calvin, believing that only a few Gnostics would be saved from Abraxas—who was associated with the evil Jewish god Yahweh—and that the rest of humanity would perish. Yet the soul alone would survive for the elect, and there was no resurrection of the body.

There were a number of smaller, rather oddball Gnostic schools, such as Carpocratianism, whose followers believed that to attain salvation, the soul must pass through every condition and experience of life—hence Carpocratians are believed to have supported all manner of sexual libertinism. One early Christian critic, Clement of Alexandria, the city in Egypt where Carpocrates was from, claimed that the Carpocratians "have intercourse where they will and with whom they will."

A major school of Gnosticism, and one that epitomized its contrarian ethos, was Sethiansim. The Sethians were opposed to apostolic Christianity—they believed they were the real Christians and that the mainstream Christians were heretics—and they took the opposite position on almost every belief you could think of: the Hebrew God, Yahweh, was bad; Adam and Eve were good; in fact, the Serpent in the Garden of Eden contributed to Eve's redemption by offering her special knowledge, symbolized by the famous forbidden fruit. For the Sethians—they took their name from Seth, a son of Adam, founder of a generation of chosen ones—the Eucharist that Christians celebrated was a sacrilege, and the Crucifixion was a particular abomination because a belief in the atonement (that God sent his Son to die for the sins of the world) was akin to child sacrifice.

Most experts believe that the Gospel of Judas, which sees Judas as a hero not a betrayer, is a manifestation of this Sethian school, or perhaps of the related Cainite school of Gnostics, whose followers worshiped Cain, notorious in the Bible for killing his brother Abel to gain their father's inheritance. "The Cainite doctrine was that you had to break every rule there was in order to have salvation," as Ehrman said.

Despite all these variations of Gnosticism, the experts do agree that the Gnostics, as we will continue to call them, do share a number of beliefs and tendencies. These tenets, which are largely agreed upon even by scholars who argue sharply over the import of the Gnostics, are often quite at odds with the popular view of Gnosticism.

Chief among them is what N. T. Wright, a retired Anglican bishop and leading New Testament scholar, calls a "deep and dark dualism," a belief that the present world and all that is in it is "evil through and through." Human beings are also inherently bad—unless they have a divine spark within them.

Second, as we saw earlier, while Gnostics hold that the world was created by the God of the Old Testament, they believe that this creator-god is a lesser, malevolent deity.

Third, the goal of wise people is to escape this wicked, material world and "outward human existence." One is saved by escaping the world to reach a higher existence with the pure, holy, true divinity.

Finally, and foremost, the Gnostics are about *gnosis*, the Greek word for "knowledge," and in their case it is a very particular and secret knowledge. Salvation came through a special knowledge, or *gnosis*, about this corrupt world and its evil creator-god, a knowledge that could be attained by the select few and were thus privileged with a secret revelation given by a divine messenger.

When you examine the cosmology of the Gnostic a bit more closely, you begin to see why you might need divine knowledge to understand it. The Gospel of Judas is a good example. The text is, as Ehrman says, "highly confusing and bizarre" and confounds even experts who are trying to figure out what the author is saying, and what his followers believe. It features a range of divine beings of varying ranks and arranged according to some inscrutable numerology.

In the Gospel of Judas, for example, it says at one point:

The seventy-two luminaries themselves made three hundred sixty luminaries appear in the incorruptible generation, in accordance with the will of the Spirit, that their number should be five for each. The twelve aeons of the twelve luminaries constitute their father, with six heavens for each aeon, so that there are seventy-two heavens for the seventy-two luminaries, and for

*each [of them five] firmaments, [for a total of] three hundred
sixty [firmaments . . .]. They were given authority and a [great]
host of angels [without number], for glory and adoration, [and
after that also] virgin spirits, for glory and [adoration] of all the
aeons and the heavens and the firmaments.*

So there. In the Gospel of Judas alone you have Barbelo, an "em-
anation" of the true God who represents God's desire and vanity
and thereby introduces the "fall," original sin, into the world—not
Adam and Eve and the forbidden fruit. It is God's own doing, though
he doesn't mean to do it. Barbelo becomes "the womb of everything,"
giving birth to other divine aspects and beings, the Aeons, who make
up the Pleroma, or Fullness, of the universe. In this complicated
Godhead, as April DeConick explains, Jesus is born of a cloud of
light, and within the Son exist the realms of the four Luminaries
(Adamas, Seth, the Generation of Seth, and Eleleth) along with a
range of angels, Aeons, and heavens.

The final Aeon to be created by the Luminary Eleleth is Sophia,
and she in turn produces a monstrous offspring, Ialdabaoth, a lion-
faced serpent with fiery eyes who is so awful that she hides him in
a cloud. However, he steals her power, descends to the lower regions—
that would be our earth—and creates a bunch of Archons, such as
Saklas and Nebruel, to rule this world.

There are innumerable other beings in this cast of characters,
all vying for dominance in a series of tricks and shifting alliances
that make the plotlines of *Game of Thrones* seem simple. De-
Conick's book *The Thirteenth Apostle* is an excellent primer on
Gnostic theology, but even her summary can make your head spin.
The main drama in the Sethian Gnosticism of the Gospel of Judas
is between Sophia and Ialdabaoth. "Ialdabaoth works to keep human beings distracted and ignorant of the supreme God and their
true nature so that the spirit will not know about the supreme

God, nor be able to find its way home," DeConick writes. "Sophia works along with an illuminator sent down from the Father to redeem the spirit and return it to God, to repair the rupture, to assist God in saving himself."

Jesus is the final Illuminator, who shares the secrets with his Gnostic followers in a ceremony of the "Five Seals." When Ialdabaoth has Jesus crucified, he discovers he cannot detain his spirit because Jesus is not a human; he is an Aeon. Jesus blazes a trail to the Upper Kingdom, destroying Archons along the way, and provides a final triumph of God over Ialdabaoth.

While some of this certainly does privilege a highly spiritualized view of Christianity over the more "incarnated" version that carried the day, it doesn't really reflect the rather simplified, even "sanitized," version of the Gospel of Judas that emerged with the papyrus in 2006.

More important, a major problem for those who say that the Gospel of Judas would undo many of the wrongs of mainstream Christianity is that the Sethians, and by extension the author of the Judas gospel, were as insistent on repudiating and vilifying the God of the Hebrew Bible as any of the Gnostics.

If that inherent antipathy to the God of the Old Testament is strongest in Marcionism, it runs through all the Gnostic texts—including the Gospel of Judas. This subverts any claim that this alternative Judas saga would reset Christian-Jewish relations by rehabilitating Judas. In fact, supplanting orthodox Christianity with the Judas gospel would be akin to "metaphysical anti-Semitism," according to Amy-Jill Levine of Vanderbilt University, one of the preeminent scholars of early Christianity and first-century Judaism: "Not only will this revised version of Judas have no impact on Christian-Jewish relations, the Gospel of Judas proclaims a theology that is not good for the Jews, and not good for Christians, either . . . I'd prefer to keep the God of Israel rather than have

Judas as a hero; I'd prefer to keep the Law and the Prophets rather than learn about enlightened aeons, and I'd prefer to honor the body rather than cast it off."

Perhaps the biggest blow to the greatest claims about the importance of the Judas gospel was not that the argument was an esoteric Gnostic text written two centuries after the canonical Gospels, or that it represented just one of many views in the tumultuous decades and centuries after the Crucifixion. No, the real problem with the Gospel of Judas was that it had been badly translated. It didn't even say what its original supporters claimed.

"OH NO, SOMETHING IS REALLY WRONG"

As a leading expert in the field of early Christian texts, April DeConick was as excited as anyone when she heard of the recovery of a copy of the Gospel of Judas. There had been only rumors about and passing references to such a manuscript, and to have a copy come to light now, after eighteen centuries, even in such a tattered state, was almost a miracle.

So as soon as she was able to download a copy on her computer at Rice University, where she chairs the Department of Religious Studies, DeConick immediately began poring over the text, translating it over several days with the expectation of finding the "good Judas" that the experts, many of them friends in the field, had been telling everyone about.

Yet that wasn't what she found. At one point she looked up and told her husband, "Oh no, something is really wrong." Indeed, as she went deeper into the Coptic lines, she found, as she said, a Judas who was "far more demonic than any Judas I know in any other piece of early Christian literature, Gnostic or otherwise." DeConick hesitated before saying anything publicly about her misgivings, but it soon became clear that other scholars shared her concerns. At academic conferences in the ensuing months, DeConick and other scholars compared notes and debated the results with experts. Then, in December 2007, she published a book on her findings, and an op-ed in the *New York Times* that summarized her arguments.

DeConick made three main points:

The first problem that she and others found was that the original translation by the National Geographic team rendered the word *daimon* as "spirit," so that Jesus addresses Judas as a "spirit," which has a positive, benevolent connotation. Yet the accepted word for "spirit" is actually *pneuma*, which is also in the Judas text. Everywhere else in Gnostic literature the word *daimon* is taken to mean "demon," as in a bad thing—a devil, an evil spirit. The translators made an exception for the Gospel of Judas, and changed the entire meaning.

The second problem was that the National Geographic team translated a phrase in which Jesus says Judas is set apart "for" a holy generation. In effect, Jesus is saying Judas is special and above all the other apostles. Yet DeConick shows that the Coptic words actually mean the opposite: the phrase actually says that Judas is "separated from" the holy generation. He is cast aside, not set above.

The third problem, she contends, is even more straightforward: the first translators said that because Jesus has singled Judas out for special treatment, the other apostles would be jealous and "will curse your ascent to the holy (generation)." In other words, Judas will be blessed by spending eternity with the true God, the good God in the upper Aeon. Yet DeConick shows that a letter was added to the original. In fact it should say the opposite. Jesus in reality tells Judas, "You will *not* ascend to the holy (generation)."

"So what does the Gospel of Judas really say?" DeConick writes in the *Times* piece. "It says that Judas is a specific demon called the

'Thirteenth.' In certain Gnostic traditions, this is the given name of the king of demons—an entity known as Ialdabaoth who lives in the 13th realm above the earth. Judas is his human alter ego, his undercover agent in the world. These Gnostics equated Ialdabaoth with the Hebrew Yahweh, whom they saw as a jealous and wrathful deity and an opponent of the supreme God whom Jesus came to earth to reveal."

"Jesus," DeConick says, "doesn't want Judas to betray him out of ignorance. Jesus wants him informed, so that the demonic Judas can suffer all that he deserves."

April DeConick ultimately argues that the Gospel of Judas is a Gnostic parody of apostolic Christianity in which Jesus's laughter is not the laughter of joy, representing a lighter, brighter Savior than the one portrayed in the New Testament. Instead, he is snickering at the apostles—though not at Judas, who now knows how dumb the others are—because they are getting it all wrong.

Her summation on the Judas gospel is spot-on: "If you are Judas, it is a story of tragedy, of a human being who became entangled in the snares of the Archons who rule this world. If you are an apostolic Christian, it is a story of ridicule, a representation of your faith as based on faithless apostles and a demon-sponsored atonement. If you are a Sethian Christian, it is a story of humor, or laughter, at the ignorance of Christians not in the know."

Scholars increasingly agree that the Gospel of Judas isn't what was originally billed. "At the end of the day the Judas character in the Gospel of Judas is not a great deal different from Judas as we [find] him on the pages of the New Testament," says Mark Goodacre. "He's not the new, sympathetic, cuddly Judas that we might want to believe in. He's actually really . . . still in continuity with the Judas who hangs himself in the Gospels in the New Testament."

"I think the author of the Gospel of Judas chose Judas as the leading figure in the text because Judas was a notorious figure," says Geoffrey Smith. "He was an attention getter in antiquity as he is today."

For Candida Moss, the Judas of this Gnostic gospel was at best a kind of ambiguous superhero, neither all good nor all bad: "If we're going to compare him to something, he's like Batman. He's sort of dark and mysterious and shadowy." This Judas "does things to protect people and save them. But he's also deeply conflicted. We admire Batman, but you wouldn't necessarily want to be friends with him."

Or pin your salvation on him.

National Geographic later acknowledged some of the translation points made by DeConick and others, and changed the text in subsequent official editions of the Gospel of Judas. Yet the popular impression was not so easily shifted, and for many, the Gospel of Judas, with its claims to challenge and even reverse everything we thought we knew about Christianity, still seems to offer a kinder, gentler—and truer—Christianity than the faith handed down by tradition.

THE REDEMPTION OF JUDAS, THE PARADOX OF CHRISTIANITY

So how should we think about the Gospel of Judas?

Some would still like to follow the route posited by the Argentine writer Borges in one of his stories about Judas and Gnosticism: "Had Alexandria triumphed and not Rome"—that is, the center of Gnosticism versus the headquarters of apostolic Christianity—"the extravagant and muddled stories I have summarized here would be coherent, majestic, and perfectly ordinary." Or as Herbert Krosney wrote in his official version of the gospel's discovery, "A reader can disagree with the themes of the Gospel of Judas. Some may think it blasphemy. But what cannot be denied is that the writer [of the gospel] accords Judas a new place in history."

Others will roll their eyes at this assertion, especially in view of the developments in the years since the gospel was revealed. For them, the Gospel of Judas represents a kind of early Christian cult that deserved to die out—something akin to the latter-day Heaven's Gate believers who, in 1997, committed suicide together in San Diego, believing that they needed to shed their earthly bodies in order to join up with a spaceship trailing the Hale-Bopp comet that was then visible in the night sky.

As Adam Gopnik put it, "By making the Gospel story more occult, one also drains it of its cosmic significance; making it more mysterious makes it less mystical." The Gospel of Judas, he wrote, "robs it of its ethical content . . . You don't have to love thy neighbor; just seek your star. The Gospel of Judas is, in this way, the dead opposite of the now much talked of Gospel of Jefferson, the edition prepared by the third president, in which all the miracles and magic stuff are deleted, and what is left is the ethical teaching."

If the arguments continue—as they surely will—even scholars who find themselves on opposite sides of the debate about the importance of the Gospel of Judas agree on several points that have been lost amid all the controversies and extravagant claims.

One is that the Gospel of Judas is invaluable for providing a clearer and more authentic picture of what was happening in the crucial early centuries of Christianity. This new old gospel is real, and important. "I am delighted that we have yet more evidence about the ancient world, and about early reinterpretations of Jesus and of the Christian faith," said N. T. Wright. "The more we have, the better we can do our history."

Another point of agreement is that even the history newly illuminated by the Gospel of Judas can take us back only so far. "It is not a Gospel written by Judas, or even one that claims to be," Ehrman stresses in his book on the papyrus. "It is not a Gospel written in Judas' own time by someone who actually knew him or who had inside information about his inner motivations. It is not a historically accurate report about the man Judas himself. It is not as ancient as the four Gospels that made it into the New Testament . . . It is not a book, therefore, that will provide us with additional information about what actually happened in Jesus's lifetime, or even in his last days leading up to his death."

Where all the experts and academics and modern-day apologists and polemicists diverge, of course, is about what the Gospel of Judas—and Judas himself, and by extension Jesus and the Christian message—means for believers today, and in no small measure, for nonbelievers as well.

The tendency in every quest for the historical Jesus, the "real" Jesus, is that we wind up finding our own reflection—a messiah who conveniently shares our preoccupations and parrots our favored opinions and solutions. Much the same could be said about the search for the Judas of history. Throughout the centuries, we have tried to explain and demystify the traitor's motives. If in fact Judas existed at all, his action was either the work of Satan or the sin of greed, or perhaps it was his love for a woman that made him do it, or his anger over a frustrated political agenda. Or, as the Gnostics had it, Judas was in fact the hero, helping the spirit of Jesus shed his corrupt flesh in order to return to the Father. There was no betrayal, no unsettling atonement theology, no crime. Case closed.

Yet hyping the Gospel of Judas to try to prove that the accepted story of Christianity is a fraud only takes us away, not into, the human condition, and such claims are far more than this tattered papyrus can truly bear.

Yet simply rejecting the Gospel of Judas as an ancient heresy that deserved to dry up and blow away in the sands of Egypt—or crumble into oblivion in a safe-deposit box on Long Island—does an injustice to the Gospel writers who kept Judas in the story, and preserved the mystery of betrayal, and the real challenge of the faith. If you believe that God writes straight with crooked lines, Judas is one of the crookedest in history.

Perhaps the real value of the Gospel of Judas is that it could prompt everyone to think more deeply—more deeply than even the canonical Gospels and Church tradition have—about who Judas was, why he was so central to the Christian story, and above all what he means today for those who are Christians, and even those who are not. Pigeonholing Judas as the "bad guy" of the New Testament, or even the "good guy" of the alternative version posited by the Sethian Gnostics, is a simplistic response that does not do justice to Judas as a real person in human history.

Scapegoating also goes against the central message of the greatest story ever told: namely, that no one is beyond hope, and even Judas may have found salvation in the end.

As it says in the old *Catholic Encyclopedia*—hardly a source of modernist pieties—if Judas's guilt cannot be questioned, neither can anyone deny that Jesus picked him as one of the twelve apostles: "This choice, it may be safely said, implies some good qualities and the gift of no mean graces." The entry continues:

> [I]t may be urged that in exaggerating the original malice of Judas, or denying that there was even any good in him, we minimize or miss the lesson of this fall. The examples of the saints are lost on us if we think of them as being of another order without our human weaknesses. And in the same way it is a grave mistake to think of Judas as a demon without any elements of goodness and grace. In his fall is left a warning that even the great grace of the Apostolate and the familiar friendship of Jesus may be of no avail to one who is unfaithful.

Christians understandably want to see themselves as Jesus on the cross, when in fact the inescapable condition of human weakness, and the high ideals of Christian doctrine, will lead believers to betray Christ's teachings. *O Felix culpa!*, as the *Exsultet* of the Easter vigil proclaims: "O happy fault that gained for us so great a Redeemer!" It is the pilgrimage back to grace that is at the heart of Christianity, and the source of hope, the ultimate paradox, that is embodied in the passion of Judas.

So instead of reading the Gospel of Judas as a literal narrative, or dismissing it as pulp fiction, perhaps it might be best to consider this remarkable text as an early marker in a long literary tradition. Maybe the author of this text was simply trying, in those tumultuous early centuries after Christ, to grapple with the mysteries of the faith rather than claiming, as some today may be tempted to do, to have discovered an alternative account of the deeds and words of Judas. Instead of clinging to a few sheets of tattered papyrus in the hope of absolving Judas, believers may be more faithful to Christian history if they read themselves into his story, and from there find a path out of despair and toward the redemption that Judas himself may have finally discovered.

FIVE

THE TRUE CROSS

Enough to Fill a Ship

The cross of Jesus, a reality and symbol of harsh Roman justice, has become the greatest brand identifier in history. *(Getty Images)*

In July 2013, archaeologists excavating a site in northern Turkey discovered a stone chest in a 1,350-year-old church that appeared to contain the greatest of Christianity's relics: a piece of the cross on which Jesus died. "We have found a holy thing in a chest. It is a piece of a cross," said Gulgun Koroglu, the excavation team leader and an art historian and archaeologist. She thought the chest served as a symbolic coffin for a holy person's relics—ones connected to Jesus's Crucifixion.

The news rocketed around the world, making headlines everywhere and displaying once again the global desire for physical evidence connected to Jesus of Nazareth, the rebellious rabbi from the hinterland who Christians believe is the Son of God.

Then, just like that, the story vanished. When contacted recently, the archaeologist backtracked, and said the stone chest, though engraved with a cross, was in fact empty. Could the archaeologists have been caught in some turbulence, either academic or political, that made their discovery a problem? How could a fragment so loudly and publicly proclaimed as present suddenly not be present?

Silence has been the answer, but even so, this dramatic reversal illustrates the nature of the most venerated and most dismissed relic in Christianity. Are fragments of the True Cross of Jesus really among us today? Or are they ethereal fakes that have more to do with faith than with history?

Anyone with some spare cash can have his own piece of the "True Cross" by visiting eBay and deciding how much he wants to spend, with prices ranging from a few dollars to thousands. The online bazaar has plentiful offerings from the Cross of Jesus, many of them sold by the Vatican itself, preserved in gilded reliquaries with letters authenticating them as, well, the True Cross.

Indeed, the expression "True Cross" has come to mean something manifestly bogus, a fantastical construct that could exist only in the most wishful imagination. As the Protestant reformer and "relic" skeptic John Calvin famously sneered in the sixteenth century, "There is not a church, from a cathedral to the most miserable abbey or parish church, that does not contain a piece. Large splinters of it are preserved in various places, as for instance in the Holy Chapel at Paris, whilst at Rome they show a crucifix of considerable size made entirely, they say, from this wood. In short, if we were to collect all these pieces of the True Cross exhibited in various parts, they would form a whole ship's cargo."

Therein lies the fundamental mystery of Christianity's identifying symbol: the True Cross has become the essential sign of a great religion and, conversely, synonymous with a great falsehood. How could the cross on which Jesus died have been preserved, given the tens of thousands of people crucified by the Romans—five hundred a day alone, reports Josephus, in 70 CE, during the Roman siege of Jerusalem? Indeed, so common was crucifixion as a capital punishment during the time of Jesus that the gospel writers saw no need to speak of its mechanics—the audience for whom they wrote would have known them intimately, for they would have seen the crucified victims lining the roads they traveled. Jesus was so insignificant to the Romans that they didn't record where they'd killed him, so how was his alleged cross found? And how did it travel from Jerusalem to Turkey, or to Spain, or to any of the other places where fragments of it are found? Could the "True Cross" possibly be true?

"THE GREATEST BRAND IDENTIFIER IN HISTORY"

Walk into any Roman Catholic or Orthodox church and at the most scared spot in the temple you'll find a crucified Jesus raised above an altar, an image that should strike the viewer as gruesome. Despite the emotional violence of representing Jesus dead on the cross on which he was killed, that very cross has evolved over time to become the most powerful image in the world's largest religion.

"You see crosses at all levels of society," says Noel Lenski, professor of classics and history at Yale University. "There are people who have crosses tattooed on their arms or people wear a cross on a chain or something. Armies have marched with crosses on their standards. You've seen crosses on military uniforms—like the German Iron Cross, which, at this point, doesn't seem to have a very Christian connotation, but ultimately that's the root of it."

The Christian cross is the greatest "brand" identifier in history, instantly proclaiming the message, and the faith, of more than a third of the world's population. At its root, though, it's a symbol of defeat.

"The cross today is an easily and universally recognizable symbol for Christianity, which is kind of ironic, because for the disciples, the cross would have been in a sense a shameful way to die," says Fr. James Martin. "So it's odd that this terrible scandal in a sense was turned into the main symbol for the Christian religion."

When steel beams in the shape of a cross were discovered in the smoking ruins of the World Trade Center in New York City shortly after the attack on the twin towers on September 11, 2001, the "Ground Zero Cross" became an instant shrine for recovery workers, and eventually, an important relic itself in the museum at Ground Zero memorializing the attack and its aftermath. When an atheist group led a court challenge asserting that the public display of this "cross" was an illegal mix of church and state, a judge declared that the cross was part of the history of the World Trade Center, not a government endorsement of Christianity. Even so, the profound cultural resonance of the Ground Zero Cross would not have been possible without the Cross of Jesus.

That same reality caused grief when a group of Carmelite nuns erected a twenty-six-foot-tall cross near the convent they had established in 1988 behind Block 11, the torture prison at the Auschwitz concentration camp. The cross was a relic from a Mass held by Pope John Paul II at Auschwitz in 1979. Though the Vatican later ordered the nuns to move their convent, the cross remains, causing great pain to the international Jewish community, who view it as a symbol of the very ideology that led to the murder of six million Jews during the Shoah, with one out of every six Jews who died murdered at Auschwitz.

So how did a barbaric Roman tool for capital punishment become a symbol that elicits such a visceral reaction from humanity? While the gospels all tell the story of Jesus's life, Crucifixion, and rebirth, none of them lingers on the cross as the defining image of the new religion that this obscure rabbi will create after his ignominious death. The important part of the story for Matthew, Mark, Luke, and John is the betrayal, trial, and death of Jesus. The cross is a detail, but not yet a symbol.

This is not surprising. Crucifixion, as practiced by the Romans, was the worst kind of capital punishment for the worst kind of criminals: traitors, murderers, pirates, and political agitators. Rarely were victims Roman citizens, for the practice was meant to brutally intimidate conquered peoples within the Roman Empire.

The Romans did not invent crucifixion, but they perfected it. The practice began in the sixth century BCE, in Asia Minor, among the Assyrians, Phoenicians, and Persians, all of whom were renowned for their appallingly imaginative forms of torturing and killing. By the time of the slave revolts led by Spartacus, the Romans had become expert at and ambitious in the punishment, crucifying six thousand victims between 73 and 71 BCE and lining the crosses on the road from Rome to Capua, a distance of 119 miles.

The Romans who crucified Jesus were part of a special detail specifically trained to kill on the cross. Each team was composed of five soldiers: the leader, a centurion, called the *exactor mortis*; and four soldiers, together called a *quaternio*. The Romans' crucifixion ground in Jerusalem was just outside the city walls, on a hill called Calvaria in Latin and Golgotha in Aramaic, the language of Jesus. In both tongues, it means "skull," likely referring to its shape and, scholars believe, to the skulls of the crucified that littered the earth.

Since the Romans killed so many on the cross, they kept the upright portion of the crosses, called the *stipes*, permanently planted in the ground. The *stipes* was only about seven to seven and a half feet high, because the *quaternio* had to nail the victim to the crossbeam (*patibulum*) and then raise the crossbeam to connect it to the *stipes*—by lifting, pulling up with a rope, or making the victim walk backward up a ladder. A high cross would have made the whole process more difficult, and less efficient.

The crossbeam was lodged in place on a mortise joint, and the victim's feet would then have been nailed to the side of the *stipes*—a far more likely practice than nailing the feet crossed, at the front of the *stipes*, which also would have been more difficult and taken more time. The victim, who would have been brutally beaten with a three-headed whip called a flagellum before carrying the crossbeam to the execution spot, usually died within a few hours, of hypovolemic shock and asphyxiation, a process helped along if the Romans broke the victim's legs to make the body sag, which put pressure on the lungs and sped the suffocation. Since the cross was low enough to the ground, wild animals could ravage the carcasses of the dead, and passersby could take note of the gruesome fate that awaited them should they transgress the laws of the Roman Empire.

So why would an instrument of such torturous death become the symbol of a faith whose essence is peace and love?

THE ANSWER LIES WITH PAUL, the first genius of Christianity. He was born Saul of Tarsus in 7 CE into what scholars believe was an affluent family of tent makers, in what was then the capital city of the Roman province of Cilicia, and which today is a town in southeastern Turkey. Saul's family was Jewish, but their Judaism was seasoned by the realities of the Diaspora in the "Hellenistic" period, which arrived in the Eastern Mediterranean in the fourth century BCE with conquest by Alexander the Great and dominated life in the Roman Empire. Paul spoke, wrote, and read in Greek as well as Aramaic, and inhaled the philosophy and culture of Greece.

The Romans had appointed Herod the Great king of Judea in 37 BCE, and ten years after his death in 4 BCE, they took direct control of the territory, renaming Judea and Samaria as Iudea. Yet the Hellenistic influence remained under a Roman political model, and it was into this world that Saul of Tarsus came when he sailed to Jerusalem around age twenty-one, to connect more deeply to his Jewish faith by studying at Judaism's physical and spiritual center, the magnificent Temple.

Jerusalem, as the center of the Mediterranean world's seven million Jews, was dominated by the great Temple, a twenty-story marvel built by Herod the Great on Mount Moriah, its plaza as big as six football fields, its gilded roof shimmering with such force as to seem a second sun to road-weary pilgrims who would come to Jerusalem during Judaism's major festivals to swell the city's population from two hundred thousand to more than a million.

Most likely helped along by family money, Saul—short, bow-legged, blue-eyed, and balding—made his way through the Holy City, where he would soon make his name as a Pharisee. As a Roman citizen, he had the right to wear a toga, but that would not have stood him in good stead as he sought the tutelage of a rabbi in the ways of the Pharisees, so he wore the black robes of the Pharisees instead. The Pharisees were one of two broad groups who made up Jewish spiritual life: The Sadducees were the elite, priestly caste who believed exclusively in the written law, the Torah. The Pharisees, considered more populist, believed in the oral tradition, the resurrection of the body, the coming of the Messiah, and in proselytizing the faith far and wide through letters and missions.

When Saul arrived in Jerusalem, Jesus had begun his ministry, but Saul was not part of it. Instead, he was deep into the Pharisaic world. In fact, by the time Jesus was killed, Saul was so profoundly opposed to the blasphemers who proclaimed the resurrected Jesus to be the Son of God that in 32 CE he took part in the stoning of Stephen, Christianity's first martyr, for his defiant, public proclamation that Jesus was the Messiah. Indeed, Rabbi Saul was so committed to eradicating the Jesus blight that he traveled to Damascus with other Pharisees, armed with letters from the high priest of the Temple, to denounce the Jesus movement in the city's synagogues.

Along the road to Damascus, Saul was blinded by a dazzling light and heard an unseen (and, he believed, angelic) voice asking him, "Saul, Saul, why are you persecuting me?" At that moment, Saul became Paul, a convert to Christianity, and the man who took his Pharisaical tradition of communicating the faith through didactic letters and preaching missions to a level that would bring the world a whole new religion.

So it was Paul who first transformed the cross from a symbol of death to one of eternal life. The thirteen Epistles of St. Paul are the earliest books that comprise the New Testament, and in his First Letter to the Corinthians, in Chapter 1 of Corinthians, which he wrote in the middle of the first century CE, Paul takes a symbol of horrible death and elevates it to one of everlasting life: "For Christ did not send me to baptize but to proclaim the gospel, and not with eloquent wisdom, so that the cross of Christ might not be emptied of its power. For the message about the cross is foolishness to those who are perishing, but to us who are being saved it is the power of God."

In Galatians, Paul considers the Cross of Jesus his mission statement: "May I never boast of anything except the cross of our Lord Jesus Christ, by which the world has been crucified to me, and I to the world."

In Philippians, the cross is a potent force in constant threat of attack: "For many live as enemies of the cross of Christ; I have often told you of them, and now I tell you even with tears."

Finally, in his Letters to the Colossians, Paul makes Jesus's death on the cross the conduit for divine reconciliation: "[T]hrough him God was pleased to reconcile to himself all things, whether on earth or in heaven, by making peace through the blood of his cross."

Less than three decades after the Crucifixion of Jesus, and with that terrible punishment still being inflicted on the worst kind of criminals under Roman law, the urbane and educated Paul—with his fluency in the language and culture of Rome, who writes in Greek to far-flung Jewish communities, and who travels to Rome to proclaim his message—has lodged the cross in the imagination of this nascent religion as liberating and militant: a signifier of the risen Jesus.

Indeed, recent work by biblical scholar Larry Hurtado has argued that early Christians were first using the cross as a visual depiction of their faith not in the fourth or fifth centuries, as previously thought, but about two hundred years before that, via the staurogram.

"In Greek, the language of the early Church, the capital *tau*, or *T*, looks pretty much like our *T*," Hurtado explains. "The capital *rho*, or *R*, however, is written like our *P*. If you superimpose the two letters, it looks something like this: ⳨. The earliest Christian uses of this *tau-rho* combination make up what is known as a staurogram. In Greek, the verb to *crucify* is *stauroō*; a cross is a *stauros* . . . [these letters produce] a pictographic representation of a crucified figure hanging on a cross—used in the Greek words for 'crucify' and 'cross.'"

The Christian cross, however, gets its first official proclamation as a symbol of power through a most unlikely source. Three hundred years after Jesus's death, Jerusalem was little more than a pagan outpost of the Roman Empire, now called Aelia Capitolina. According to legend, a woman considered to be the world's first archaeologist headed a dramatic excavation on the site of Christ's Crucifixion. She was looking for the truth—and her name was Helena.

"FROM THE DUNG TO THE ROYALTY"

In 293 CE the emperor Diocletian, a noted persecutor of Christians, divided the Roman Empire into four regions, to be ruled over by four emperors, later known as the Tetrarchy. Diocletian appointed Constantine's father, who had risen swiftly through the military ranks, as a "caesar," or junior co-emperor. He was eventually promoted to "Augustus," or senior co-emperor, and when Diocletian died in 306 CE, his son Constantine was acclaimed his successor by Constantine's own troops.

For the next eighteen years, the Tetrarchy was roiled by civil war, with Constantine finally emerging victorious in 324 CE. However, it was a battle in 312 CE that brought the cross into focus as Paul had intimated: as a force to use against enemies.

The fourth-century CE Christian historian Eusebius writes that before the Battle of the Milvian Bridge, where Constantine launched his attack against the superior forces of the emperor Maxentius, Constantine "saw with his own eyes in the heavens a trophy of the cross arising from the light of the sun, carrying the message *In Hoc Signo Vinces*, or 'With this sign, you will conquer.'"

Or he saw the cross as a symbol of victory in a dream the night before the battle—but the end result was the same: Constantine's soldiers, most of them pagans, went into battle with the sign of the cross adorning their shields. Outnumbered by as many as four to one, Constantine's army nonetheless won the battle and chased Maxentius into the Tiber, where he drowned. Constantine then entered Rome in triumph.

The following year, Constantine's Edict of Milan allowed religious freedom throughout the empire for Christians and other faiths, and he banned crucifixion, the most degrading of capital punishments. Constantine made the cross his official symbol, something as extraordinary, as Thomas Cahill has wittily observed, "as a governor of Texas electing to wear a tiny electric chair or poison-filled hypodermic needle on a chain around his neck."

Capital punishment, however, may well have been the impetus for the discovery of the "True Cross," launching Constantine's mother, Helena, on a world-changing pilgrimage to Jerusalem in 326 CE, when she was nearing eighty years old.

Helena is one of the most compelling characters in the story of early Christianity. She was likely born in 248/9 CE in the city of Drepanum (later renamed Helenopolis), in what is today northeastern Turkey. By most accounts, Helena was of humble origin, a *stab-*

ularia, or maid in an inn or tavern, when she met the Roman soldier Constantius and became his wife or concubine.

One account of Helena's imperial origins reveals that Constantius was sent on a mission to Persia and stopped at an inn in Drepanum, where he took a fancy to the innkeeper's daughter Helena and spent the night with Helena the *stabularia*. While this does not make her a prostitute, it certainly underscores St. Ambrose's take on her as rising "*de stercore ad regnum*"—"from the dung to the royalty." When Constantius went on his way the morning after, he gave Helena an embroidered purple robe, one that was recognized by another imperial emissary years later, who encountered Helena and her son, a dead ringer for Constantius and wearing the regal purple robe.

What is for certain is that Helena gave birth to Constantine in 272 CE. Shortly before his father, Constantius, was promoted to become one of the empire's four rulers in 289, Constantius had to divorce or leave Helena, for political reasons, to marry Theodora, the stepdaughter of his imperial boss, Maximian. So Helena and her seventeen-year-old son, Constantine, recede from the tale, living together in exile and developing a deep and powerful bond, until Constantine is proclaimed his father's successor by the army in 306 CE.

In 326, two extraordinary events happened that may explain why Helena makes the arduous pilgrimage to the Holy Land at a time in life when a chair by a fire with Holy Scripture in hand should have been spiritual journey enough. Constantine, like his father before him, also married a daughter of Maximian. When he wed Fausta in 307, he was already father to a son, Crispus, whom he'd sired with a concubine. The boy grew up as the heir apparent in the empire's northern region, in the palace at Trier (in western Germany, near the Luxembourg border), under the adoring watch of his grandmother Helena.

Fausta, however, had sons of her own, and here the story takes a dark and dramatic turn. Fausta approached her stepson, Crispus, and suggested they begin a love affair, a move that shocked the young emperor-in-waiting. Seeing his repelled reaction, Fausta quickly switched gears and reported to Constantine that Crispus had attempted to rape her, and was planning to overthrow his father. Constantine, whose temper was a short as his realpolitik was large, had Crispus dispatched into exile on an island—and then dispatched by poison.

Helena was heartbroken by the murder of her grandson by his father. She told Constantine how Fausta had plotted against him, and the emperor now set his vengeance on the mother of his other three sons. One day, while Fausta was in the steam room, Constantine had the doors barred and the heat turned up so high that she roasted to death. A suicide, officially, but even so, the empire was as stunned by this brutal death of the empress as of that of Constantine's successor.

With the death of Fausta, Helena was now regent at the side of her son, and what better way to cleanse the emotional debris of a little family homicide than by sending the elderly dowager on a pilgrimage to the Holy Land? "She may herself have wanted to be involved in this Holy Land venture because the meaning of this Holy Land venture is really about repentance and redemption," says Kate Cooper, professor of ancient history at the University of Manchester and an expert in the role of women in early Christianity. "Now Constantine has been killing people, they've been dropping like flies in the 320s, so what better as a gesture of the imperial family than to go to the place where Jesus died on the cross for the salvation of sinners. It's a perfect PR move, if you like."

In 325 CE, Constantine had convened a council of Church Fathers at Nicaea, to resolve pressing theological issues and consolidate Christian unity. One of the Nicene Council's accomplishments was the Nicene Creed, which describes, among other things, the last days of Jesus: "He suffered, died, and was buried. On the third day he rose again . . . he ascended into heaven."

There's no mention of the cross until the creed is revised at the First Council of Constantinople in 381, but there was restlessness in the Eastern part of the empire with Constantine's Christian agenda. So Helena's trip could also have been a diplomatic mission to smooth troubled imperial waters.

Lending credence to that theory is the fact that pilgrimages for penitential reasons did not begin before the Middle Ages, so Helena's journey to the Holy Land was not as a humble pilgrim in search of sacred relief. She went as an empress.

Helena went not only with an imperial blank check in hand from her son, but with her own image on the coin of the realm. Before 324 CE, Helena's official title was *nobilissima femina*, meaning she was a member of the imperial house, a fact borne out by surviving bronze coins depicting her image and the words "Helena NF." After 342 CE, Helena became "Augusta," and coinage reflected her exalted imperial status. Now her image bore the inscription *"Securitas Reipublice"* [*sic*], which announced to all that Helena was at the very pinnacle of Constantine's rule.

In late 326 or early 327 CE, Helena embarked for the Holy Land to "worship at the place whereon his feet have stood," according to Eusebius, Bishop of Caesarea, and Helena's companion and chronicler. The *stabularia*-cum-empress had set out in her eightieth year on a journey that would if not save the empire, then change the world. Indeed, she was the first Roman empress to make the journey without the company of consort or son, and while she wasn't exactly sleeping in stables, a journey to the Holy Land, as recounted seven years later by an anonymous traveler who followed the same route as Helena, covered 3,250 miles, with stops at 190 way stations and 360 changes of horse.

"I think Helena's cavalcade would have made the most extraordinary impression on the people who came out to witness it," says Annelise Freisenbruch, author of *The First Ladies of Rome: The Women behind the Caesars*. "You've got to imagine vehicles loaded with treasures that she was planning on giving out to local communities. You've got to imagine pack horses maybe loaded with furniture and creature comforts from home. There would be a military escort to clear the road for her to go ahead and make sure that the path was clear. And you've got to imagine people lining the route to see this extraordinary sight of the empress's litter going by."

As she and her litter made their way to Jerusalem, Helena dispensed imperial largesse to a diverse and important constituency: citizens, soldiers, the poor, the oppressed, and the politically exiled. Eusebius records that "she bestowed abundant proofs of her liberality as well on the inhabitants of the several cities collectively, as on individuals who approached her, at the same time that she scattered largesse among the soldiery with a liberal hand. But especially abundant were the gifts she bestowed on the naked and unprotected poor. To some she gave money, to others an ample supply of clothing: she liberated some from imprisonment, or from the bitter servitude of the mines; others she delivered from unjust oppression, and others again, she restored from exile."

Helena's largesse was born of Christian charity—and Constantinian calculation. If the emperor hadn't suggested that she dispense imperial funds, he certainly approved of it. His aged mother on a pilgrimage to the restless outposts of empire was the perfect political emissary.

"Helena's journey is the ancient equivalent of a good photo op for Constantine," says Freisenbruch. "She is going there to advertise her son's newfound Christianity. She's going to meet local people. She's going to be Constantine's mouthpiece, in a way. And this is very much a public journey as well as one that is motivated by personal piety."

Helena arrived in a Jerusalem that had been profoundly changed by two catastrophic wars with Rome. After the brutal four-year siege of the city ended in 70 CE, the Romans had burned down and destroyed the Temple, the center of Jewish spiritual life. A little more than half a century after that, when the emperor Hadrian finally vanquished the Jewish insurgency led by Simon Bar-Kokhba, he was so shaken by the near defeat of the mighty Roman Empire by a band of guerrilla fighters, that he decided to solve the Jewish problem once and for all.

Hadrian murdered Jewish scholars, and burned the Torah in a public ritual on the Temple Mount—symbolically razing the Temple again with flame. He renamed the country Syria Palaestina, after the Jews' historic enemies, the Philistines. So the Palestinians began from a disastrous Jewish defeat, one where Jews were forbidden to enter Jerusalem save for one day of the year: Tisha B'av, which commemorates the destruction of their temple. "Jerusalem is the theological center of the Jewish people and for centuries had been the political center of the Jewish people," says Rabbi Joshua Garroway. "So to not be permitted to go into Jerusalem but once per year in order to lament the destruction of the Temple was tremendously devastating for the Jewish community."

Hadrian also renamed Jerusalem: Aelia Capitolina. Aelius was Hadrian's *nomen gentile*, a rough equivalent to a surname, while Capitolina referred to the Romans' chief god, Jupiter Capitolinus.

By the time Helena arrived, the Roman colony that had been Jerusalem was just called Aelia, though the temple to Venus that Hadrian had built on the site of Jesus's Crucifixion was now demolished, and a new building was under way. Shortly after the Council of Nicaea, Constantine had commanded construction of a Christian basilica (which became the Church of the Holy Sepul-chre) on the spot where Jesus died and was entombed. So when Hel-ena arrived in Jerusalem, she went to inspect the site.

"Jerusalem at the time of Helena would have been, to our eyes and ears and noses, a crowded, dark, smelly place," says archaeolo-gist Byron McCane, who has spent many years excavating the Holy Land. "The streets were more like alleys. Buildings were crowded very close together. People lived in very cramped quarters by our standards. And most of all it stank."

According to legend, while supervising the excavation for the new church, Helena unearthed three crosses. According to the Gos-pels, Jesus was crucified with two brigands, so the three crosses, to a Christian audience hearing the tale, would have resounded. Also, because the *titulus*—the plaque nailed to the Cross of Jesus pro-claiming, "INRI," or *Iesus Nazarenus Rex Iudeaorum*—had been detached from Jesus's purported cross, thus preventing easy identi-fication, a means had to be devised to discover which cross was that of Jesus.

One of the most entertaining accounts of that enterprise comes fifteen hundred years later, via Mark Twain's *The Innocents Abroad*, which recounts his great journey through Europe and the Holy Land—and which is the greatest-selling of all his books. Twain vis-its Jerusalem, and while in the Church of the Holy Sepulchre, he relates the story of how Helena detected the "True Cross" from the trio that she had discovered:

> A noble lady lay very ill in Jerusalem. The wise priests ordered that the three crosses be taken to her bedside one at a time. It was done. When her eyes fell upon the first one, she uttered a scream that was heard beyond the Damascus Gate, and even upon the Mount of Olives, it was said, and then fell back in a deadly swoon. They recovered her and brought the second

cross. Instantly she went into fearful convulsions, and it was with the greatest difficulty that six strong men could hold her. They were afraid, now, to bring in the third cross. They began to fear that possibly they had fallen upon the wrong crosses, and that the true cross was not with this number at all. However, as the woman seemed likely to die with the convulsions that were tearing her, they concluded that the third could do no more than put her out of her misery with a happy dispatch. So they brought it, and behold, a miracle! The woman sprang from her bed, smiling and joyful, and perfectly restored to health. When we listen to evidence like this, we cannot but believe. We would be ashamed to doubt, and properly, too. Even the very part of Jerusalem where this all occurred is there yet. So there is really no room for doubt.

Despite Twain's tongue-in-cheek belief, doubt is the proper response, thinks Byron McCane. "The challenges in the search for the True Cross are overwhelming," he says. "The thought that we might be able to pick out one cross out of all of those crucifixions from the Roman Empire—the odds are staggering. No one really paid much attention to the True Cross when it mattered most— that is, right after Jesus was taken down from it. By that time there are only about four Christians left—four followers of Jesus are still watching—and they follow the body, not the cross. The Roman soldiers on that unit took the nails out, took the cross down, and put it back wherever they stored those things. By twenty-four hours later, nobody could've told you which one was the True Cross of Jesus."

Helena, on the other hand, after determining which cross was true, pretty much destroyed it by cutting it into three pieces—one for her son, one for herself, and one for Jerusalem. She then returned to Constantine in Rome laden with portions of the True Cross, and the *titulus*, the nails from the cross, the crown of thorns, and the

Scala Santa, or "holy steps," which Jesus climbed as he went to his death. Helena may well be considered one of the first archaeologists, but she could also be considered a looter of imperial proportions.

Despite her holy haul from Jerusalem, the story of Helena's discovery of the True Cross first took hold at the end of the fourth century CE, more than sixty years after Helena died. St. Ambrose, preaching at the funeral of the emperor Theodosius on February 25, 395 CE, declared of Helena, "The Spirit inspired her to search for the wood of the Cross. She drew near to Golgotha and said, 'Behold the place of combat: where is thy victory? . . . Why did you hide the Wood, O Devil, except to be vanquished a second time?'"

Eusebius, Helena's enthusiastic companion and chronicler, tells a different story. In his account, Helena founded a church on the spot where Jesus was born, which became the Church of the Nativity in Bethlehem, and she "raised a stately structure on the Mount of Olives also, in memory of his ascent to heaven who is the Savior of mankind, erecting a sacred church and temple on the very summit of the mount," which became the Eleona Church. Nowhere does Eusebius suggest that Helena found the True Cross of Jesus.

"The idea that Helena finds parts of the real True Cross that Jesus was crucified on is extraordinarily unlikely. There isn't a snowball's chance in hell," says Candida Moss. "We have to be a little bit skeptical of Eusebius because he certainly wanted to position himself as an imperial biographer, as favored by Constantine. He was politicking himself, and so when we think about what Eusebius tells us about Constantine, we have to bear in mind that he's really quite pro-Constantine even before he sits down to write."

One theory for omission of the True Cross argues that Eusebius, as Bishop of Caesarea, had professional interest in not publicizing Jerusalem too much, lest it reduce his own power. "The fact is that Eusebius had good reason to keep silent about the discovery of the True Cross on several levels," says Noel Lenski. "First of all he was not the bishop of Jerusalem, he was the bishop of neighboring Cae-sarea, which had formerly been the more powerful bishopric in that diocese, so he doesn't want to give any more glory to Jerusalem than he absolutely has to. And the second issue is that Eusebius was very concerned about a spiritualized version of Christianity that avoids the interest in relics and in physical connections to the spiritual past."

The holy Jewish city of Jerusalem had become a Roman garri-son backwater, and from the early second century CE and for an-other two hundred years, there was hardly any pilgrimage to Jerusalem, because there was no tangible construct of the "Holy Land." Eusebius could see that this sudden transformation of Jeru-salem into "all things Jesus" would be bad for the pilgrimage po-tential of Caesarea, and his own influence on Christian matters.

Even so, in 350 CE, just a decade after the death of Eusebius, Cyril, the Bishop of Jerusalem, suggested that the Cross of Jesus, or what was left of it, was in fact in Jerusalem, by proclaiming in his "Catechetical Lectures" that "the wood of the Cross confutes me, which has from hence been distributed piecemeal to all the world."

Three decades later, in 383 CE, Egeria, a devout woman from Galicia (in present-day Spain), made her own pilgrimage to Jerusa-lem and declared that the Cross of Jesus was not only in Jerusalem, but was a central part of Christian liturgy. In a long letter to her Christian "sisters" back home, known as the *Itinerarium Egeriae*, or the "Travels of Egeria," she explained that the Cross of Jesus was a central part of the Holy Week events preceding Easter Sunday at the Church of Holy Sepulchre, and venerated with elaborate ritual— along with some Christian muscle:

> Then a chair is placed for the bishop in Golgotha behind the Cross, which is now standing; the bishop duly takes his seat in the chair, and a table covered with a linen cloth is placed

before him; the deacons stand round the table, and a silver-gilt casket is brought in which is the holy wood of the cross. The casket is opened and (the wood) is taken out, and both the wood of the Cross and the title are placed upon the table.

Now, when it has been put upon the table, the bishop, as he sits, holds the extremities of the sacred wood firmly in his hands, while the deacons who stand around guard it. It is guarded thus because the custom is that the people, both faithful and catechumens, come one by one and, bowing down at the table, kiss the sacred wood and pass through. And because, I know not when, some one is said to have bitten off and stolen a portion of the sacred wood, it is thus guarded by the deacons who stand around, lest any one approaching should venture to do so again.

As both these sources predate St. Ambrose's proclamation of Helena's discovery of the True Cross, is it possible that there was a cross found on the site where Constantine built the Holy Sepulchre?

"I think Helena found something, or those around Helena found something, and there was some kind of miraculous healing, because something must have happened to make everyone go 'Ah, wow, that really is the wood of the Cross,'" says archaeologist Joan Taylor. "If nothing had happened, if Helena or someone else had just said, 'I think we're just going to call this the wood from Jesus's Cross,' and there was nothing that made everyone surprised or wonder, then I don't think it really would have worked in terms of the mentality of the time."

One thing is for certain: at last count, 1,150 pieces of the Cross of Jesus were out there in the world. What can science tell us about their provenance? And what can science say about that divine intangible—that one of these pieces of ancient wood has a possible connection to Jesus Christ?

"THE ONLY CONCRETE EVIDENCE OF ROMAN CRUCIFIXION IN EXISTENCE"

In 1870, the French architect Charles Rohault de Fleury set out to test Calvin's theory that so many pieces of the "True Cross" had been sliced up and sent into the world that they could have filled a ship. De Fleury, as the architect of the Natural History Museum and two opera houses in Paris, had credibility, as did his results. He calculated that the cross on which Jesus was crucified would have been between nine and thirteen feet high, with a crossbeam six and a half feet wide. He then painstakingly catalogued all the pieces then known to be in existence of the True Cross and created a kind of jigsaw puzzle that put the pieces back together. Amazingly, according to de Fleury's calculations, the known fragments of the True Cross amounted to only a third of the cross on which Jesus died, directly contradicting Calvin and those who echoed his skepticism.

One of the perplexing realities for archaeologists is the lack of residual wood from the massive archive of Roman crucifixion. Despite the fact the Romans killed tens of thousands of people through crucifixion, the only piece of evidence connected to this terrible punishment was discovered in 1968. In the Israel Museum in Jerusalem, Professor Israel Hershkovitz, who teaches anatomy and archaeology at Tel Aviv University, has the only concrete evidence of Roman crucifixion in existence. It's the heel bone of a man crucified in the first century, with the nail still stuck in the bone. "This was found in a Jewish burial tomb in Giv'at ha-Mivtar," says Hershkovitz, referring to a northern suburb of Jerusalem. "I would say that Giv'at ha-Mivtar is between five hundred and a thousand meters [or sixteen hundred to nearly thirty-three hundred feet] from Golgotha—from the hill of the 'skull' where the Romans used to crucify people."

The man, whose ossuary, or burial box, identifies him as Yeho-hanan, was in his mid-twenties when he died on the cross. His good teeth and lack of heavy musculature meant that he most likely came from a wealthy family, for most crucifixion victims were far too humble to wind up in tombs—save for Jesus, who was laid in one by the wealthy Joseph of Arimathea. Others buried in the same tomb as Yehohanan had connections to the Temple, so it's possible that he was killed by the Romans for some political transgression.

The Romans were great recyclers, and reused not just the up-rights and crossbeams, but also the crucifixion nails. Those nails that the Romans didn't recover were used as talismans by the Jews and Christians to ward off illness or heal wounds, and indeed, "a nail from [the gallows of] an impaled person as a cure [for various conditions]" was one of the few things Jews were permitted to carry on the Sabbath.

Hershkovitz agrees, and argues that the only reason the cruci-fixion fragment survives is because someone wanted the nail as a talisman and failed to extract it. "We have this case because the tip of the nail was bending backwards, and somebody was trying to pull it out, but it stuck. Like a fish hook."

Yehohanan was cut down from the cross with a 4.5-inch nail still in his right heel bone, and with part of a board still attached to the head of the nail. Hershkovitz believes that the relative short-ness of the length of the nail reveals much about Roman crucifix-ion methods. "The nail was too short [to go through] two heel bones, so sure enough each foot was hammered separately to the cross."

Yehohanan's legs had been nailed to the side of the *stipes*, or up-right beam, and the board had been hammered into the outside of his ankle—like a "washer," says Hershkovitz—to prevent him from tearing his leg away from the cross. The wood on the outside of the ankle and that of the cross, says Hershkovitz, "were made of to-tally different trees."

The tests done on the fragment concluded that the cross was made of olive wood, but Israel Hershkovitz is convinced that this is wrong—first, because the people depended on the olive tree for food, and wouldn't have slashed them down to make crosses, and second, because of the structure of the tree itself. "Olive trees don't grow tall and straight; it has branches everywhere, and there are a lot of holes in the wood," he says. This would have made it difficult to support the nails against the weight of the victim. "The olive tree is the least appropriate tree. We have different types of local oaks that better serve the purpose."

Hershkovitz tested a five-millimeter (0.19-inch) sliver of wood on the heel bone nail with an electron microscope, which uses electrons instead of light to "see" into an object. A beam of high-voltage electrons is formed (usually a heated tungsten filament) and aimed through a vacuum toward the object. This beam is focused onto the sample using a magnetic lens. The response inside the irradiated sample is then collected by the microscope and presented as a three-dimensional image to present a study of the "microstructure," or the geometry, of the wood, which will then reveal its type.

"There's a lot of distortion," due to the hammering on the wood, and time, says Hershkovitz, "but luckily we're dealing with wood, which keeps its general microstructure. If it was something like earth, like soft tissue, then you're in big trouble. Still, there is a lot of distortion." Too much for Hershkovitz to determine exactly what type of wood clung to the heel bone of the crucified man.

So a sliver of a cross bought in the Old City of Jerusalem was taken to a sophisticated Nano Lab to determine its type of wood, and the results came back suggesting more likely than not that the wood, as Hershkovitz theorized about that in Yehohanan's heel bone, was oak.

ONE OF THOSE PIECES of the True Cross of Jesus is tucked in the Cantabrian Mountains of northern Spain, in the hilltop monastery of Santo Toribio de Liébana, an eighth-century outpost of Christianity that stands with Jerusalem, Rome, Santiago de Compostela, and Caravaca de la Cruz as one of Roman Catholic Christianity's five Holy Cities. With this extraordinary distinction comes a papal honor dating to the sixteenth century, as the Gothic monastery has been granted permission to celebrate its jubilee every seven years, when the name day of its saint falls on a Sunday. Santo Toribio's next jubilee will occur on April 16, 2017, and pilgrims passing through the monastery's Romanesque "Door of Forgiveness" on that day will be absolved of all sin—a "perpetual indulgence" granted by the Catholic Church.

In the meantime, intrepid pilgrims will take tour buses up the winding, narrow foothill roads—the braver ones will walk—to venerate the reason for Santo Toribio's exalted holy status in the first place: a piece of the *lignum crucis*, or "True Cross" on which Jesus was crucified and died almost two thousand years ago, and which the monastery has housed since the eighth century.

Santo Toribio claims to have not only a piece of the True Cross, but also the world's largest piece, measuring 25 inches long, with a 15.5-inch crossbar, and a thickness of 1.5 inches. According to its keepers, the fragment comes from the "left arm" of the cross on which Jesus died, an arm that was sawed off and turned into its present form, retaining the hole in the wood from a nail that was pounded into Jesus's hand. The "True Cross" is protected by an ornate seventeenth-century gold-plated reliquary, itself in the shape of a cross, decorated with lily drawings, which leaves a piece of the wood exposed so that Christian pilgrims might kiss the cross on which their Savior died.

This cross migrated to Spain with Toribio—Turibius, in Latin—of Astorga, a town in northwest Spain. Toribio was a devout fifth-century CE defender of Nicene Christianity, which was being opposed by the doctrine of Priscillianism—a combination of Gnostic and Manichean beliefs that argued that the world is divided into two kingdoms, darkness and light, with humans imprisoned in their bodies and therefore separated from God. For his zeal in opposition to this perceived heresy, Toribio received a letter of support from Pope Leo the Great.

He also, somehow, received a piece of the "True Cross" while in Rome, and this relic was transferred with his body to the monastery of Liébana in the eighth century, to protect it from the invading Moors. In 1817 the Bishop of León went to the monastery and asked the Benedictine monks in charge of it for a remarkable favor. He wanted to remove two pieces of the cross to make another cross, which he then gave to Joachim and Felix Columbus, descendants of Christopher Columbus, for the family chapel in their castle in northern Spain.

Then the tale of this True Cross takes an interesting American turn—the Columbus family chapel moved to the United States. Theodore Davis Boal, a member of the founding family of Boalsburg, Pennsylvania, traveled to Europe in the 1890s to continue his study of architecture, and there he married Mathilde de Lagarde, a descendant of Christopher Columbus. When her aunt Victoria Columbus died in 1908, she bequeathed the chapel from the Columbus Castle to the Boal family, and Theodore Davis Boal imported it in 1909 as the centerpiece for his modifications to his family estate in Boalsburg, reconstructing it all, complete with the relic of the True Cross.

The story of how this piece of the "True Cross" traveled from Jerusalem to Europe is representative of how other fragments and sacred relics made their journeys from a dusty outpost of the Roman Empire to the great churches and monasteries of the world. Yet another migration of the True Cross leads to a fragment in the medieval museum of Waterford, Ireland. This relic is composed of five pieces of cedar wood, encased in a seventeenth-century silver reliquary whose Latin inscription reads, "This piece of the wood of the Most Holy Cross belongs to the Cathedral Church of the Most Holy Trinity Waterford." The relic was likely taken from Palestine during the First Crusade of 1096 and given to Muircheartach O Briain, King of Munster, in 1110, by Pope Paschal II. O Briain then gave it to Malchus, who became Archbishop of Cashel in 1111 CE. Today, the Waterford Cross, as it is called, has allowed science access to the evidence that it wouldn't otherwise have gotten. So what can science tell us about this piece of wood that allegedly touched Jesus's blood, sweat, and tears?

Professor Thomas Higham has traced the relic's journey from Jerusalem to Spain to Brussels. Higham visited the Cathedral of St. Michael and St. Gudula and took a tiny slice of the Brussels "True Cross" to test back in the lab in Oxford to see how old it truly was. The sliver—at five milligrams, about two and half times the weight of a grain of salt—is barely enough to be seen by the naked eye, but Higham, who is deputy director of the Oxford Radiocarbon Accelerator Unit, has what he needs.

"So we need about five milligrams in order to give us a sufficient amount to have a good shot," says Higham. "The unknown is really in how the material reacts with the chemicals that we use to clean and pretreat this wood, because sometimes the wood can be fully preserved, and it can mean that we end up with a lot of material that's lost during the process, the chemical pretreatment."

The three possible outcomes of the Oxford tests are all of value: that the wood is indeed from the first century CE, and possibly connected to the Cross of Jesus; that the wood is from the fourth century and connected to Helena's epic expedition; or that the wood is more recent, which is perhaps the most unlikely of the three possibilities because of the documented provenance of the cross. All results, one way or another, will deepen the desire to know more about the last object to touch the living Jesus.

SHORTLY AFTER HER RETURN from the Holy Land, Helena died, and less than a decade later, in 337 CE, Constantine became ill and was baptized a Christian around Easter, which fell on April 3 that year. On May 22, the Feast of Pentecost, Constantine died, wearing the white robes of a Christian neophyte. The cross had been transformed from a symbol of death into one of divine salvation and imperial power.

Ironically, Helena became a relic herself. Five hundred years after her death, one evening during prayers, a light-fingered monk stole some of her remains from her tomb in the mausoleum at Saints Marcellino and Pietro in Rome. Three centuries later, Pope Innocent II ordered what was left of Helena's corpse, including her head, to be moved for safekeeping. As with the True Cross, everyone wanted a piece of the woman who became venerated for finding the True Cross—something she never did—and whose power is a testament to what the Cross so quickly became just a few centuries after the Crucifixion of Jesus.

Indeed, as Helena's remains were being reinterred, Christian forces would soon be marshaling for their Second Crusade, ostensibly to liberate the Holy Land from Muslim rule. In truth, the Crusades were consolidating land and power for the rulers of Europe, but no matter to the hundreds of thousands of men, women, and even children who went forth to the Holy Land to slaughter infidels in the name of Jesus, with the symbol of his cross on their tunics and shields—and eventually as the symbol of Jerusalem itself. In the course of a thousand years, the Cross of Jesus had come full circle: from a symbol of violent death, to divine salvation, to that of a sword, one sanctioned to bring violent death to those who did not believe in the divinity of Jesus.

Over the next thousand years, it would repeat this cycle, one that the Romans who nailed Jesus to the cross would find incomprehensible. To Christians, however, the truth of the Cross is not a fragment, but personal: "The cross is a symbol, of course, of Jesus's suffering, his death on the Cross, and also the Resurrection," says Fr. James Martin, "but also for the Christian, it's a symbol of suffering in general. So when Jesus tells us in the gospels to take up our cross, it's to accept the fact that suffering is part of everyone's life."

SIX

THE SHROUD AND THE SUDARIUM

Jesus of History, Jesus of Mystery

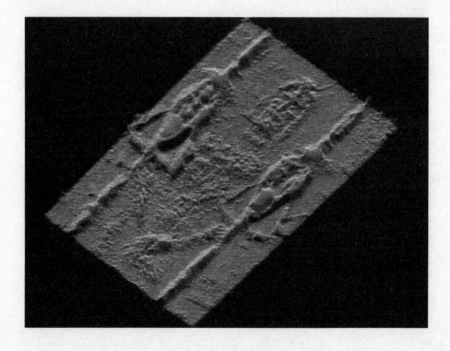

This 3-D image of the Shroud of Turin—revealing the contours of the man who was wrapped within it—is proof, some scientists argue, that the Shroud is not a faked photograph. *(© 1997 Barrie M. Schwortz Collection, STERA, Inc. All Rights Reserved.)*

In the northern Italian city of Turin, a specially built chapel with temperature controls and bulletproof glass enshrines the most famous relic in Christendom, if not all of history: the burial shroud that some believe wrapped the broken body of Jesus of Nazareth nearly two thousand years ago, far away in a rock-hewn tomb outside Jerusalem.

The Shroud of Turin is a rectangular linen cloth measuring a little more than fourteen feet long by three feet and seven inches wide, bearing the image of the body of a crucified man. Yet the shroud isn't famous simply because it may once have enwrapped the body of Jesus. It is famous because Christians believe the tomb did not hold Jesus.

When he emerged from the tomb that first Easter morning, as the gospels of the New Testament recount, he left behind not just the linen wrapping but also an almost photographic impression of himself on the cloth—a stunning, unique image that would be not only the sole physical evidence that Christ existed but also the only image of the true face of the Son of God.

No wonder the shroud has beguiled believers and provoked doubters for centuries. "The shroud's a fascinating object whether it's real or fake, because it tells the story of Jesus's Passion in one object," says Duke University's Mark Goodacre. "So you see in it not just that Jesus has been flogged but that there are marks of the Crucifixion. There are marks from the crown of thorns. There are marks from where he's been beaten around the face. So, in one object, in one image, you're getting a story told of the Passion. And I think that's one of the reasons it has such an appeal as a relic."

For believers, it's much more than a relic; it's tangible evidence of the miracle of Jesus rising from the dead. "First of all I would say that my faith does not rise or fall on the authenticity of the Shroud of Turin," says Fr. James Martin. "But I would say that it's most likely the image of Jesus at the moment of the Resurrection."

Yet is there any evidence that the shroud is authentic? How could it be?

In March 2013, just two weeks after Francis was elected Roman pontiff, the shroud was brought out for papal veneration for little over an hour. On that occasion, Francis sent a video message to the faithful in the cathedral of Turin that poignantly evoked the power of the shroud—while carefully avoiding any pronouncement on whether it was authentic. The "unique and supreme Word of God comes to us" through the shroud, the pope said, making clear that it had real power whether or not it was the actual burial cloth of Jesus.

That has been more or less the official position of the Roman Catholic Church for decades, since 1988, when three laboratories used radiocarbon tests that dated the cloth to between 1260 and 1390 CE. That seemed to settle the matter, and the Catholic Church, which owns the shroud, did not want to fall into the "Galileo trap" again and become bogged down for centuries defending the scientifically indefensible. So the Church's basic position has become that the shroud is an icon, much like any other, worthy of contemplating inasmuch as it leads a person to faith, but of no inherent sacred or divine nature.

Like every piece of new research connected to the shroud, the detailed findings from the 1988 radiocarbon tests raised doubts: the swath of cloth that was tested was not from the original shroud, but came from an edge of it that had been patched, and touched by many grimy fourteenth-century hands as the icon was moved from place to place. Subsequent experiments cast further doubts on a medieval origin for the burial cloth.

Then, in recent years, the pace of revelations picked up. In 2011, scientists at Italy's National Agency for New Technologies, Energy, and Sustainable Economic Development found that the markings on the shroud could have been created only by a "blinding flash of light." Other, new experiments detected the ancient version of a "death certificate" on the shroud, while a recent study showed that the blood patterns on this "Man of Sorrows" indicated he was crucified on a Y-shaped cross—not the traditional T-shaped one that is the central icon of Christian art, and so central to Western civilization.

The Catholic Church this time followed the lead of the scientists in making greater claims for the authenticity of the Shroud of Turin. "For science, the shroud continues to be an 'impossible object'—impossible to falsify," *L'Osservatore Romano*, the Vatican's daily newspaper, wrote in a lengthy article on the new findings. Then, in 2013, the Vatican released Shroud 2.0, an app available at iTunes that allows users to zoom in on the shroud via their smartphones or tablets and take a closer look.

Indeed, the shroud image was, as a modern art scholar recently put it, the first "selfie" and the one that not only inspired virtually every picture of Jesus from the Middle Ages on, but also prompted artists, and now owners of smartphones, to put themselves in the picture, to put themselves in the place of Christ, to seek some sort of immortality.

So whose image has been made immortal—or even divine—on the shroud?

"THE MAN OF THE SHROUD"

If the Shroud of Turin's man is not Jesus, there are plenty of other theories as to who he might be. He might be someone else who was crucified—perhaps the Good Thief or the Bad Thief, the two criminals crucified on either side of Jesus. Or he could be one of the untold thousands subjected to the Roman Empire's harsh version of cruel and unusual punishment. Some theorists suggest that the image on the shroud might be of someone who died—maybe was murdered—in the thirteenth century and whose body was used for artistic and religious reasons to create a fake.

As humanity seems to make exponential leaps in science and discovery, with tests that are more sophisticated than ever, why is it that the Shroud of Turin continues to remain beyond the reach of our understanding? The one thing we know for certain about the shroud is that of all the Jesus relics in existence, it is the best documented. The burial cloth of Jesus that was divinely imprinted with the image of the Son of God—or the tattered rag that is the cleverest forgery in human history—is mentioned in all four gospels and in the Apocrypha (those accounts of Jesus not considered the "official" version of his life).

There would be no shroud to investigate at all, however, if not for Joseph of Arimathea, the man who bought the fine linen in which to wrap the body of the executed rabbi from Nazareth, and then buried him. So who was he, and why did he do it?

The first version of Joseph's story comes from the Gospel of Mark, written around 70 CE, when Jerusalem was in a disastrous four-year war with Rome that would see the center of Jewish spiritual life, the Holy Temple, destroyed and hundreds of thousands of Jews perish in the conflict. As such, the writer(s) of Mark were closest in time to the life of Jesus, and there has been much scholarship devoted to whether Mark's author or authors knew Jesus, or were the interpreters for Peter, the chief disciple and first "pope." What is certain, though, is that Mark's wartime gospel is the earliest of the four books of the New Testament. In it, he reveals that Joseph of Arimathea, "a respected member of the council, who was also himself waiting expectantly for the kingdom of God," went to Pontius Pilate and asked to claim Jesus's body. Pilate agreed. "Then Joseph bought a linen cloth, and taking down the body, wrapped it in the linen cloth, and laid it in a tomb that had been hewn out of the rock. He then rolled a stone against the door of the tomb."

The next account in the synoptic gospels of the New Testament comes from Matthew, which was written about a decade after that of Mark, by a highly educated Jew deeply immersed in the history of his religion. It adds that Joseph was wealthy, so we get a deeper picture of this man: he can afford to buy fine linen, he's a disciple of Jesus, and he's a member of the council. This "council" would have been the Sanhedrin, the group of respected, scholarly, influential Jewish men who met in an inner chamber of the Temple in Jerusalem to administer the law of the land, both political and religious.

Though Israel was under Roman rule, the Romans gave the Jews a large degree of autonomy, but the obligations of obeisance varied: to anyone from the emperor in Rome to the procurator, or governor, on the ground in this remote, fractious outpost of the empire. As a result of both policy and tradition, the Sanhedrin—the term first appears in the fourth century BCE, from the Greek *synedrion*—had their own police force, and the right to make arrests. They also judged legal cases, including those that could result in the death penalty, a sentence requiring the confirmation of the Roman procurator—who, at the time of Jesus, was Pontius Pilate.

Matthew's statement that Joseph was a disciple of Jesus and yet not under arrest himself provokes the question "why not?" The two later gospels, Luke and John, written between 80 and 100 CE, give an answer. Luke reveals that Joseph hadn't been part of the council that condemned Jesus to death, while John adds that Joseph was "a disciple of Jesus, though a secret one because of his fear of the Jews," and that he had an accomplice named Nicodemus, "bringing a mixture of myrrh and aloes, weighing about a hundred pounds," to help with the shrouding of Jesus.

By the time the Gospel of John came into existence, signs of how far the followers of Jesus had come from their origins were readily apparent. Joseph is explicitly not part of the Jesus death panel, but he's definitely a "secret" disciple of Jesus, out of fear of his fellow eminent Jews who have just worked with the Roman ruler to kill the rabbi from Nazareth—and who are now on the hunt for his followers.

While the Gospel of John will be used in the Middle Ages, and tragically onward, as the divine authorization for terrible persecution of the Jews, it reminds us that Joseph is indeed a Jew and, in fear of his fellow Sanhedrin or not, needs and wants to obey a fundamental law of his faith: the dead must be buried, even those who have been executed. He would have known the words of Deuteronomy that tell an observant Jew what to do with an executed body dangling from a cross or a tree: "When someone is convicted of a crime punishable by death and is executed, and you hang him on a tree, his corpse must not remain all night upon the tree; you shall bury him that same day, for anyone hung on a tree is under God's curse. You must not defile the land that the Lord your God is giving you for possession."

There is another reason Joseph could have wanted to remove the body of Jesus. "For me it's easier to see why Joseph of Arimathea would have gotten involved in the first place: an encounter with Jesus must have been transformative," says Fr. James Martin. "Everyone who encounters Jesus in the gospels is in some way transformed. They're either healed or they want to follow him, and so simply meeting Jesus even for one time probably changed Joseph's life."

While Joseph felt compelled to retrieve the body of Jesus for several reasons (as an observant Jew, as a secret disciple of Jesus), why would Pontius Pilate have released it?

The Romans might have left the bodies of crucified criminals on the cross as fodder for wild animals and birds, and as further deterrence to troublemakers, but it was highly unlikely that Pilate would have wanted to provoke Jerusalem at Passover, the city's population having swollen from ten thousand to possibly a million people stoked with religious fervor to celebrate their liberation from another tyrannical epoch, when they were slaves in Egypt.

Pilate had already backed down in the face of Jewish opposition when he first took over as procurator in 26 CE. While his predecessors respected the Jewish prohibition against graven images and removed these from their standards when they entered the Holy City of Jerusalem, Pilate did not. He allowed his soldiers to bring statues of Tiberius Caesar into the city at night and lodged these statues, along with gilded shields inscribed with dedications to the gods, in the Palace of Herod, which was his Jerusalem base during high-traffic, potentially violent Jewish festivals.

As a result of this provocation, outraged Jews traveled seventy-five miles up the Mediterranean coast to the procurator's headquarters in Caesarea and demanded that he remove the images. The historian Josephus recounts that the Jews refused to back down even when threatened with death, and lay down on the ground prepared to die, dramatic resolve that impressed Pilate enough that he had the offending statues removed. Philo of Alexandria wrote a less cinematic but more plausible account, reporting that when the Jews saw that Pilate regretted what he had done but didn't want to lose face by giving in to their demands, they wrote to the emperor Tiberius, pleading their case. Tiberius chastised Pilate, and made him remove the cause of offense.

"If you're the Roman governor and you have two legions,

right—two, four thousand troops plus auxiliaries, max—to cover the whole of Judea, Samaria, and Galilee, and you've got five hundred thousand Jews coming to town for Passover, you are nervous in the service," says Ben Witherington. "You are worried that some little incident could light a powder keg and cause a huge uproar in Jerusalem."

Pilate had already crossed into dangerous territory by pushing back against the Pharisees when they wanted to crucify Jesus, but after Jesus was on the cross, Pilate faced another delicate issue. The Gospel of John reveals that while Jesus and the two criminals crucified with him were dying, Pilate received a delegation of pious Jews asking him to take away the bodies of the executed because the Sabbath was at hand—and if the three criminals were still alive, to break their legs to hasten death and then remove them from the crosses.

When the Roman soldiers arrived at the crucifixion site to do as ordered by Pilate, they broke the legs of the two brigands killed alongside Jesus, but they saw that Jesus was already dead, so a soldier simply pierced his side with a spear. As the Gospel of John recounts, "one of the soldiers pierced his side with a spear, and at once blood and water came out . . . These things occurred so that the scripture might be fulfilled, 'None of his bones shall be broken.'"

In condemning this power-usurping "King of the Jews" to death, Pilate had already given the Temple priests what they wanted, and was likely relieved to have someone offer to take the body of the troublesome rabbi off the cross and bury it before the Sabbath sundown came—especially at the politically charged time of Passover.

"I think this is pretty shrewd of Pilate to allow Joseph of Arimathea to have the body of Jesus," says Ben Witherington. "In doing that, he's not handing it over to Caiaphas. He's not handing it over to the high priest. He's handing it over to somebody who is a Jesus sympathizer at the least, right? So this could be another example of Pilate tweaking the high priest's nose. The last thing that the high priest would have wanted is some independent party taking the body off and burying the body, and then it being out of the control of Caiaphas."

Taking a body down from a cross was easier than putting one up. According to forensic pathologist Frederick Zugibe, who devoted his extensive scientific talents to studying the Crucifixion of Jesus, the remover would tap the points of the nails protruding through the crossbeam. As the nails were wedge-shaped and square, they would come out easily.

Jesus's body would have been in a state of rigor mortis, and therefore in the same angle as when he took his last breath. It would also have been naked. The Romans crucified their victims naked, the only difference being that women were nailed to the cross facing the beam, and men facing out. Jewish burial custom required that people who died violently be buried in the garments in which they died, as the blood shed into the clothing would be reunited with the body in the afterlife. Jesus, bloody though his body was, died naked, and thus was wrapped in the burial shroud—as was the man whose image appears on the Shroud of Turin.

John's gospel reveals that Joseph had help burying Jesus, when Nicodemus brought one hundred pounds of myrrh and aloe (the volume befitting the burial of a king) to the cave that Joseph had recently had dug out as a family tomb in a garden very close to the crucifixion site. Nicodemus was another wealthy Jerusalem sage, who the Gospel of John tells us was "a Pharisee . . . a leader of the Jews" who had come to see Jesus under the cover of night and said to him, "Rabbi, we know that you are a teacher who has come from God; for no one can do these signs that you do apart from the presence of God."

The Pharisees, part of a political-theological strand of Judaism whose followers claimed to be the true and more fluid interpreters of the Law of Moses, as opposed to their rivals the Sadducees, an elite, priestly caste that invoked their lineage to the days of King Solomon in 1000 BCE and were staunchly fundamentalist.

Not only would Joseph and Nicodemus, two powerful members of the Jerusalem establishment, have rendered themselves ritually unclean for seven days after the burial (and so, for most of Passover), but they would have vividly shown that there were conflicting forces in the Sanhedrin who disagreed with the high priest Caiaphas's fatal strategy in dealing with Jesus—that and the fact that the rabbi's disciples, who less than a week earlier had entered Jerusalem in triumph with him, had now effectively vanished, to escape the same fate.

With the Sabbath coming fast, Joseph and Nicodemus washed Jesus's body and anointed it with spices and oils, then laid it on the bottom half of the fourteen-foot-long piece of fine linen that Joseph had bought. They then pulled the top half of the linen over Jesus's head and matched it to the bottom half of the linen at his feet. Then they folded the sides of the shroud toward the middle, the way one does when swaddling an infant. As they needed something to hold the shroud in place, they likely improvised, cutting a lengthwise strip of cloth from the edge of the linen and tying it around the body. (This would account for the strip of cloth that runs along the side of the Shroud of Turin, which scientists say was reattached to the linen, perhaps after binding the body of Jesus.) Then Joseph and Nicodemus rolled a stone to close the mouth of Jesus's tomb and hurried off before the sun set.

The Gospel of Matthew tells us that the next day, Pilate had some visitors who were worried about the man inside the tomb, his messianic promise to rise again after three days, and the potential for a hoax on the part of Jesus's followers. The chief priests and Pharisees begged Pilate to prevent any more nuisance from the Nazarene rabbi and his rabble. "Command the tomb to be made secure until the third day; otherwise his disciples may go and steal him away, and tell the people, 'He has been raised from the dead,' and the last deception would be worse than the first." Pilate said to them, 'You have a guard of soldiers; go, make it as secure as you can.' So they went with the guard and made the tomb secure by sealing the stone."

The gospels all agree that when Mary Magdalene, along with another Mary—perhaps Jesus's mother, or her sister-in-law—went to visit the tomb three days after the Crucifixion, it was empty. Only Matthew mentions that the guards were still there and that they shook "like dead men" when an angel of the Lord appeared to the women and rolled back the stone to show them the empty tomb.

It is the last gospel, John, that mentions what was left behind in the empty tomb, and it is here that the story of the shroud undergoes its own transformation. The women run to tell the disciples that the body of Jesus is not in the tomb, and Peter and Simon Peter, still lying low in fear of the Romans, emerge to have a look and see "the linen wrappings lying there, and the cloth that had been on Jesus's head, not lying with the linen wrappings but rolled up in a place by itself."

The disciples had found the burial linens of Jesus, the very items that would become celebrated as the Shroud of Turin and the Sudarium of Oviedo, the handkerchief that was wrapped around Jesus's head after he died.

The world would not see either of these items again for more than a thousand years—or would it? The mystery had begun.

THE SHROUD OF HISTORY

One of the things that skeptics of the shroud's authenticity point to is its debut on the European stage in the Middle Ages. They see this as evidence of its being a medieval fake: something so precious could not have been kept under wraps for thirteen hundred years. However, if the shroud is not a fake, then how did it get to Turin?

The shroud that allegedly wrapped Jesus's dead body first surfaced (or reappeared) in France in the middle of the fourteenth century, in the possession of Geoffroi de Charny, under rather vague circumstances. De Charny was a gallant knight in the service of King Jean II, a founding member of the chivalric Order of the Star (similar to England's Order of the Garter, and founded at the same time) and admired to the point where he was entrusted with carrying the royal standard into battle. Indeed, it was that honor, and the enemy attention the standard attracted, that would lead to de Charny's death in the Battle of Poitiers in 1356.

De Charny had built St. Mary of Lirey, a church in his ancestral home of Lirey, about one hundred twenty miles southeast of Paris, in gratitude to the Virgin Mary, who he believed answered his prayers for a miraculous escape while he was prisoner of the English after the Battle of Morlaix in 1342. After de Charny's death, his wealthy widow, Jeanne de Vergy, began showing a "Holy Winding Sheet" to pilgrims, who flocked to see it at a time when both the Black Plague and the Hundred Years' War were ravaging France.

Indeed, so popular was the exhibition that special souvenir medallions were struck, featuring an image of the shroud and the coats of arms of the de Charny and de Vergy families. This attracted the notice of Henri de Poitiers, the Bishop of Troyes, who in 1359 charged that the shroud was a fraud, because it wasn't mentioned in the gospels. It was also taking a lot of pilgrimage money away from his diocese.

Aside from the irony of this quick accusation of fraud not long after the shroud saw the light of day in Europe, its exhibition in Lirey in the mid-fourteenth century is the first reliable appearance of it since it was last seen on the floor of Jesus's empty tomb in the

Gospel of St. John—that, however, is not to say that it had completely disappeared from the Jesus story for thirteen hundred years.

About thirty years after the death of Jesus, those Jews who followed his message began a migration eastward, trekking across the Jordan River and into the hardscrabble lands of Syria and Egypt, to establish communities of believers. It's why we find the Gnostic gospels in Egypt. These works written to reveal the life of Jesus didn't make it into the "official version" that became the New Testament, but are nonetheless tantalizing. It is in such a Gnostic gospel that we reconnect with the shroud.

It comes in a fragment of the Gospel of the Hebrews, a text composed early in the second century CE, believed to have been used by Greek-speaking Jewish Christians in Egypt. Fragments of the gospel survive only in quotation by the "Fathers of the Church"—so called because they are the earliest interpreters of Christianity and attained their "paternal" status by virtue of their seminal theological work.

The earliest commentary on the shroud appears in the fourth-century CE work of Church Father St. Jerome, who translated the New Testament from Hebrew, Aramaic, and Greek to create the Latin Vulgate Bible. In one of his commentaries he writes, "Also the gospel which is named according to the Hebrews, and which was recently translated by me into Greek and Latin . . . refers after the resurrection of the savior: 'But the Lord, when he had given the shroud to the servant of the priest, went to James and appeared to him. James indeed had sworn that he would not eat bread from that hour when he had drunk the chalice of the Lord until he saw him risen from among those who sleep.'"

So the custodian of the shroud, according to the gospel, is Jesus himself, who hands it off to the "servant of the priest" before making an appearance before his brother James. In the third-century

CE Gnostic text known as the Acts of Thomas, the "Hymn of the Soul" now had Jesus seeing the shroud as a luminous garment with mirror-like properties: "But I remembered not the brightness of it; for I was yet a child and very young when I had left it in the palace of my Father, but suddenly, [when] I saw the garment made like unto me as it had been in a mirror. And I beheld upon it all myself (or saw it wholly in myself) and I knew and saw myself through it, that we were divided asunder, being of one; and again were one in one shape."

In a pilgrim's account dated 570 CE, there is a reference to "the cloth which was over the head of Jesus," which was kept in a cave convent on the Jordan River. A century later, another pilgrim described having seen the shroud of Christ exhibited in a church in Jerusalem.

The burial shroud of Jesus could be considered both unclean and dangerous by first- and second-century Judeo-Christians under threat of persecution—a reason to keep it hidden. By the end of the eighth century such fears were largely gone, and Church officials convened a council to discuss the preservation and promotion of such Jesus relics, the second Council of Nicaea (in present-day Iznik, Turkey), held to determine the shape of the evolving Church, and one of the most significant events in the history of Christianity.

The first Nicene Council had been convened in the same city, in 325 CE, by Constantine the Great, who would eventually make Christianity the state religion of the Roman Empire. In that council, bishops gathered to hammer out uniform Christian doctrine, its essence expressed in the Nicene Creed—at the core of the Catholic Mass today and which states the basic tenets of Catholic belief (Catholicism equaling Christianity at the time, with the Great Schism that split the Church into Roman Catholic and Orthodox coming in 1054).

The second council convened in 787 CE to restore the use and veneration of icons, which had been banned by imperial edict earlier in that century. At the seventh session of the second council, on October 13, the clerics issued a declaration that said that relics were to be placed in all churches and (to make sure everyone got the message) that no church was to be consecrated without such relics.

As a result, relics became not only legal but necessary. They exploded into the Christian world to the point that by the time the shroud arrived in the mid-fourteenth century in France, bishops were complaining about relics' fraudulent sale to the pope, and by the end of that century, Geoffrey Chaucer was using them as the basis for satire in *The Canterbury Tales*.

Yet how did the shroud get to France? One potentially profound answer to that question comes from historian Ian Wilson, who, like other scholars, was puzzled by the creases in the shroud, which indicated that it had been folded up. It was Wilson who shone a bright light on where the shroud had been by first advancing the theory that it might be linked to another early Christian icon, the Mandylion of Edessa.

The word *mandylion* comes from the Arabic *mandil*, which means "handkerchief" or "head cloth." Edessa was the name of present-day Urfa, a city in southeastern Turkey, which, at the time of Jesus, was a kingdom tucked between the Parthians to the east and Romans in the west. Its population was mixed: there were speakers of Syriac, Greek, Armenian, and Arabic, and a strong Jewish community. Christianity was a growing force in Edessa by the late second century CE, with a Christian church there dating from 201 CE. However, it was King Abgar V, a contemporary of Jesus, who invited Jesus to come to Edessa.

Jesus did not go to Edessa, but around 40 CE a cloth that was said to have received the miraculous imprint of Christ's face was taken to Edessa by the disciple Thaddeus. According to legend, the

"Image of Edessa" (which was just the face of Jesus, not his entire body) was hidden in a wall during a persecution in 57 CE and redeployed (or rediscovered, depending on the story) during a siege by the Persian army in the middle of the sixth century.

The primary document for this is Evagrius's *Ecclesiastical History*, written about 595 CE. In it, he recounts the Edessans fighting off a fierce Persian siege in 544. The Persians had built a large wooden ramp from which to overrun Edessa's walls. The Edessans, in their desperation, mined beneath it, stacking wood that they planned to set alight to burn the ramp down. However, there wasn't enough air to kindle a fire, so the Edessans brought out the divinely created image that "human hands had not made"—the one that Thaddeus had delivered to King Abgar. "Then, when they brought the all-holy image into the channel they had created and sprinkled it with water, they applied some to the pyre and the timbers. And at once . . . the timbers caught fire."

Another version of the story sees the wind suddenly shift on the Edessan plateau and the flames blow back on the Persians, destroying their war machines. The result in both stories was that the Persians ended their siege, and the Edessans, at some point in the reinforcement of their ramparts for war, found the carefully folded image of Jesus that had been high above the city gate.

While the latter story is less dramatic, the Mandylion was clearly present in Christian lore by the end of the sixth century. According to Wilson's theory, the image of Christ from the shroud is also at the heart of all Christian art depicting the face of Jesus, after some unknown artist studied the shroud face and then circulated copies of it to Christian communities. The large pilgrim influx to the Holy Land and the migration of Syrian-trained monks to distant places ensured that what was current in the East would be known everywhere.

A compelling example of that theory can be found in the sixth-century depiction of Jesus in St. Catherine's monastery in Egypt, in the icon known as Christ Pantocrator. When shroud researchers Dr. Alan Whanger and his wife, Mary, overlaid an image of the Shroud of Turin on that of Christ Pantocrator, they discovered two hundred fifty points of congruence on the face—when forty-five to sixty points are sufficient to prove identity using such a method in a legal case.

The story of how the Mandylion/Shroud of Turin could have traveled to Europe from Edessa is the story of the rise of the Byzantine Empire, and of its strife. In 330 CE the emperor Constantine had moved the seat of the Roman Empire to the site of the ancient Greek city of Byzantium, located on the trade routes between Europe and Asia and between the Mediterranean Sea and the Black Sea. He called it Nova Roma; the world called it Constantinople. By the end of the seventh century, the Byzantine Empire's principal enemy was Islam. Edessa had come under Muslim control in 639 CE, and Constantinople itself endured a devastating four-year siege, repelling Arab invaders in 678 CE but suffering a vast reduction in size (from five hundred thousand people to one-tenth that) as citizens fled for safety.

The eighth and ninth centuries saw more conflict, both on the battlefield and in the Church. The "iconoclasts" of the Eastern, or "Patriarch-led orthodox," Church opposed the worship of icons, while the Western, or "Pope-led Roman," Church embraced it. It would take the Second Council of Nicaea to clarify the notion that veneration and worship were not the same thing when it brought icons back into the fold in 787.

The issue roiled the Church and society for the next seventy years, furthering the divide between "Eastern" and "Western" branches of Christianity, and seeing the destruction of many icons—the Greek word *iconoclasm* means "image breaking"—by the imperial police of the Byzantine Empire, as well as injury, death, and banishment to those who supported icons.

When the last iconoclast emperor, Theophilos, died, the *iconodules*, or those who believed in the power of icons, finally won the day. On February 19, 842 (the first Sunday of Lent for that year), the emperor's widow, Theodora, and the patriarch Methodios made a triumphal procession through the bustling streets of Constantinople to the glorious cathedral known as the Hagia Sophia, bearing icons aloft, to the cheering of the people. Icons were officially back in holy business.

Once again, statues and pictures of saints were venerated in homes, churches, and monasteries. The imperial family was well aware of the power and influence that the possession of major icons and relics would bring to the empire. In 943 CE, to celebrate a century of the "Triumph of Orthodoxy," the seventy-three-year-old Byzantine emperor Romanos Lekapenus (just a year away from being deposed, and looking for a lifeline) sent an army to take the Mandylion of Edessa away from the Muslims and onward to its rightful place in Christian Constantinople.

The military might of Islam was, at that point, in decline, so the Byzantine forces in search of the holy image were not going to meet with a fight. Instead they met with a commercial problem: even though Islam was also iconoclastic, the emirs and caliphs had enjoyed the lavish revenue from Christian pilgrimage to venerate the religion's holy icons. So, the Emir of Edessa wanted to make a deal: in exchange for money, the return of prisoners, and the promise of no future attack, he'd hand over the Mandylion of Edessa.

The Byzantines agreed, but the local Christian community was furious. With no small irony, given the "shroud authenticity" wars to follow, they tried to pass off not one but two fake versions of the holy image to the Byzantines before a visiting bishop who had seen the original verified the true one that the crusaders wanted to retrieve. The outraged local Christian community considered the Byzantine seizure of the holy image a great robbery and harangued the crusaders out of the city as the latter made their escape.

Constantinople, on the other hand, saw the Mandylion as a magnificent prize. As the greatest city in Europe, glittering on the sea with its treasury of churches, art, shrines, and palaces, and driven by the power of a mighty commercial engine, it now had the most superlative holy image in Christendom: the face of Jesus imprinted on a shroud.

Soon after arriving in Constantinople in August 944 CE, the image was paraded through the crowded streets in mass celebration, with hymns, torchlight, and the weeping of the faithful in thanks for and in wonder at this divine gift.

So could the Mandylion have been the Shroud of Turin? A telling detail about the Mandylion's connection to the shroud is recalled by the tenth-century writer Symeon Magister, who reported that during a private audience with the holy image, the emperor's two sons "could see nothing but a [faint] face," while their brother-in-law and future emperor Constantine VII (an artist) could see various facial features.

In 1203, a Flemish knight named Robert de Clari, fighting with the Fourth Crusade then camped in Constantinople, noted that a church within the city's Blachernae Palace put on a very special exhibition every Friday. On display wasn't just the holy image of the face of Jesus, but the actual cloth in which Christ had been buried. In 1205 de Clari composed a more detailed account: "There was a Church which was call My Lady Saint Mary of Blachernae, where there was the shroud (syndoines) in which Our Lord had been wrapped, which every Friday, raised itself upright so that one could see the form (figure) of Our Lord on it, and no one either Greek or

French, ever knew what became of this shroud (syndoines) when the city was taken [by the Crusaders]."

The theory advanced by Ian Wilson is that the Mandylion had been unfolded in Constantinople and had suddenly become the shroud, which would explain the creases that can be seen so clearly in the linen. The following year, de Clari and his crusaders sacked Constantinople, and just as suddenly, the holy image/burial cloth of Christ disappeared in the fog of war—or into the possession of Othon de la Roche.

A powerful Burgundian nobleman, Othon de la Roche emerged as a leading figure of the Fourth Crusade. The crusaders had won control of the Byzantine government on April 14, 1204, and Othon de la Roche was among those following Henry of Flanders. He and his fellow crusaders were garrisoned in Blachernae Palace, the very place where Robert de Clari said he had seen the shroud exhibited on Fridays.

By the summer of 1204, Othon had emerged as the right-hand man to Marquis Boniface de Montferrat, who very nearly had become the first Latin Byzantine emperor, but after losing the election to Baldwin of Flanders, he took possession of Thessalonica as his prize. For his devoted service, Othon de la Roche was rewarded with the title Lord of Athens in November 1204.

In 1207, Nicholas of Otranto was in Athens as translator for the newly seated Latin patriarch. In a report on Communion bread—indeed, bread from the time of Jesus that the Byzantines said had been stolen by the crusaders—he wrote, "When the city was captured by the French knights, they entered as thieves, even in the treasury of the Great Palace where the holy objects had been kept, and they found among other things the precious wood, the crown of thorns, the sandals of the Savior, the nail [sic], and the burial linens, which we [later] saw with our own eyes."

Scholars believe that "with our own eyes" refers to Nicholas witnessing the burial linens of Jesus in Athens, and most probably in the possession of the Lord of Athens, Othon de la Roche. When the Lord of Athens returned to his home in eastern France, the shroud went with him, and ended up in his Château de Ray-sur-Saône, near Besançon, and near the Cathedral of St. Etienne, where it was sometimes on view. Although Othon died in 1224, papal politics made Besançon—part of France, yet so close to Germany—an important place.

From 1309 to 1377, a period that has become known as the "Babylonian Captivity" of the papacy, in reference to the enslavement of Jews in biblical times, the pope lived not in Rome but in Avignon. The "captivity" was a result of the refusal of Pope Clement V, a Frenchman, to move to Rome. The next five popes after him, all French, followed his lead in holding the papal court in southeastern France.

The location of Besançon, straddling France and the Holy Roman Empire of Germany, made it a focal point for those campaigning for the legitimacy of the French popes, and for those Germans who wanted to bring Besançon into the orbit of papal Rome. The de Vergy family, power brokers in Besançon for two centuries as seneschals (or royal officers in control of the administration of justice) in southern France, supported the French popes.

Out of this family came Jeanne de Vergy, who was a descendant of Othon de la Roche and who became the second wife of the knight Geoffroi de Charny sometime between 1351 and 1354. Although the Cathedral of St. Etienne had been destroyed in a fire in 1349, the "Holy Winding Sheet" was safe in Jeanne de Vergy's ancestral home, the Château de Ray sur Saône, and she brought it with her as part of her dowry when she married de Charny.

After de Charny's death, and his widow's contretemps with the local bishop who objected to her exhibition of the shroud, the holy icon more or less remained out of sight in the de Charny family castle, Montfort. After Jeanne de Vergy's death around 1388, her son Geoffroi II exhibited the shroud again, and this time fell afoul of another Bishop of Troyes. This one complained to the antipope Clement VII at Avignon that the shroud was a fraud and, indeed, that he knew the man who'd painted it.

In all likelihood, Jeanne de Vergy had commissioned a painting of the shroud to replace the one she'd taken as her dowry, the one believed destroyed in the fire of 1349. The cathedral in Besançon, unaware of the replacement, had exhibited its shroud as the authentic icon, thus raising the bishop's holy ire.

Fortunately for Geoffroi II, the antipope happened to be his cousin, and told the Bishop of Troyes to remain silent upon pain of excommunication. In 1390 the antipope helped his cousin out again, declaring special indulgences (pardons from sin) for all those pilgrims who visited the Holy Winding Sheet at Lirey.

For the next two centuries, the shroud survived litigation (when Geoffroi's daughter Marguerite refused to return it to the Lirey church), war, bandits, and the fickle whims of the aristocracy as it journeyed around Europe. In 1502 it found a home in the High Chapel of Chambery Castle, thanks to Margaret, Duchess of Savoy. Margaret placed it in a silver casket that she had commissioned from the Flemish artist Lieven van Latham in 1509, at a cost of roughly three million dollars. Made of solid silver with gold decorations, the casket saved the shroud from total destruction when fire broke out and melted part of the casket on December 4, 1532.

The shroud continued its continental trip, arriving in Turin from Chambery in September 1578, to spare the Archbishop of Milan, Cardinal Charles Borromeo, a trip over the Alps to venerate it in thanks for freeing Milan from the Plague. On Sunday, October 12, 1578, the Holy Winding Sheet was carried in a grand procession from the cathedral to the Piazza Castello. Once it was in the piazza, Cardinal Borromeo (along with another cardinal, the archbishops of Turin and Savoy, and six other bishops) displayed the burial linen of Jesus to a crowd estimated at forty thousand people.

The crowd was astonished, but it is important to realize that the onlookers, and even those who could inspect the shroud up close, had to take the image largely on faith.

Through close inspection, one could discern the image of a corpse, but it was a vague impression that over the centuries had faded into the increasingly yellowed and smoke-infused linen cloth. Jesus was steadily disappearing into what was possibly the very evidence of his Resurrection from the dead.

THE SHROUD OF SCIENCE

In the Age of Faith, the word of Church authorities and the power of relics were enough to keep the cult of the shroud alive. A modern age, however, wanted more—and had the tools to provide firmer answers.

The first of those answers, still the most stunning of all shroud discoveries, came on the evening of May 28, 1898, when an amateur Italian photographer, Secondo Pia, was allowed to take a picture of the shroud using then-cutting-edge technology. The image that emerged from the negative plate in Pia's darkroom was startling: a *positive* image of the man in the cloth popped out at Pia, indicating that the image on the shroud was some sort of photographic *negative*. At that moment, almost nineteen centuries after Jesus died, the Shroud of Turin was born—not just as a relic of devotion, but also as an object of scientific obsession.

The new image produced by Secondo Pia's camera was so clear, detailed, and powerful that Pia was at first accused of perpetrating some kind of hoax. Then, in 1931, another photographer, a professional, took pictures of the shroud and found the same results. In

1978 the image was further enhanced, and confirmed, by ultraviolet photography. Then came the radiocarbon testing results of 1988 that seemed to deflate the expectations of the faithful. The shroud appeared to come from the late Middle Ages, which was centuries after it was first mentioned in historical records.

It was that 1988 test that prodded art historian Nicholas Allen into action. He believes that the shroud is not only a fake, but one that pushes the history of photography back by about five hundred years. "The Shroud of Turin is in fact a very primitive form of photography," says Allen, a professor of art history at North-West University in South Africa. "Quite frankly, if this had been a picture of a tree and not a picture of Jesus, we would have worked it out a long time ago."

Allen decided to work it out for himself, and his theory turns on the intersection of the camera obscura with the advent of crystal lenses. The camera obscura—in Latin, "dark chamber"—is a box with a hole on one side to admit light, whose properties were understood by the Chinese and the Greeks centuries before the birth of Jesus. The light then projects off an external image through the aperture and onto the rear of the box, and reproduces that image visually, on paper or linen.

"We know that optical technologies passed through the West from China via Islamic East, and we know that by the twelfth and certainly by the thirteenth centuries, the Western people were making use of crystal lenses," says Allen. "We know that because there was even a guild that made crystal lenses and because they were a relatively new phenomenon in Europe in the thirteenth century. They had to find a name for them, and because they were lentil shaped, they came up with the word lens."

To make the shroud, according to Allen, you would need a camera obscura about the size of a room, large crystal lenses, and a linen sheet immersed in silver nitrate, to capture the light, along with the "crucified" subject. "You would need a figure which would be hanging up in the sun such that it received early morning and afternoon sun in equal measure, which means at noon the sun would be directly above the figure; this is positioned opposite the lens," says Allen. "Inside the camera you would stretch a piece of linen that had been previously dipped in a silver salt on a frame, you would open up the aperture, and you would just simply leave it to expose, and after eight hours' exposure, you will notice a discoloration on the linen, and that discoloration would be a negative image of what was outside the camera."

To stop the linen from continuing to be exposed in light, the silver nitrate had to be washed out with ammonia. Allen thinks that if the Vatican allowed a noninvasive test on the fibers of the shroud, traces of silver would be discovered. He also believes that, through a process of trial and error, along with an intimate knowledge of the gospel accounts of the Crucifixion of Jesus, some medieval genius created the shroud.

"For me, personally, the Shroud of Turin has been grossly misrepresented as being an important relic or icon of the Church, but it is more than that," Allen says. "It is an incredible artifact that embodies both the cultural dynamics and the highest level of technology at that period in time."

While Allen believes the shroud is the work of a medieval photographic genius, photography has also been used to look deep into the shroud and cast doubt on the notion of it as a forgery. In 1975, U.S. Air Force Academy physicist John Jackson and his colleague Eric Jumper used image enhancement analysis designed for the U.S. space program to study the shroud. The VP-8 Image Analyzer is used to examine "image density," which manifests as the light and dark areas in an image, which it then converts into a vertical relief of terrain, as one would see on a topographic map. When Jackson and Jumper applied this analysis to a regular photograph, the result was a distortion of lights and darks, but when they used it to examine the shroud, they discovered that the image there contained 3-D data that revealed an image of a human form, something that would not be found in ordinary reflected-light photographs. They concluded that a real human had been wrapped in the shroud at the time the image was produced on the linen.

Jackson went on to cofound the Shroud of Turin Research Project (STURP), and in 1978 forty scientists were given unprecedented access to the shroud to see if they could use the tools at the forefront of science to reveal the truth behind it. Working around the clock for five consecutive days, the scientists came up with conclusions that both advanced the authenticity of the shroud and deepened its mystery.

Jackson and the team looked at the shroud as an archaeological document whose map was described by the story of Jesus's Crucifixion. One of the things they needed to determine was whether the stains on the shroud had come from blood or paint. "We brought samples back to the United States, where they were analyzed microchemically," says Jackson. "The conclusion was that the blood was not red paint, for example, but it was derived from actual blood contact to make the blood features that we see on the shroud."

The shape of the bloodstains also told a story, one that corresponded to the gospel accounts of Jesus's violent death. The Gospel of Mark states, "So Pilate, wishing to satisfy the crowd, released Barabbas for them; and after flogging Jesus, he handed him over to be crucified." John Jackson says the shroud reveals that Mark's account understates the intensity of that flogging, something the Romans also used as a capital punishment. "When we look at the dorsal image on the Shroud and see this pattern made of blood residues on the Shroud, I think the only way that we can make sense of this, or at least I do, is that this represents a savage whipping event on the man of the Shroud. And when the body was laid on the

Shroud, the blood residues from that whipping event then were transferred to the cloth."

So, too, was the evidence of just how the man was crucified. Jackson and his fellow scientists did not have the gospels to guide them, for the gospel writers had no need to explain the mechanics of crucifixion to their first-century audience, who would have known its cruel reality as part of life in the Roman Empire. One of the things the shroud reveals about crucifixion is that artistic depictions of the death of Jesus are full of artistic license. In religious art, "you'll invariably see the wounds in the palm of the hand," says Jackson. However, a nail through the palm could not support the weight of a body on the cross. "Nailing in the wrist, however, is supported by bony structures that are held together by ligaments. And experiments have shown that, yes, you can actually affix somebody to a cross with the way you see on the shroud. So art gets it wrong, the shroud gets it right."

After STURP's final meeting in October 1981, the group released a statement to the media that ended, "We can conclude for now that the Shroud image is that of a real human form of a scourged, crucified man. It is not the product of an artist. The bloodstains are composed of hemoglobin and also give a positive test for serum albumin. The image is an ongoing mystery and until further chemical studies are made, perhaps by this group of scientists, or perhaps by some scientists in the future, the problem remains unsolved."

Yet in the decades since the groundbreaking tests of STURP, advances in technology might be measured more in light-years than in leaps and bounds. These innovations have provided experts the means to find traces of pollen on the shroud, pollen that could have come only from the Holy Land. This was the conclusion of Israeli botanist Avinoam Danin, who, in several studies, has matched faint images of flowers from the shroud to types of flora that are native only to the Jerusalem area. Danin and colleagues also found traces of pollen on the shroud that could have come only from plants that flower in Israel in March or April—the time of Passover and the Crucifixion.

Also, in the 1980s, using a high-resolution microprobe, researchers Joseph Kohlbeck, from the Hercules Aerospace Company in Utah, and Richard Levi-Setti, of the Enrico Fermi Institute, independently matched dirt particles from the shroud with the kind of limestone residue found in tombs from around Jerusalem.

In 2009, in the Vatican Secret Archives, shroud expert and respected paleographer Dr. Barbara Frale discovered writing on the surface of the shroud. Computer analyses of photographs of the shroud had exposed faint Greek, Aramaic, and Latin script, which Frale deciphered to read, "In the year 16 of the reign of the Emperor Tiberius, Jesus of Nazarene, taken down in the early evening after having been condemned to death by a Roman judge because he was found guilty by a Hebrew authority, is hereby sent for burial with the obligation of being consigned to his family only after one full year."

It was nothing less, Frale claimed, than the death certificate of Jesus of Nazareth. The Romans issued death certificates so that relatives of the crucified could identify bodies. Low-ranking Roman officials would write on a piece of papyrus and attach the document to the burial shroud with a flour-based glue, allowing the ink to seep into the cloth.

Frale's discovery has been challenged, with many scholars doubtful that such writing can be seen on the Shroud by anything. Frale's computer work was based on photographs taken in 1931 by Giuseppe Enrie with "orthochromatic" film, which captures images in black and white, with gray ranges rendered in silver grain patters. Critics claim that the high definition required to see such writing is absent from these photos.

Despite skepticism toward particular studies of the Shroud, other studies pick up momentum as scientists hope to use the latest technology and thinking to find the perfect proof for establishing the Shroud's authenticity—or forgery—once and for all.

Four Italian professors recently conducted a detailed study of the physical injuries revealed on the body image from the shroud. Their research led them to an uncompromising conclusion, published in April 2014 in *Injury*, the scholarly and prestigious International Journal of the Care of the Injured: "from correspondences . . . detected between [the Turin shroud man] and the description of Jesus's Passion in the Gospels and Christian Tradition, the authors provide further evidence in favor of the hypothesis that Turin Shroud Man is Jesus of Nazareth."

The in-depth scientific study of the image by the four professors—Matteo Bevilacqua of the Hospital-University of Padua; Giulio Fanti of the Department of Industrial Engineering, University of Padua; Michele D'Arienzo of the Orthopedic Clinic at the University of Palermo; and Raffaele De Caro of the Institute of Anatomy, at the University of Padua—reveals striking correspondences between the evidence for the various injuries suffered by this man and the accounts of the Passion in the gospels. The crucified man suffered a dislocation of the humerus, paralysis of one arm, and violent trauma to the neck and chest; also there is evidence of double wrist-nailing. The violent trauma to the neck and chest suggest that the man of the shroud collapsed under the weight of a heavy object, falling forward and suffering a "violent knock while falling to the ground," causing neck and shoulder muscle paralysis; the "right eye is retracted in the orbit," consistent with the weight of a cross. At this point it would have been impossible for the cross bearer to go on holding it—bringing to mind the passage in the gospels that describes how soldiers force Simon of Cyrene to pick up Jesus's cross—an act not of compassion, but of necessity.

"The Romans, when they see that Jesus is struggling and that he can't carry the cross himself, they seize one of the bystanders, someone called Simon, who is from Cyrene, which is absolutely miles away, who happens to be in Jerusalem," says Mark Goodacre. "Maybe he's a pilgrim in Jerusalem that day. And he takes over the carrying of the cross for Jesus."

The crucified man's hands show clear signs of having been double-nailed, causing a retraction of the thumb. This explains the absence of thumbprints, and suggests that his executioners were unable to nail his hands into the holes already punched into the cross and had to drive in the nails a second time, lower down, between the two rows of carpal bones (the eight small bones that make up a human wrist).

Analysis of the imprint of the sole of the right foot also reveals that two nails were driven into it. This method of nailing would have led to breathing impairment: with the arms raised, the lungs have difficulty expiring, reducing air flow. Each deep breath the man took to speak or catch his breath would have put a strain on the lower limbs, causing intense pain.

The study also concludes that the stains of blood from the chest are consistent with stabbing by a spear, as stated in the gospels, while serum stains were the result of bleeding in the lungs, which may have started before the crucifixion, caused by the same violent fall.

At Liverpool John Moores University, new research by Dr. Matteo Borrini into the pattern of bloodstains on the Shroud of Turin brings into question the very image we have of the Crucifixion. Attaching tubes filled with donated blood, replicating veins, to the arms of a member of his team, Dr. Borrini demonstrated that the pattern of bloodstains on the image on the shroud match those that would have resulted from a real crucifixion—but with a surprising twist: the pattern of blood flowing along the arms of the figure on the shroud, from the nails in his hands, could have come only from crucifixion on a Y-shaped cross, with the arms extended and nailed close together above the head, rather than a crucifixion with outstretched arms that has become the symbol of Christianity.

One other tantalizing piece of evidence connected to the shroud that confounds the skeptics is not new at all: "the cloth that had been on Jesus's head, not lying with the linen wrappings but rolled up in a place by itself." The Gospel of John refers to the bloodstained cloth—now known as the Sudarium of Oviedo, *sudarium* meaning "sweat cloth" in Latin and Oviedo the city in northern Spain where the Sudarium has been enshrined in the Cathedral of San Salvador since the ninth century CE—as about three feet long and two feet wide. Mark Guscin, an art historian, has spent nearly twenty years studying the Sudarium. As part of a team of Spanish scientists, he believes that the stains on the shroud are consistent both with the gospels and with the science of crucifixion. Guscin says that the Sudarium contains bloodstains "formed by some kind of sharp object that had penetrated the scalp at the back of the head. Now, sharp objects penetrating the scalp immediately remind us of a crown of thorns used on . . . the body of Jesus of Nazareth. Again the stain cannot say 'this was a crown of thorns,' but it can say that they were made by sharp objects penetrating the scalp. Again it's perfectly compatible with crucifixion. And this was the line of studies that we followed when we started analyzing the cloth."

"After Jesus's arrest, he is taunted by the Roman guards, who place a crown of thorns on his head to mock him," says Fr. James Martin, referring to the accounts in the Gospels of Matthew and John. "Who stick a reed in his hand as a sort of scepter to mock him and put a purple cloak around him and say, 'All hail King of the Jews.'"

Guscin and his fellow Sudarium scholars created a head to pump blood consistent with that exuding from a crucifixion victim, which they wrapped with a cloth the same size and composition as the Sudarium. "When we reproduced the stains in the laboratory [we saw that the cloth] was used on a male body with long hair, a beard, and a moustache who had died in an upright position with his arms outstretched," he says. "It was the only way that the liquid could come out through the nose and the mouth and form this particular stain; so immediately we're talking about somebody who died in that position that we can say is absolutely compatible with crucifixion—in an upright position with the arms outstretched."

When the Sudarium was overlaid with the shroud, the relationship was startling. When they compared the stains on the back of the head of the [image on the] shroud with those on the Sudarium, the match is . . . almost perfect," Guscin says. "Which has led various eminent hematologists to say that the only possible conclusion is that the two cloths, the Sudarium of Oviedo and the Shroud of Turin, were used on the same body." The bloodstains on both the shroud and the Sudarium are identical in another way, one that further makes the case for authenticity. "Then it gets even better in a way, because we see that the bloodstains are made up of blood of the same group, which is the group AB."

As for those who remain convinced that the 1988 carbon-dating tests place the shroud as an artifact created between 1260 and 1390 CE, Guscin points out that the Sudarium's kinship with the shroud trumps carbon dating, and that one of the most significant documents to prove the shroud's provenance is housed in the cathedral in Oviedo. "It's the Book of Testaments, which dates from the late eleventh century," Guscin says, "and it tells us right at the beginning of the book how the ark with the holy relics came to Oviedo from Jerusalem. And it tells the story of how it left Jerusalem in 614 and came into Spain before 621. And at the end of the text, it gives a list of everything that was contained in the ark. And we can see very clearly, it says the Sudarium of the Lord, which leaves no room for doubt."

Still, Guscin points out that, in the end, the authenticity of the Sudarium and the shroud will never be fully proven. "I think science and history take us to a certain point where everything points in the direction that they could very well be genuine. After that point, it's just a question of everybody's personal faith as to whether they believe or not that these cloths covered the body of Jesus of Nazareth."

Yet is this an either/or situation? Must the shroud and Sudarium be authentic—or their supporters frauds? What is really at stake here?

The answer is almost two thousand years of religious art, for one, plus a theology that sees Jesus as truly God incarnate for all—a man of a particular place and time who can be represented in any culture or tribe as one of their own, every bit as much as he was a Jew in the ancient Roman Empire.

Yet the Shroud of Turin and the Sudarium of Oviedo, more than any relics, illuminate so much about our eternal fascination with sacred objects that may have touched the divine. Be they baseballs supposedly thrown by a star pitcher or a portrait allegedly depicting Shakespeare, relics are unmatched in their potential to connect us physically to the past, and to a mystery—one that we desperately want to solve even as we fear what we may find on the other side of that wall of space and time.

Both the scientist and the cleric come to the same conclusion about where the Shroud fits in the story of mankind. "Personally, from my involvement in research on the shroud for almost forty years," says physicist John Jackson, "and the wealth of scientific data that we did acquire, I do think that this is the historical burial cloth of Jesus." Fr. James Martin says, "When we look at the authenticity of the shroud, my gut tells me that it's real." At the same time, he ventures that the story will continue: "It is a relic that produces more questions than answers . . . I don't think we'll ever get to the heart of the mystery of the Shroud of Turin."

ACKNOWLEDGMENTS

Many hands have helped to make this book, and the CNN television series to which it is a companion. We are most grateful to Lynne Kirby and Aynsley Vogel of Paperny Entertainment; to Neil Sieling for his knowledge and wisdom; to Jane Root, Ben Goold, Simon Breen, Carl Griffin, and the team at Nutopia; and to our splendid agents Stephen Hanselman, Richard Pine, and Eliza Rothstein. We'd also like to thank Nichole Argyres and Laura Chasen at St. Martin's Press for being so great to work with—all writers should be so lucky.

BIBLIOGRAPHY

Bartlett, Robert. *Why Can the Dead Do Such Great Things? Saints and Worshippers from the Martyrs to the Reformation*. Princeton, NJ: Princeton University Press, 2013.

Brown, Raymond. *The Death of the Messiah: From Gethsemane to the Grave*. New Haven, CT: Yale University Press, 1998.

Burleigh, Nina. *Unholy Business: A True Tale of Faith, Greed, and Forgery in the Holy Land*. New York: HarperCollins, 2008.

Cahill, Thomas. *Mysteries of the Middle Ages: And the Beginning of the Modern World*. New York: Anchor Books, 2008.

Calvin, John. *A Treatise on Relics*. Edinburgh: Johnstone, Hunter and Co., 1870. Trans. Count Valerian Krasinski. E-book #32136, http://www.gutenberg.org/files/32136/32136-h/32136-h.html.

Carroll, James. *Constantine's Sword: The Church and the Jews, a History*. New York: Mariner/Houghton Mifflin, 2002.

Chilton, Bruce. *Rabbi Jesus: An Intimate Biography*. New York: Doubleday, 2002.

———. *Rabbi Paul: An Intellectual Biography*. New York: Doubleday, 2004.

Coletti, Theresa. *Mary Magdalene and the Drama of Saints: Theater, Gender, and Religion in Late Medieval England*. Philadelphia: University of Pennsylvania Press, 2004.

Crossan, John Dominic, and Jonathan L. Reed. *Excavating Jesus: Beneath the Stones, Behind the Texts*. New York: HarperSanFrancisco, 2001.

Cyril, Archbishop of Jerusalem. Trans. Members of the English Church. *The Catechetical Lectures of S. Cyril, Archbishop of Jerusalem.* Oxford: John Henry Parker, 1839. http://babel.hathitrust.org/cgi/pt?id=hvd .ah3x2a;view=1up;seq=5.

de Clari, Robert. *La Conquête de Constantinople,* cited by Peter F. Dembowski, Letters to the Editor. Reprinted from *Biblical Archaeology Review,* March/April 1999. www.shroud.com/bar.htm#article.

DeConick, April. *The Thirteenth Apostle: What the Gospel of Judas Really Says.* New York: Continuum, 2007.

de Voragine, Jacobus. *The Golden Legend: Readings on the Saints.* Princeton, NJ: Princeton University Press, 2012.

Drijvers, Jan Willem. "Helena Augusta, the Cross, and the Myth: Some New Reflections." *Millennium: Yearbook on the Culture and History of the First Millennium C.E.* 8 (Oct. 2011): 125–74.

Egeria. "Egeria's Description of the Liturgical Year in Jerusalem." "Holy Week and the Festivals at Easter: Veneration of the Cross," 1–2. http:// users.ox.ac.uk/~mikef/durham/egetra.html.

Ehrman, Bart. *Did Jesus Exist? The Historical Argument for Jesus of Nazareth.* New York: HarperOne, 2012.

———. *The Lost Gospel of Judas Iscariot: A New Look at Betrayer and Betrayed.* New York: Oxford University Press, 2006.

———. *Lost Scriptures: Books That Did Not Make It into the New Testament.* New York: Oxford University Press, 2003.

———. *Misquoting Jesus: The Story behind Who Changed the Bible and Why.* New York: HarperSanFrancisco, 2005.

Eusebius. *The Church History.* Trans. Paul Maier. Grand Rapids, MI: Kregel Academic and Professional, 2007.

———. *Life of Constantine.* Trans. Ernest Cushing Richardson. Nicene and Post-Nicene Fathers, Second Series, vol. 1. Ed. Philip Schaff and Henry Wace. Buffalo, NY: Christian Literature Publishing Co., 1890. http://www.newadvent.org/fathers/25023.htm.

Francis, His Holiness Pope. "Exposition of the Holy Shroud Video Message of His Holiness Pope Francis." March 30, 2013. http://w2.vatican.va/content/francesco/en/messages/pont-messages/2013/documents/papa-francesco_20130330_videomessaggio-sindone.html.

Freeman, Charles: *Holy Bones, Holy Dust: How Relics Shaped the History of Medieval Europe.* New Haven, CT: Yale University Press, 2012.

Goodman, Martin. *Rome and Jerusalem: The Clash of Ancient Civilizations.* New York: Alfred A. Knopf, 2007.

Griffith-Jones, Robin. *The Four Witnesses: The Rebel, the Rabbi, the Chronicler, and the Mystic.* New York: HarperSanFrancisco, 2001.

Guirgis, Stephen Adly. *The Last Days of Judas Iscariot.* New York: Faber and Faber, 2006.

Hadas-Lebel, Mireille. *Flavius Josephus: Eyewitness to Rome's First-Century Conquest of Judea.* New York: Macmillan, 1993.

Haskins, Susan. *Mary Magdalene: Myth and Metaphor.* New York: HarperCollins, 1993.

Hegesippus. "Fragments from His Five Books of Commentaries on the Acts of the Church." Early Christian Writings. http://www.earlychristianwritings.com/text/hegesippus.html.

James, M. R. trans. *The Infancy Gospel of Thomas.* New York: Clarendon Press, 1924. http://gnosis.org/library/inftoma.htm.

Johnson, Elizabeth. *Truly Our Sister: A Theology of Mary in the Communion of Saints.* New York: Continuum, 2004.

Josephus, Flavius. *The Antiquities of the Jews.* Trans. William Whiston. E-book 2848. http://www.gutenberg.org/files/2848/2848-h/2848-h.htm.

———. *The Jewish War.* Trans. G. A. Williamson. New York: Penguin, 1981.

Kasser, Rodolphe, Marvin Meyer, and Gregor Wurst. *The Gospel of Judas.* Washington, DC: National Geographic, 2006.

Kienzle, Beverly Mayne, and Pamela J. Walker, eds. *Women Preachers and*

Prophets through Two Millennia of Christianity. Oakland: University of California Press, 1998.

King, Karen. *The Gospel of Mary of Magdala: Jesus and the First Woman Apostle*. Salem, OR: Polebridge Press, 2003.

———. *What Is Gnosticism?* Cambridge, MA: Belknap Press/Harvard University Press, 2005.

Krosney, Herbert. *The Lost Gospel: The Quest for the Gospel of Judas Iscariot*. Washington, DC: National Geographic, 2006.

Levine, Amy-Jill. *The Misunderstood Jew: The Church and the Scandal of the Jewish Jesus*. New York: HarperOne, 2006.

Long, John. "The Shroud of Turin's Earlier History: Part One: To Edessa." Associates for Biblical Research, March 14, 2013. http://www.biblear chaeology.org/post/2013/03/14/The-Shroud-of-Turins-Earlier -History-Part-One-To-Edessa.aspx.

Martin, James. *Jesus: A Pilgrimage*. New York: HarperOne, 2014.

Meeks, Wayne A., ed. *The Harper Collins Study Bible: New Revised Standard Version*. New York: HarperCollins, 1993.

Meier, John P. *A Marginal Jew: Rethinking the Historical Jesus, Volume II: Mentor, Message, and Miracles*. New Haven, CT: Yale University Press, 1994.

———. *A Marginal Jew: Rethinking the Historical Jesus, Volume III: Companions and Competitors*. New Haven, CT: Yale University Press, 2001.

Meyer, Marvin, and Esther De Boer. *The Gospels of Mary: The Secret Tradition of Mary Magdalene, the Companion of Jesus*. New York: HarperOne, 2006.

Olsen, Ted. "Israeli Officials Say James Ossuary, Joash Tablets Are Fakes." *Christianity Today*, June 1, 2003. http://www.christianitytoday.com /ct/2003/juneweb-only/6-16-31.0.html.

O'Reilly, Bill, and Martin Dugard. *Killing Jesus*. New York: Henry Holt and Company, 2013.

Pagels, Elaine. *The Gnostic Gospels*. New York: Random House, 1979.

Pagels, Elaine, and Karen King. *Reading Judas: The Gospel of Judas and the Shaping of Christianity.* New York: Penguin Books, 2007.

Patterson, Stephen, and Marvin Meyer, trans. "The Gospel of Thomas." The Gnostic Society Library. http://www.gnosis.org/naghamm/gosthom.html.

Rubenstein, Richard E. *When Jesus Became God: The Struggle to Define Christianity during the Last Days of Rome.* New York: Harcourt, 1999.

Scavone, Daniel. "Besançon and Other Hypotheses for the Missing Years: The Shroud from 1200 to 1400." http://www.ohioshroudconference.com/papers/p41.pdf.

Schaberg, Jane. *The Resurrection of Mary Magdalene: Legends, Apocrypha, and the Christian Testament.* New York: Bloomsbury Academic, 2004.

Shanks, Hershel, and Ben Witherington III. *The Brother of Jesus: The Dramatic Story and Significance of the First Archaeological Link to Jesus and His Family.* New York: HarperSanFrancisco, 2003.

Sheler, Jeffery L. *Is The Bible True? How Modern Debates and Discoveries Affirm the Essence of the Scriptures.* New York: HarperSanFrancisco, 1999.

Stark, Rodney. *The Rise of Christianity: How the Obscure, Marginal Jesus Movement Became the Dominant Religious Force in the Western World in a Few Centuries.* New York: HarperSanFrancisco, 1997.

"The Staurogram: The Earliest Images of Jesus on the Cross." *Bible History Daily*, March 26, 2013. http://www.biblicalarchaeology.org/daily/biblical-topics/crucifixion/the-staurogram/.

Twain, Mark. *The Innocents Abroad.* New York: American Publishing Company, 1869. E-book 3176. http://www.gutenberg.org/ebooks/3176?msg=welcome_stranger.

Waugh, Evelyn. *Helena.* 1950. Reprint. Chicago: Loyola Classics, 2005.

Wilson, Ian. *The Turin Shroud.* Revised edition. London: Penguin, 1979.

Wright, N. T. *Judas and the Gospel of Jesus: Have We Missed the Truth about Christianity?* Grand Rapids, MI: Baker Books, 2006.

Wright, Tom. *The Original Jesus: The Life and Vision of a Revolutionary.* Oxford: Lion Publishing, 1996.

Zugibe, Frederick T. *The Crucifixion of Jesus: A Forensic Inquiry.* Lanham, MD: M. Evans and Company, 2005.